NC Foundations of Reading
Preparation for the North Carolina Foundations of Reading Exam

Mary DeSouza Stephens

Contents

Chapter 4:

Reading Comprehension Concepts and Strategies 125

Chapter 5:

Theories for Teaching Reading Skills 197

Introduction

PrepForward's Foundations of Reading material is designed to give candidates the knowledge and skills needed to pass North Carolina's Foundations of Reading licensing test. The lessons provide targeted instruction closely aligned to the exam objectives of phonological and phonemic awareness; print, alphabetic principle, and phonics; word analysis; reading comprehension strategies; theories for teaching reading skills; and assessment. The six main chapters are divided into twenty lessons. Practice problems with detailed explanations accompany each lesson. Chapter reviews consolidate learning and prepare candidates for the full-length test simulation. A glossary defines domain-specific terms essential to comprehending the tasks and to producing high quality constructed response answers. PrepForward's Foundations of Reading book builds the fluency and mastery necessary for success on test day.

About the Authors

PrepForward is a leader in content review for current and future teachers, offering effective test prep books and online test prep as well as courses for continuing education. PrepForward has helped thousands of teaching candidates pass licensure exams and has partnered with educational institutions across the US. Teachers who apply PrepForward strategies develop a deep understanding of fundamentals through material with proven results. Please visit our website, www.prepforward.com, to find out more about our teacher preparation solutions. PrepForward was founded by Mary Stephens, who graduated from MIT with a bachelor's degree and a master's degree in Computer Science and Electrical Engineering. She has over 15 years of teaching experience, including designing courses and teaching as an adjunct faculty member at UMASS Boston; TAing discrete math at MIT; and developing curriculum for and teaching classes in high school computer science, LSAT, algebra, geometry, science, humanities, and K-12 math and computers. Outside of teaching, Mary worked in engineering, product management, and strategy for companies including Edusoft and Oracle. In the past few years, Mary has spoken at international education conferences and has served as adjunct faculty at UMass, professional math consultant at Merrimack College, founder of Omega Teaching, board member of Alpha Public Schools, and research and development manager at Houghton Mifflin Harcourt. She currently serves as the CEO of PrepForward (www.prepforward. com) and can be contacted at mary@prepforward.com.

PrepForward's expert team of authors includes teachers, professors, and curriculum developers with extensive experience and qualifications in teaching English language skills. They have degrees ranging from PhDs in Language and Literature to Masters in Special Education. In addition to their years of teaching in K-higher ed classrooms, they have served as ELL coordinators, writers, editors, school board members, founders of ed tech companies, and curriculum developers.

How to Use the Book

This book is designed to help you succeed on the North Carolina Foundations of Reading test. Each test area is given its own separate section in the book so you can follow a study path that works best for you.

It is recommended that you work through all chapters of the book at least once. Read each lesson to get a comprehensive review of key learning objectives. Practice your testing skills with the practice questions following each lesson. The questions are designed to provide practice in confronting both the knowledge and types of questions candidates are likely to encounter on the Foundations of Reading test. Read the detailed explanations for every problem, including questions you answered correctly. The explanations complement the content of the lessons. Each of chapters 1 through 6 is followed by a quiz that will help you to gauge your level of preparedness and see which concepts require further study. Then, Chapter 7 provides guidelines, sample answers, and strategies for the Open Response section.

If you start with the comprehensive diagnostic exam, the results will highlight your personal strengths and weaknesses, allowing you to personalize your learning path. You may also want to save the diagnostic for after you have reviewed all chapters. Then, based on your results, go back and review any areas of weakness that remain. Take the final exam two weeks before your test date. Use the final exam as a simulation for the actual test and be conscious of time. Make sure to use the test-taking strategies outlined in the book. Review explanations of final exam answers. Consider the time used to answer each question. Evaluate which questions presented the greatest challenge and required the most time. Continue your preparations accordingly.

Passing the Foundations of Reading test is critical for your future role as a licensed teacher, but understanding the concepts is just as important. With this book and your commitment, you can achieve both goals. Good luck!

About the Test

Candidates applying on or after October 1, 2014, for North Carolina Elementary Education (K-6) and Exceptional Children: General Curriculum (K-12) licensure must pass the Foundations of Reading test. This testing requirement pertains to in-state and out-of- state initial licensure.

It is a computer-based test that is administered on a first-come, first-served basis, Monday through Saturday by appointment at specified testing centers. You are given 4 hours to complete the exam, plus an additional 15 minutes to complete a tutorial on the computer-based system. You might find that you need less time, but be prepared to stay for the entire 4 hours. Use any remaining time to check your work for accuracy.

There are 100 multiple-choice questions and 2 open-response item assignments. The open response questions test your ability to relate concepts from several different areas. The content is broken down as follows:

Subarea	Approx Percentage of Score	Approx Number of Questions
Foundations of reading development	35%	44
Development of reading comprehension	27%	34
Reading assessment and instruction	18%	22
Integration of knowledge and understanding	20%	2 Open Response

You must achieve a score of 229 or higher to pass the test. You will not be deducted any points for incorrect answers, therefore, be sure to leave no blanks, even if that means guessing.

For current information regarding test framework, registration, scheduling, and other pertinent notices, please visit www.nc.nesinc.com.

Test Taking Tips

There are several things you can do prepare yourself for success on the Foundations of Reading exam:

- ⊙ **Read all of the directions.**
  Take the time to read, listen and carefully review all directions on each section of the test.

- ⊙ **Read through the entire question and all of the answers before making your final selection.**
  Make sure to take the time to read through all of the possible choices - remember, you are asked to determine the "best answer". At a first glance, though Choice A may appear to be a good answer, it is possible another Choice will be better.

- ⊙ **When in doubt, take a guess.**
  Because unanswered questions are considered incorrect, it is important to answer every question even if you are unsure of a particular answer.

- ⊙ **Pace yourself.**
  Remember, you have four hours to complete the exam. While you should not race through the test, you should also take care not to spend too much time on any one question. Keep in mind you also need to leave time to answer two open response questions. Should you find yourself struggling on a question, there will be an option to "Flag for Review". Make a selection, flag the question, and if you have time at the end of the exam, come back for further review.

- ⊙ **Respond to all parts of the Open Response questions.**
  Make sure you read the Open Response questions with care and if applicable, respond to all parts of the question when answering.

Chapter 1:
Phonological and Phonemic Awareness

Lessons

1.1 Phonological and Phonemic Awareness

When people think of reading, they visualize books and written letters. However, reading is a complex process that requires awareness of the connections among spoken and written sounds and words. Before people begin to read aloud written letters, they must first understand how those letters' sounds combine to create meaning.

Phonological Awareness

The ability to recognize written words begins with an understanding of how spoken language works. The development of **phonological awareness**, the awareness that oral language is composed of smaller units, such as words and syllables, is key to the reading and writing process.

For example, a student who can recognize that spoken words can be divided into syllables, or who can clap or count the number of syllables in a word, has developed (or begun to develop) phonological awareness.

3 syllables:

al pha bet

Phonological awareness involves being able to **identify and manipulate sounds** in
- ⊙ Words
- ⊙ Syllables
- ⊙ Phonemes

onset	rime
ch	op
b	at
h	ouse
fl	ight

Rhyming is one of the first ways students demonstrate phonological awareness. Students in the beginning stage who can recognize and make rhymes usually do so using the part of the word known as the **rime**. In a one-syllable word, the onset is the first letter(s) before the vowel. The rime is the last part of the word. For example, in the word **run**, the onset is "r-" and the rime is "-un." In the word **chin**, the "ch-" is the onset and the "-in" is the rime. With multisyllabic words, rhyming can be a greater challenge that requires strong skills.

Phonemic Awareness

Whereas phonological awareness is the umbrella term denoting one's ability to hear and manipulate spoken sounds, **phonemic awareness** is a division of phonological awareness that denotes one's ability to hear and manipulate phonemes, or smaller sound units.

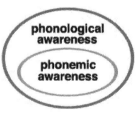

Phonemes, the most basic units of language, alone have no meaning; but when combined, they create syllables and words. For example, the word **cat** can be broken into three phonemes: /k/ /a/ /t/.

Together, these phonemes make a word, but when each phoneme is isolated, meaning is lost—/k/ becomes just a sound. Phonemes are building blocks that are combined to create meaning.

cat: /k/ /a/ /t/

rat: /r/ /a/ /t/

Phonemic awareness involves understanding that changing one of these blocks also changes a word's entire meaning. For example, if we replaced /k/ with /f/, the word **cat** becomes **fat**. We could then change the /f/ to /r/ and make it /r/ /a/ /t/, or rat.

Forty-four phonemes in English represent letter sounds and letter combinations. The phoneme /f/ can represent the letter "f" in the word **farm**, and it can stand for the "-ph" in "morph" and the "-gh" in **tough**.

To summarize, phonemic awareness encompasses the ability to hear and identify phonemes in a word as well as the ability to manipulate them to change the meaning.

Importance of Phonological and Phonemic Awareness

Phonological awareness is critical to developing reading comprehension skills. Recognizing and pronouncing written words require basic understanding of phonemes and the corresponding of sounds with letters.

Studies have concluded that phonological awareness strongly indicates a child's ability to read. One study shows that weak phonological and phonemic awareness levels predict reading difficulty in kindergarten (Lyon 1995). Another study concludes that phonemic skills can predict spelling and long-term reading difficulties (Gillon 2004).

Teachers should also note common difficulties seen in reading development among English Language Learners. To begin, many students might not be exposed to English outside school; they might not speak or use it at home. Even when they become immersed in the language at school, many barriers continue. For example, some phonemes might not exist in a student's native language, making it difficult to hear or use those sounds when reading, writing, or speaking. Using games, rhymes, and songs to teach particular sounds and teaching them in context with vocabulary and pronunciation can be helpful and make learning more meaningful.

Although children enter school with varying levels of phonological and phonemic awareness, many activities can be done to help them develop these skills, significantly affecting their success in school. Such skills are typically taught and gained in preschool and the early elementary years. However, if a child is weak in these areas, schools might choose to target these skills in small group or 1:1 settings. Such interventions are often helpful, and they can provide the basic building blocks for reading, writing, and language success for years.

Phonological processing

Auditory processing refers to the skills used by the brain to recognize and interpret information presented orally. An auditory processing disorder means that something is interfering with the information the child hears. Phonological processing refers specifically to the detection and discrimination of differences in phonemes or speech sounds. Phonological processes are the patterns of sound errors common in development of children or language learners. They may include such errors as /w/ for /r/ (wabbit for rabbit) and cluster reduction (poon for spoon). A phonological disorder occurs when the errors extend past the normal age of development. Phonological processing difficulties can interfere with reading development.

PHONOLOGICAL AND PHONEMIC AWARENESS PRACTICE

1. **What is a phoneme?**
   A. A speech sound
   B. A syllable
   C. The name of written letters
   D. A word

2. **What is the relationship between phonemic awareness and phonological awareness?**
   A. They mean the same thing, and they can be used interchangeably.
   B. Phonological awareness deals with reading print letters whereas phonemic awareness deals with manipulating sounds in words.

C. Phonological awareness concerns reading letters, and phonemic awareness concerns writing letters.
D. Phonological awareness describes the ability to understand that words are made of sounds. Phonemic awareness refers specifically to the ability to manipulate individual sounds in words.

3. **Which of the following might be predicted by difficulties with phonological and phonemic awareness?**
   A. Difficulty spelling
   B. Poor reading skills later in life
   C. Difficulty reading in kindergarten and first grade
   D. All the above

4. **Which of the following would be a strategy that promotes phonemic awareness skills?**
   A. Ask students to sound out each letter in a printed word.
   B. Ask students to trace written letters on paper.
   C. Have students say a word and count the number of sounds they hear.
   D. Write a word and repeat it, and then ask students to read it.

5. **How many phonemes are in the word bass?**
   A. 1
   B. 2
   C. 3
   D. 4

6. **Which of the following would not be a strategy that primarily promotes phonological awareness skills?**
   A. Point to letters on a chart, say a word that starts with that letter, and stress the first sound. Ask students to repeat the initial phoneme.
   B. Ask students to change the onset to make a rhyme.
   C. Ask students to repeat a word and count the number of sounds.
   D. Read a word aloud, and ask students to write it.

7. **Which of the following skills could a child with phonological awareness do?**
   A. Sound a one-syllable print word.
   B. Transcribe in writing a rhyme using onset and rime.
   C. Write the alphabet.
   D. Hear and repeat rhymes using onset and rime.

8. **Which part of the word sport is the onset, and which part is the rime?**
   A. "Sp" is the onset and "ort" is the rime.
   B. "S" is the onset and "port" is the rime.
   C. "Ort" is the onset and "sp" is the rime.
   D. There is no onset in one-syllable words, and "ort" is the rime.

9. **A student has been assessed as having moderate phonemic awareness skills. Which of the following is most likely the highest skill a student with moderate phonemic awareness could demonstrate?**
   A. The student can make rhymes using the rime of a word.
   B. The student can identify that the word "bat" starts with /b/ and ends in /t/ but cannot identify all of the individual sounds.
   C. The student can identify all of the sounds in the word "mailbox."
   D. The student can hear a letter and write the letter on paper.

10. **An English Language Learner in a first-grade class has been assessed as having weak phonemic awareness skills. Which activity would be most beneficial for this student?**
    A. Model print directionality
    B. Teach the student common rhymes
    C. Introduce phonemes that may not be in the student's first language
    D. Present the student with a list of common onsets

PHONOLOGICAL AND PHONEMIC AWARENESS EXPLANATIONS

1. **A** A phoneme is the basic unit of speech. There are approximately 44 phonemes in English—all letter sounds and sounds created by letter combinations, such as /sh/ and /th/. Individual phonemes have no meaning; they must combine with other phonemes. For example, in **clock**, you can hear four different phonemes: /k/ /l/ /o/ /k/. However, those four phonemes make only one syllable. Phonemes are like building blocks that make syllables and words, which make sentences.

2. **D** Phonological awareness describes the ability to understand that oral language is made up of smaller sounds such as words and syllables. Phonemic awareness refers to the specific type of phonological awareness involving the ability to distinguish separate phonemes in a spoken word.

   Phonemic and phonological awareness are frequently and incorrectly used interchangeably; they do not have the same meaning.

   Phonological awareness is a general term that describes the ability to understand that oral language is made up of smaller sounds. It also describes the ability to manipulate spoken language and break spoken words and syllables into smaller units. Phonemic awareness refers specifically to the ability to manipulate individual sounds, or **phonemes,** in words. Phonemic awareness falls under the umbrella of phonological awareness.

3. **D** Phonological and phonemic awareness contribute greatly to a student's ability to read, write, and comprehend. Several studies have concluded that a weak level of phonological awareness can lead to reading and spelling difficulties in kindergarten and first grade and further affect a child's educational career.

4. **C** Remember that phonemic awareness deals only with the phoneme, the most basic speech sound. Choices A, B, and D involve reading and writing print words. Answer C, therefore, is the best answer; saying a word, asking students to repeat it, and then having them count the number of sounds they hear allows students to practice breaking words into smaller units to hear different phonemes.

5. C   Remember; English has 44 phonemes—each letter sound and letter combination. Phonemes are basic sound units that are building blocks. A syllable, for example, can be made of more than one phoneme. If you think about how many sounds are in bass, you can eliminate choices A and B: / bass -- /b//a//s/

    If you were tempted by choice D because of the double consonants at the end, ask yourself how many sounds you hear when you say the. /s/ of bass. Spelling and phonemes do not always match; it is the number of sounds, not letters, that counts.

6. D   Phonological awareness skills deal with spoken language. Choice A allows students to hear and repeat a phoneme or sound, which promotes phonological awareness. In choice B, rhyming is a basic component of phonological awareness and is one of the first skills children learn. Finally, choice C encourages students to distinguish different sounds in a word—an important step in learning how to read and a component of phonological awareness. Choice D deals with written language, requiring students to spell and transcribe a word—skills that do not directly target phonological awareness.

7. D   Phonological awareness is the backbone of reading skills. It deals with the ability to recognize and manipulate sound structures. Choice A involves reading a word, and C involves writing, which phonological skills ultimately enable one to do after mastering sounds. Choices B and D deal with onset and rime, a common way of making rhymes. However, B requires the child to rhyme (a good indicator of a student's phonological awareness skills) and write, a skill that involves more advanced understanding. Answer D is the best answer as it involves hearing spoken words and orally repeating rhymes, something a child with phonological awareness should be able to do.

8. A   The onset-rime is a way of describing how children make rhymes with one-syllable words. In one-syllable words, the onset is the first letter(s) before the vowel. The rime is the last part of the word. The rime is the vowel and everything after it. Therefore, in the word sport, "sp" is the onset, and "ort" is the rime.

9. B   This student can identify the first and last consonants but not the medial vowel, which reflects a healthy level of phonemic awareness skills. Strong phonemic awareness skills mean that a student can identify all

the sounds in a word, especially a multi-syllabic one, like in Choice C. Choice A is incorrect because rhymes tend to be one of the first learned components of phonological awareness. Additionally, the rime may contain multiple phonemes, the focus of phonemic awareness. Choice D requires knowledge of letter and sound correspondences and a grasp of the alphabetic principle, whereas phonemic awareness is based on spoken language.

10. C Since this student is having difficulty hearing and manipulating phonemes or basic sound units, it may be that the student is not familiar with these phonemes, which makes comprehension more difficult. Choice A is too advanced. Print directionality involves written language whereas phonemic awareness deals with spoken language. Rhymes, choice B, may be an implicit strategy, but this student needs explicit instruction that is more focused on identifying individual sounds. Common onsets, choice D, is an example of explicit instruction, but again, the student may need help with phonemes rather than onsets and rimes.

1.2   Strategies for Assessing & Teaching

It is important for teachers to understand how children develop phonological and phonemic awareness so they can appropriately assess and plan instruction. Typically, children develop awareness in a predictable pattern. For example, word comparison and rhyming generally come before blending, segmenting and phoneme deletion. Each of the following skills builds upon each other, preparing children to learn to read.

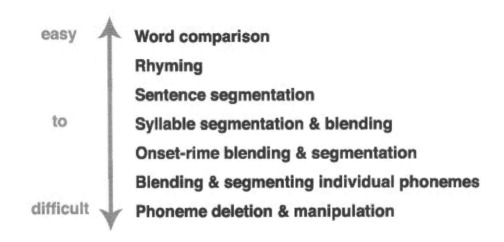

In this section, you will learn more about each of the aforementioned skills, including activities that may be used for practice and assessment. You'll learn both explicit and implicit strategies.

- ⊙ Explicit instruction means that the teacher provides a lesson on a specific skill and an activity to complete based on this instruction. For example, a teacher may provide instruction on rhyming, model rhyming, and then have the students try.
- ⊙ Implicit instruction looks at skills in context, without overt teaching of a concept. Popular nursery rhymes like "Row, row, row your boat" may be an implicit instruction strategy for practicing rhyming.

Studies show that both explicit and implicit strategies together are the most effective for the development of phonological awareness.

Word Comparison & Rhyming

As children begin to develop phonological awareness, one of the first things they are typically able to decipher is beginning sounds and rhyming words. By exposing children to activities that allow them to hear, say, manipulate words and rhyme, they will be better prepared to later understand more complex phonological awareness skills.

Strategies & Methods to Assess

Typically, as children manipulate individual sounds within words to create rhymes, they simultaneously gain an understanding of beginning sounds. Following are possible activities that can be used for assessments or for children to practice word comparison and rhyming skills:

- Word comparison activities - provide students with a group of words and ask them to identify which words within the group are similar. For example:

   Say the following words aloud: **sit, sip, bug.**

   Ask the student(s): **Which words sound alike** or **which words begin with the same sound?**

- Provide opportunities for students to practice identifying the various sounds within a word. Note that students often first learn the beginning sound, then the end sound, then medial sounds, until they can identify all phonemes.

   What is the first sound in **phone**? /f/

   What is the last sound in **book**? /k/

   What is the middle sound in **tip**? /i/

   What are all the sounds in chip? /ch/ /i/ /p/

- Read nursery rhymes aloud to children, have them read/say the rhymes to allow them to hear rhymes and rhythm within the writing.

- Sing songs that use rhyming words, such as **Row, Row, Row Your Boat**. Once children are familiar with the song, rhyming words can be left out for them to say on their own and attention can be drawn to rhyming words within songs.

- Read books that rhyme, such as those by Dr. Seuss. Allow children to come up with their own rhyming word possibilities while reading.

- Oddball Activities – provide students with three printed words, three spoken words or three pictures. Within each set, two words should rhyme and one should not. Have students identify the "oddball" in the set.

- Matching Games – Have students match picture cards or word cards that rhyme or play rhyming memory.

Segmenting

Segmenting refers to the ability to break sentences into words, words into syllables, and syllables into phonemes. Children begin by recognizing that sentences are made up of words and often practice counting words in a sentence, pulling the words apart and putting the words in order to create a sentence. Next, they typically progress to identifying the number of syllables in a word and eventually learn to break words into phonemes, citing each sound they hear.

Strategies & Methods to Assess

Children can be taught to segment through both implicit and explicit teaching methods. Following are examples of how segmenting can be taught, practiced and assessed:

- ⊙ Clap the words of a common rhyme or song, such as **Jack and Jill Went Up the Hill,** to teach sentence segmentation.
- ⊙ Provide students with a printed sentence and individual word cards for each word used in the sentence. Have students count the number of words in the sentence. Next, using the word cards, ask them to build the sentence and then touch each word as they read the sentence aloud.

    My dog is nice.

    Note this activity may also be used for words using individual letter/sound cards such as the following:

    Chip

- ⊙ String 6-8 beads onto a pipe cleaner. Tie both ends and push all of the beads to the left side of the pipe cleaner. Say a sentence aloud. Have students repeat the sentence. Each time they say a word, students should slide one bead to the right. When they are finished saying the sentence, the number of beads should match the number of words in the sentence. This may also be used to count syllables or phonemes within a word.

- ⊙ Clap or tap the syllables in a student's name or sounds within a word.

- ⊙ Segment using visual cues. For example, provide students with pictures such as the following:

Tell students that on the board there are four pictures, one of which starts with /l/. A teacher says the sound /l/. The student identifies that **lamp** starts with /l/. Repeat for other beginning, ending and medial sounds.

- ⊙ Elkonin Boxes may be used to teach children to segment words into phonemes. Provide students with a picture and a box for each phoneme represented in the word (important note: boxes should be for phonemes and not individual letters). As students say each sound within the word, they push one counter into place, such as with the example to the right.

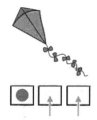

Blending

Blending, often understood as the opposite of segmenting, is the ability to sequence sounds together to form words. For example, after saying the individual sounds /d/ /o/ /g/, those sounds can be said quickly to form the word **dog**. When students have difficulties blending sounds smoothly and cohesively while reading, comprehension may be at risk. For example, while reading a paragraph imagine hearing multiple words as single phonemes (i.e. the word **mat** as /m/ /a/ /t/ instead of **mat**) rather than as blended words.

When children are provided with enough exposure and practice opportunities, their blending skills are more advanced by the time they begin to read. Below are several suggestions that can be used to teach, practice and assess blending skills (note that often activities used to promote blending are similar to those that target segmenting):

- ⊙ Stretch Words/Bubble Gum Words - Say a word (example: **flat**). Repeat the word slowly, "stretching it out" like bubble gum, (ffff-llll-aaaaa-t). Students can repeat, saying both the word and the "stretched out" version. It is important to note that when stretching the sounds within a word, some sounds such as /t/, /k/, /d/, /b/, etc. are "short" or "quick" sounds. They do not stretch, but rather they should be said (even when being said while stretching a word) in a short, quick manner. Otherwise, it becomes difficult to decipher the word being stretched (i.e. **flat** becomes ffff-llll-aaaa-t-t-t-t-t with the **t** being accented several times as the sound cannot be held).

- ⊙ Practice making words – provide students with a picture or say a word aloud. Using letter tiles, cards or magnets, have them stretch and create the word. Create blending charts that allow children to segment each sound heard within a word and then say the word fast. For example:

- ⊙ Use visuals to reinforce awareness that sounds and words carry meaning. Provide students with pictures, such as those below. Say a word slowly (beeeeee), emphasizing each sound, while students guess the correct picture.

To make the activity more challenging, use pictures corresponding to words that begin with the same sound, such as the following:

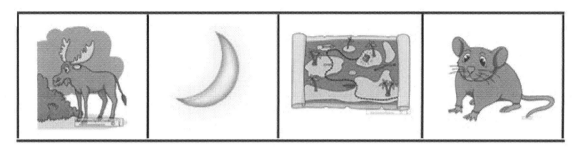

Deletion

Deletion, a more complex activity, requires an understanding that when a sound is omitted, the rest of the word and/or sounds remain. For example, if the /p/ were omitted from the word **pat,** the word **at** would remain. Deletion is typically a precursor to a child's ability to substitute sounds or letters within words.

Strategies & Methods to Assess

⊙ An excellent way to introduce deletion is through compound words. For example, ask students the following:
> Say **mailbox**. Now say it again without saying **mail.** [box]
> Say **hotdog**. Now say it again without saying **hot**. [dog]

⊙ When students are able to confidently delete using compound words, they should progress to deleting phonemes through questions such as the following:
> Say **mat** without the /m/ sound. [at]
> Say **mat** without the /t/ sound. [ma]

⊙ Have students identify the deleted sound. For example:
> What is missing from **feet** when I say **eat**? /f/
> What is missing from **ball** when I say **all?** /b/

⊙ Double consonants, such as those in the word **stalk**, can be challenging for students. Provide exposure to questions such as the following:
> What happens to the word **stalk** if you take out the /k/? [stall]

Provide students with picture cards such as those below. Ask the following: What does **train** becomes when you leave out /t/?

Substitution

Substitution, changing a sound or combination of sounds in a word to create a new word, is one of the more difficult phonological awareness tasks. For example, if the first sound in **bet** were changed from /b/ to /l/, the word would become **let**. As with the other skills, the first sound is the easiest to manipulate. The last sound and the medial sounds can be more difficult.

Because of the challenging nature, modeling, instruction and practice opportunities are beneficial.

Strategies & Methods to Assess

When introducing substituting, pictures or letters can show how new words are formed when one sound is changed. For example, a student sees a picture of a bat and the word bat printed on the board. The teacher says the word bat aloud and asks what the word would be if the /b/ sound changed to /k/. After students identify the word **cat**, the instructor repeats it and a picture of a cat is shown. The teacher then says cat and asks what the new word would be if the /k/ sound changed to an /h/. After students identify the new word, a picture of a hat is shown, etc.

⊙ Word Ladders can be excellent activities to encourage children to manipulate words using substitution. Word ladders may be done as a group or independent activity. Students may begin with one word or may be given a beginning word as well as an ending word. Below are two examples of word ladders:

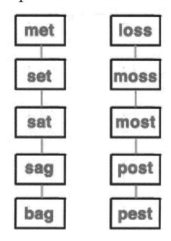

⊙ Depending on students' age, songs and games are another enjoyable way to work on phonological skills and more specifically, substitution. One method is to have a volunteer say his or her name aloud. Students can clap syllables of the name, stretch it out, say it fast, and generate a rhyme by substituting a different phoneme. Also, several songs such as the following exist where students can substitute specific sounds. Students begin by learning the basic song/chant:

I like to eat, eat, eat apples and bananas, apples and bananas.

Next, they substitute one particular long vowel sound each time they come across a vowel:

Substitute /ā/:
I like to āte, āte, āte, āpples and bānānās, āpples and bānānās

Substitute /ē/:
I like to ēte, ēte, ēte, ēpples and bēnēnēs, ēpples and bēnēnēs...

Conclusion

Utilizing a variety of phonological awareness activities to assess and provide practice opportunities for students is crucial. The more exposure students have, the easier it will be for them to use decoding strategies when they stumble upon difficult text while reading. As a result, reading will likely be easier and more enjoyable.

STRATEGIES FOR ASSESSING & TEACHING PRACTICE

1. **What skill does a child who can clap the number of syllables in a word demonstrate?**
   A. Phonological awareness by segmenting
   B. Phonemic awareness by blending
   C. Phonemic awareness by segmenting
   D. Phonological awareness by substituting

2. **Knowledge of onset/rime can best benefit a student in reading which word?**
   A. Plate
   B. Where
   C. Said
   D. Ice

3. **Which of the following skills is generally considered the most difficult?**
   A. Segmenting words in a sentence
   B. Blending phonemes into words
   C. Deleting phonemes from a one-syllable word
   D. Substituting one phoneme for another in a one-syllable word

4. **How do blending skills influence reading comprehension?**
   A. Blending is an important practice skill, but not incorporated into reading text.
   B. Difficulty with blending can result in choppy reading skills, which interferes with comprehension.

C. Blending difficulty can pose problems for learning letter names and sounds.

D. Students who can segment and blend sounds well do not need deleting and substituting skills.

5. **Mark can easily count the number of phonemes in a word. He also can accurately blend sounds to make a word. What would be the next logical skill for him to work on?**
   A. Reading print
   B. Recognizing rhymes in isolation activities
   C. Deleting phonemes from one-syllable words
   D. Segmenting syllables

6. **Sara is a kindergartener who can identify the first sound in the word log, but she cannot identify the three individual sounds. The next instruction should be in ___.**
   A. Generating rhymes
   B. Segmenting sounds of a syllable
   C. Deleting part of a compound word
   D. Substituting one sound for another

7. **Chris is a kindergartener who can easily clap the number of words in a sentence. He can somewhat count the number of syllables in a word, but he has great difficulty distinguishing the number of sounds in a syllable or word. Which statement best describes Chris?**
   A. He has highly developed advanced phonological and phonemic awareness skills.
   B. He has developed phonemic awareness skills, but he needs to work on phonological awareness skills.
   C. He has developed some phonological skills, but he needs to work on phonemic skills.
   D. He is ready for phonics.

8. A teacher displays four images: a web, a bus, a bike, and a rake. She then says bus slowly, emphasizing each sound and its connection to the next. She asks students to point to the appropriate picture. Which skill is the teacher practicing?
    A. Segmenting
    B. Blending
    C. Deleting
    D. Rhyming

9. Which of the following activities is an effective means of practicing deleting?
    A. Showing a picture of a cat and saying cat slowly to emphasize each sound.
    B. Showing a picture of a snake and asking students to clap the number of sounds they hear.
    C. Showing a picture of a cat and asking what would happen if you changed the last sound in cat to /p/.
    D. Showing a picture of a dog and asking what would be left if you took off the initial /d/ sound.

10. Which activity is appropriate for assessing phonemic awareness?
    A. Clap the syllables in mailbox.
    B. What word do these sounds make /h/ /op/?
    C. Do these words rhyme? Chair/Bear
    D. What sounds are in the word block?

STRATEGIES FOR ASSESSING & TEACHING EXPLANATIONS

1. A   The child is not being asked to identify or manipulate phonemes; thus clapping syllables is a phonological awareness skill. The ability to hear and identify different syllables in a word is the phonological awareness skill (not phonemic awareness—C) of segmenting. As the name indicates, segmenting involves breaking and distinguishing the syllables in a word or the phonemes in a syllable. Blending (B) can be thought of as the

opposite of segmenting. It involves the ability to correctly blend sounds. Substituting (D) involves swapping sounds to create new meaning, and it can be thought of as the most difficult task out of the above choices.

2. A   Plate has an onset (pl-) and a common word family rime (-ate), where (B) and said (C) are sight words not decoded with onset/rime skills. Ice (D) does not have an onset (because there are no consonants preceding the vowel).

3. D   Although each child has individual strengths and weaknesses, the above skills are presented in order of difficulty according to how the typical brain processes language. Segmenting, or breaking words, is the simplest (A), followed by blending (B), or the ability to coherently combine sounds in a word. Deleting (C), or taking out sounds to make new words, is an advanced concept, but it is simpler than the most complex, substituting (D), which entails manipulating sounds by changing them with other sounds to make new words.

4. B   Blending problems affect how well students can form words from phonemes. Choppy sounds slow reading and impede the ability to understand what is read, particularly with longer words and sentences. All skills associated with phonological and phonemic awareness influence reading skills and reading comprehension, which makes choices A and D incorrect. Difficulties blending (C) do not pose a problem learning letter names and sounds because learning the names and sounds typically precedes blending.

5. C   Mark can blend, so the next skill would be deleting. It is important to consider the order in which skills are developed. The test asks about the next skill given in a specific situation to assess your understanding of how phonological and phonemic skills vary in difficulty. If Mark can count the number of phonemes, he likely has already developed the ability to recognize rhymes (B) and segment syllables (D). The student would likely benefit from further awareness instruction and phonics instruction before reading text (A).

6. B   Segmenting is the ability to count and identify words in a sentence, syllables in a word, and phonemes in a word. Most reading programs recommend work with rhymes (A) before segmenting. Because deleting, which is omitting a word part or phoneme (C), and substituting, which is substituting one phoneme for another (D), are more complex skills, they follow segmenting.

7. C Phonemic awareness deals specifically with the most basic unit, the phoneme (the smallest unit of language). The ability to segment into words and syllables is a phonological awareness skill. If he could segment phonemes, Chris would have phonemic awareness (B). Chris has not developed advanced phonological and phonemic awareness (A) He would benefit from further instruction on phonemic awareness before beginning phonics (D).

8. B Blending is the ability to join sounds in a word coherently and smoothly. Modeling the blending of a word by stretching the sounds can be an effective strategy to promote the development of blending skills. Segmenting (A) is a similar skill, but a student practicing segmenting would give the response in separate phonemes. Deleting (C) requires removing a sound in bus. Rhyming (D) is generating or recognizing a word with a similar sound from the last vowel onward.

9. D Deleting is the ability to understand what sounds are left or how a word changes if a particular sound is deleted. Blending (A) is stretching the sounds; clapping syllables is segmenting (B); changing one sound for another (C) is substitution.

10. D Identifying phonemes in a word is a phonemic awareness skill. Identifying syllables (A), blending onset-rime (B), and rhymes (C) are phonological awareness skills.

1.3   Chapter Review

1. How does phonological awareness impact reading development?
- A. In order to be able read print words, students must understand that print letters correspond to sounds, and that sounds carry meaning.
- B. Reading print can be easier when a student demonstrates phonemic awareness skills.
- C. Students who are strong readers must demonstrate phonemic awareness skills. Phonological awareness skills are less important.
- D. Students who are strong readers must demonstrate phonological awareness skills. Phonemic awareness skills are less important.

2.   A teacher designs the following lesson plan:

1. Sing "Row row row your boat"
2. Say aloud stream, dream
3. Ask students to repeat
4. Oddity activity: Do these words rhyme: dream, team, stream, strap?

The lesson plan would be most appropriate in conjunction with which of the following activities in order to promote phonological awareness?
- A. Model how to divide stream and dream into onset and rime.
- B. Ask students to draw a picture that represents a stream and a dream.
- C. Ask students, "Who remembers a dream they have had?"
- D. Model how to identify all of the phonemes in the words "stream and dream."

3.   A teacher has recently worked on segmenting words into syllables in a kindergarten class. Which of the following would be a logical skill to introduce next?
- A. Blending phonemes
- B. Blending syllables
- C. Substituting medial vowels
- D. Deleting first consonants

4. A student with strong phonemic awareness skills can demonstrate which of the following?

A. The student can identify the consonant sound at the beginning of the word **hat**.

B. The student can tell the two parts in the word **rainbow**.

C. The student can identify the medial vowels in the word **skate**.

D. The student can accurately segment a sentence.

5. Clapping each word in a sentence would promote which of the following phonological awareness skills?

A. Deleting

B. Substituting

C. Blending

D. Segmenting

6. Which of the following skills demonstrates the highest level of phonemic awareness?

A. Name all of the sounds in the word "supper."

B. Name the medial vowel sound in the word "time."

C. Name the initial consonant sound in the word "jam."

D. Name the final consonant sound in the word "roof."

7. A teacher wants to promote substituting skills in a first-grade class. Which of the following activities would promote substituting of phonemes?

A. The teacher shows an image of a dog, a desk, and a duck. The teacher slowly says "duuuuu……" and waits for students to indicate the picture of the duck.

B. The teacher says aloud, "I went to the beach and I took a blanket." Students take turns replacing "blanket" with their own object.

C. The teacher shows an image of a fan, a man, and a ham. The teacher says, "What if I change the first sound in the word "ran" to /f/ ? The students then point to the image of a fan.

D. The teacher reads aloud a list of compound words and asks students to jump up and down each time a different syllable is said.

8. A teacher writes up the following report of a kindergartener's phonological awareness skills: "Samantha can identify onsets of monosyllabic words, but she is unable to correctly indicate initial consonants." Which of the following skills could Samantha most likely do according to this assessment?

    A. Samantha can hear that "stop" starts with "st-".
    B. Samantha can clap each phoneme in the word "stop."
    C. Samantha can identify that "stop" ends in "p."
    D. Samantha can identify the medial vowel in the word "stop."

9. A first-grader with average phonemic awareness skills shows difficulty deleting final consonants. Which of the following would be the first thing the teacher should do?

    A. Determine if the student can identify medial vowels.
    B. Determine if the student can segment the syllables in a word.
    C. Determine if the student can delete the initial consonant in a word.
    D. Determine if the student can substitute final consonants to make new words.

10. What is a possible explanation for a proficient reader's comparatively easy, rapid beginning reading development?

    A. Students are able to convert phonological awareness to the phonological processing needed for reading.
    B. Students have benefited from intervention from specialists.
    C. English phonemes are not in the student's native language.
    D. Metacognitive comprehension strategies are being used effectively.

11. A student is struggling with hearing rhymes and he requires one-on-one explicit instruction. Which of the following activities would a teacher use?

    A. The teacher sings "Row row row your boat"
    B. The teacher says the nursery rhyme "Little Miss Muffet"
    C. The teacher breaks the word "frog" into onsets and rimes and models how to make new words by changing the onset.
    D. The teacher plays "Miss Mary Mack" with the student.

12. **A teacher provides students three pictures: a bed, a cat, and a sock. The teacher says, "Which of the following words has the sound /e/ in it?" Based on the teacher's question, the students most likely have already worked on which of the following?**
    A. identifying initial and final consonant sounds
    B. segmenting medial vowel sounds
    C. blending compound words
    D. deleting initial sounds

13. **A teacher uses pictures when teaching blending skills. Which of the following is a reason for doing so?**
    A. Reinforces that words and sounds have meaning
    B. Promotes phonological awareness skills
    C. Promotes phonemic awareness skills
    D. Encourages phonics skills

14. **During an assessment of blending skills, a teacher shows a student pictures of a house, grass, and a car. The teacher says aloud "hou......." and the student quickly points to the house. Which of the following would be a logical next step?**
    A. The teacher puts up images of a ball, a wall, a mall, and a frog. The student indicates which word does not belong.
    B. The teacher asks the student to segment "house" into phonemes.
    C. The teacher puts up images of a hat, a house, and a ham, and asks the student to identify the first consonant sound.
    D. The teacher does the same activity, but this time using images of a hat, a house, and a ham.

15. **A first-grade teacher is starting to introduce deleting skills. Where would be a good place to start?**
    A. Say aloud the word "football" and ask them what happens if you take away "ball."
    B. Say aloud the word "tall" and ask them what happens if you take away the /t/ sound.

C. Say aloud the word "mat" and then model what happens when the /m/ sound becomes the /k/ sound.

D. Say aloud the word "spark" and divide the onset and rime.

16. **A teacher asks a first-grader to substitute the /t/ in "tip" with /l/. The student accurately produces the new word, "lip." The teacher then asks the student to replace the /p/ in "lip" with /d/. The student accurately says, "lid." The teacher then asks the student to identify the first sound in the word "mother." The student says /m/. The teacher asks the student to replace the /m/ in "mother" with /br/. The student is unable to find the new word. Which of the following assessments would be accurate of this student's skills?**

A. The student has advanced phonemic awareness skills.

B. The student needs practice substituting phonemes in multisyllabic words.

C. The student works well with initial and final consonants of monosyllabic and multisyllabic words.

D. The student works well with monosyllabic words but needs to work on segmenting multisyllabic words.

17. **Students are given index cards with different letters written on them. The teacher then puts up on the board an index card that says "PART." The teacher asks one student to take away the /p/ and say the word left. Next, students take turns putting up different letters in front of "ART," each time saying aloud the new word. What is the pedagogical reason for doing this activity?**

A. The teacher wants to promote word identification skills.

B. The teacher wants to promote deleting and substituting skills.

C. The teacher wants to promote segmenting and substituting.

D. The teacher wants to promote word identification and deleting skills.

18. **An English Language Learner has shown an ability to identify and manipulate the individual sounds in a word. However, the student has difficulty indicating the appropriate visual cue for an activity where the teacher asks students to point to the picture of the word created when the /p/ in "pail" becomes /t/. Which of the following should the teacher work on with this student to promote phonological awareness skills?**
    A. Teach letter names in addition to phonemes that may not exist in the student's first language.
    B. Teach common rimes that may not exist in the student's first language in conjunction with segmenting skills.
    C. Teach vocabulary in conjunction with phonological awareness skills.
    D. Teach songs that model rhyming in addition to presenting print cues.

19. **Which of the following is an example of how skills on the phonemic awareness continuum contribute to reading development?**
    A. Automaticity in reading sight words contributes to fluency.
    B. Blending oral sounds promotes using letter-sound knowledge to blend printed words.
    C. Environmental print awareness contributes to internalizing the alphabetic principle.
    D. Segmenting syllables promotes the ability to analyze multi-syllable words

20. **Which of the following students is demonstrating phonemic awareness?**
    A. While pretending to read a book he's written himself, a student appropriately tracks text from left to right.
    B. A student correctly states opposites for each of the following words: stop, up, yes.
    C. A student is consistently able to identify the first and last sounds in CVC words.
    D. A student is able to clap the syllables in multi-syllable words.

CHAPTER REVIEW EXPLANATIONS

1. **A** Phonological awareness, which encompasses phonemic awareness, is necessary in order for students to be able to move on to phonics and reading print. Students who have difficulty hearing and manipulating sounds may seriously struggle with reading and reading comprehension. Choice B is worded in a way that suggests phonemic awareness is helpful but not necessary. It is, however, necessary in order for a child to continue developing strong reading skills. Choice C is incorrect because phonemic awareness is a type of phonological awareness. Choice D is also incorrect because both phonological and the subset phonemic awareness are important to students' reading development.

2. **A** This teacher is using an implicit activity, a popular song, to work on rhyming. Another way to work on rhyming is to encourage segmenting and playing with words by dividing them into onsets and rimes. Students can then practice rhyming by changing the rime, or the part of a word that encompasses the vowel and remaining sounds (dr-eam, str-eam). Choices B and C would reinforce that words and sounds carry meaning, and they would also engage students, but they wouldn't necessarily work on promoting phonological awareness. Choice D, identifying all of the sounds in those words by segmenting phonemes, is a complex phonemic awareness skill that would probably be too advanced for a class still working on rhyming.

3. **B** This class is working on segmenting syllables, such as dividing "mother" into "mo-ther." The question does not mention if the students have worked on segmenting phonemes, or the individual sounds:"m-o-th-r". Since working on the level of phonemes is more advanced than working on the word level, jumping to the blending of phonemes, choice A, may be too quick. Segmenting sounds would be a logical step before going on to blending phonemes. It'd be more effective for students to learn choice B, blending syllables, since they've learned segmenting syllables. Choices C and D involve the more complex tasks of substituting and deleting phonemes, and are therefore too advanced.

4. **C** Phonemic awareness is a type of phonological awareness that deals strictly with phonemes, or sound units. Choice B deals with syllables and word parts, which may not necessarily entail phonemes. Choice D is

segmenting a sentence, which is part of phonological awareness skills, but not phonemic awareness skills. In general, the initial sound like in choice A is the first students encounter. Next is the final consonant, and then the medial vowels are the most advanced.

5. D Segmenting words means that students can identify each separate word in a sentence. For example, they can separate out each word in the sentence "I-have-a-sister." Deleting, choice A, involves looking at a word and removing a sound or part in order to create a new word. Similarly, choice B is substituting a sound or part in order to make a new word. Blending, choice C, is fluidly combining sounds or words to make words and sentences. Blending is sort of the opposite of segmenting; it works on accurately pronouncing and blending different sounds and words, while segmenting divides sounds and words.

6. A The most difficult phonemic awareness skill in terms of identifying sounds is to name all of the sounds in a word. Choice C is the easiest, since students often learn to identify the initial sound first. Choice D, the final consonant sound, would be next after the initial consonant sound. After the final sound, the medial vowel can be explored, leading up to the ability to name all of the sounds in a word, which would be demonstrating advanced phonemic awareness skills.

7. C Substituting involves replacing a phoneme or group of phonemes with another in order to make new words. For example, in choice C, the student must make "fan" from "ran." Choice A is a blending activity since the student must predict what word will be said by hearing the first few sounds stretched out. Choice B works on substituting words, not phonemes or individual sounds. Choice D works on identifying and segmenting syllables, but again, a syllable could be made up of numerous phonemes, and it also is not a substituting activity.

8. A This student has started to develop phonological awareness by being able to hear onsets of monosyllabic words, like in choice A. Choice B involves phonemic awareness skills since it requires Samantha to clap each individual sound. Given her ability, choices C and D are unlikely, since they deal with more complex skills. Choice C is identifying the final consonant, which usually comes after identifying the initial consonant, a skill Samantha has not yet grasped. Choice D is even harder since it involves the medial vowel, which often is learned after the initial and the final.

9. C If the student is unable to work with final consonants, the teacher would first look at what the student is able to do. Medial vowels, choice A, are more difficult than final consonants, so that would be illogical. Choice D deals with substituting, which is more difficult than deletion, so that also would be illogical. Choice B involves identifying syllables, whereas this question asks about phonemes, or final consonants. It would not be logical to be working on individual sounds and to then go back to the question of syllables, since phonemes are harder to manipulate than syllables and word parts.

10. A Phonological processing is a complex process that integrates such skills as phonological awareness and knowledge of the phonemic code to enable a child to become a proficient reader. Choice B is illogical since a beginning proficient reader would likely not have received intervention. English phonemes missing from a native language would be an explanation for a struggling reader, not a proficient reader (C). Metacognitive strategies for comprehension (D) are not an explanation for beginning reading success.

11. C Explicit instruction is an important part of reading instruction, especially for struggling students. Choices A, B and D all are tailored to promote students' ability to hear and repeat rhymes, but the activities are implicit because they do not provide overt and direct instruction. Explicit instruction means that the teacher provides an explanation and models the concept, then providing practice. Implicit, like nursery rhymes, is less obvious. Students may work on rhyming without even knowing it. In explicit activities, students know what to look for and have an example to model.

12. A If the teacher is asking students to identify the /e/ sound or the medial vowels, the students are working on one of the more difficult parts of sound identification. The initial and the final consonant sounds tend to be tackled before medial vowels, all of which comes before being able to identify each individual phoneme. Choice B, segmenting medial vowels, is more difficult than identifying those vowels, although the two abilities work together. It would make more sense to first work on identifying in order to move on to segmenting. Choices C, and D are more advanced skills than identifying vowels. Blending compound words, choice C, is more difficult than monosyllabic words, too. Deleting tends to be one of the more difficult tasks along with substituting phonemes.

13. **A**   Visual cues can be helpful for many reasons. They engage students, thereby promoting active learning, but they also can reinforce that the sounds and words they make have meaning. While print awareness is part of the reading development process, the pictures themselves would not promote phonological and phonemic awareness skills. The pictures would have to be followed with an activity on sounds. Similarly, phonics deals with letter-sound correspondences, and thus is not connected to the role of visuals in this activity.

14. **D**   Since the teacher is working on blending skills in this assessment as the question indicates, the choice should include blending. This question involves blending and visual identification with words that are all distinctly different. Choice D does the same, but with words that all start with the same sound, making it more complex. Choice A works on word identification skills, not blending. Choice B deals with segmenting. Choice C promotes phonemic awareness skills and identification of initial consonants, which is not necessarily blending.

15. **A**   Compound words like hotdog, mailbox or football can be good starting points since it's easier to see what happens when numerous sounds are removed. Choice B is more difficult because it targets deleting an initial consonant, whereas choice A is a distinct group of words. Choice C is more for substituting sounds to make new words. Choice D, onsets and rimes, is usually learned before deleting. Plus, it would be more difficult to take away the onset than an entire word like in choice A.

16. **B**   The student shows an ability to substitute initial and final consonants in monosyllabic words (words that contain only one syllable, like "top"). The example also tells us that the student can identify the initial sound in a multisyllabic word (words that contain more than one syllable, like "mother"). Given that the student is unable to substitute the initial sound, it is most likely that the student needs practice substituting, or changing sounds to make new words, in multisyllabic words. This student doesn't show an ability to fully manipulate sounds, making choice A incorrect. Choice C is incorrect because we are not given evidence that the student works well with the final consonant of multisyllabic words. In the example, the student only identifies the initial sound in "mother"--not the final. Choice C thus makes an assumption. Choice D discusses segmenting, which is possibly true. The student may need segmenting help in multisyllabic words, but the question more clearly points to difficulty with substitution.

17. B This activity works both deleting and substituting skills. When the teacher asks the student to take away "p" and say "art," the student is deleting a sound in order to make a new one. By substituting "p" with another letter, students are working on making new words by changing sounds. Choice A, word identification, involves identifying words that do not belong with others in some way. For example, a student picks out the word that doesn't rhyme in "hound, found, round, over." Segmenting, choice C, would require the students to divide the different phonemes in "part" or their new word. Since word identification is not correct, choice D is also not the right answer.

18. C This student is able to identify sounds, but the visual cues are what prove confusing. This is most likely due to a lack of vocabulary, which some ELL learners may demonstrate. Vocabulary, choice C, would be helpful for this student. Choice A involves letter names, which is most likely too complex for the student at this point. Letter names often come after phonological awareness skills instruction. Common rimes, choice B, like "-art" or "-ar" could be helpful, but since the student has shown phonological awareness, rimes are most likely too easy. Similarly, choice D would be beneficial for reinforcing that print and sounds carry meaning and are related, but this student can probably rhyme.

19. B Blending is a phonemic awareness skill that is important in reading development. While reading sight words (A), environmental print awareness (C), and segmenting syllables (D) all contribute to reading development, they are not phonemic awareness skills.

20. C Phonemic awareness refers to a child's ability to identify and manipulate individual phonemes within words. The student who is able to identify the first and last sounds within words is demonstrating phonemic awareness, making Choice C the best answer. While the skills demonstrated in the other choices are also important for children to acquire, they are not indicative of phonemic awareness. Pretending to read a book and track text (Choice A) demonstrates the student's understanding that text is read from left-to-right, also known as concept of print. Choice B shows a student's understanding of opposites, and the student in Choice D demonstrates phonological awareness but not phonemic awareness because the task does not require the student to identify or manipulate phonemes.

Chapter 2:
Print, Alphabetic Principle and Phonics

Lessons

2.1   Print Basics

In literate societies, the written word has major significance. Print carries meaning in our daily lives as communication and self-expression. Diaries, journals, letters, and to-do lists transmit personal and interpersonal meaning. The professional world of contracts, signatures, newspapers, and documents also supports the power of print in our society. So how do we begin to understand the function of print?

The Importance of Print

Before children begin to learn about sounds and letters in the classroom, they have been surrounded by print. In the home, children see notes, magazines, cards, books, and many other types of print. Outside, they also see print on signs and on storefronts in ink and in other materials.

TARGET

Environmental print is the print of everyday life, and a print-rich environment is one in which different forms of print surround the child. As young children become aware of the print, they begin to recognize signs and labels and "read" them. Similarly, children begin to write squiggly lines under their drawing and "read" their stories. Their reading and scribbles demonstrate print awareness, meaning that the child is aware that print carries meaning, that speech can be translated into print, and that print can be translated into speech. They are attempting to interact with that print. This child understands that reading is tied to the print on a page and is not the same as talking about an illustration.

In the classroom, assessment of print awareness can conducted formally and informally. In creative play, does the child "write" a menu with squiggly lines? Does he "write" notes to friends or family and retell the meaning of his scribbles? Does he pretend read books with attention to the print in addition to the illustration? All of these activities suggest that the child is distinguishing print and other graphics and understands that print is used to encode speech.

Print awareness also includes an understanding that words convey thoughts, words are made of letters, and spaces appear between words. The learner comprehends that writing can happen with pencil, marker, chalk, and other media and that print has different functions including stories, greeting cards, calendars, and menus.

Researchers know that environmental print contributes to emergent reading or to the pretend reading that children do when they see familiar signs and labels around them. However, whether environmental print awareness directly predicts later literacy levels is contested. Whitehurst and Lonigan (1998) concluded that environmental print awareness did not influence one's long-term reading ability. Even so, while children develop print awareness in and outside the classroom, explicit instruction can help children of all environments learn to read. The following strategies are guidelines for how teachers can promote print awareness in the classroom:

- Label objects such as the door, window, and desk.
- Put nametags on students' desks.
- Have toys based on letters and words with which children can play.
- Have large books that emphasize letters.
- Designate and label parts of the classroom, i.e. the "class library."
- Read predictable text books where the illustrations are closely tied to the text and vary from page to page.
- Scribe student words either as a class activity or one-on-one. The teacher can write verbatim the words of a student as the student speaks and then read the words back to the child, demonstrating that speech can be encoded in to writing and later decoded into speech.

Book Handling Skills

Learners also need book handling skills which include holding a book upright, being able to identify the cover and back, identifying the title, beginning, middle, and end of a book, and knowing to begin reading on the first page.

The best strategy for promoting book handling skills and print directionality is regular modeling of how books and print are read. During story time, engage students in page turning and ask them to point to the cover and back.

Print Directionality

In addition, readers must understand print directionality in English. Whereas some traditional Asian languages were written from right to left, English print
moves from left to right and from top to bottom. Readers must also perform what some call a "return sweep."
Reading involves moving from left to right to the last
word on the line and then returning to the left to continue to the next line in a book.

One of the most common methods for teaching print
directionality is to follow the text with your finger during story time to model to
students that we read from left to right. Students in a 1:1 or small-group setting
can also be encouraged to follow with their finger in books during reading. The
more often children see how adults read, the more prepared they will be when
tackling print words.

One strategy to promote an understanding of print directionality is the use of a
pointer. The teacher can use a large pointer to show 1:1 correspondence between
spoken and written words. While reading, the teacher naturally moves from
left to right. Students can be invited to take a turn with the pointer and demonstrate 1:1 correspondence and print directionality.

PRINT BASICS PRACTICE

1. **Print awareness does not include which of the following?**
   A. Understanding that printed numbers carry meaning
   B. Understanding that printed words carry meaning
   C. Understanding that in English print moves from top to bottom and
      from left to right.
   D. Understanding that spoken language can be broken into sounds

2. **What is print directionality?**
   A. A way to describe how print reads from left to right and top to bottom
   B. The way directions to activities are worded to ensure
      comprehension
   C. The method for teaching the direction of letters
   D. The method for following text with your finger

3. **Which of the following is not an example of a way to promote book handling skills?**
   A. Engaging the child in page turning
   B. Pointing out the cover and back
   C. Showing that page numbers increase
   D. Using a pointer to practice one-to-one correspondence of spoken and written words on a pocket chart

4. **Which of the following is <u>false</u> about environmental print?**
   A. Environmental print includes words and print that surround children daily.
   B. Children often show emergent reading by pretending to read familiar signs or visible print.
   C. Environmental print has a clear correlation to one's later reading abilities.
   D. Environmental print contributes to children's print awareness skills.

5. **Which of the following is an example of good book handling skills?**
   A. Claire picks up a book, turns it to the cover, and reads from the last page.
   B. Pat picks up a book, turns to the cover, and begins to read on the first page.
   C. Henry picks up a book, turns to a random page, and begins to play read.
   D. John picks up a book, identifies the cover and the back, and reads from the back.

6. **Which of the following scenarios would be an effective strategy to promote print awareness?**
   A. A kindergarten teacher labels objects and areas such as the door, window, and math center.
   B. A kindergarten teacher claps a gong while sounding each syllable in a word.

C. A first-grade teacher asks students to substitute the first letter of their name with a letter of their choice.

D. A first-grade teacher hands out letter tiles and asks students to spell their name.

7. **In the dramatic play center, a preschool child creates a menu by drawing a pizza and writing a scribbled line below it. He asks his classmate what kind of pizza he wants. This type of play suggests that the child**

A. understands that speech can be encoded into writing.

B. understands that print is distinct from pictures.

C. understands that words are made of separate phonemes which can be written in graphemes.

D. understands that the English is an alphabetic language.

8. **A child looks at a book and turns to the back. She looks at the last page and begins to pretend to read what is on the page. Which of the following would be an accurate assessment of this child's skills?**

A. The child has developed phonics skills.

B. The child has developed phonological awareness and print awareness.

C. The child shows a basic understanding of print awareness, but she has not mastered book handling skills.

D. The child has basic print awareness skills and advanced book handling skills.

9. **A first-grader is having difficulty tracking print in connected text. What is one strategy a teacher can use to promote reading development in tracking?**

A. The teacher can read the sentence and follow with her finger to model the direction it is read.

B. The teacher can point out the title, beginning, middle, and end of a book.

C. The teacher can place toys dealing with words and letters in the classroom.

D. The teacher can clap each time a word is read aloud.

10. **A young child has seen a note with her mother's phone number on the fridge for months. She looks at the note and pretends to punch the numbers into her play phone.**
   What is she demonstrating?
   A. The child is showing awareness of environmental print.
   B. The child is showing phonological awareness.
   C. The child is showing phonemic awareness.
   D. The child is showing book handling skills.

PRINT BASICS EXPLANATIONS

1. D   Print awareness is the understanding that written language (both letters and numbers) carries meaning. It includes print directionality from top to bottom and left to right, which makes A, B, and C all correct. Choice d deals with spoken language, or phonological awareness. Test questions often ask you to distinguish between skills and awareness for print or spoken language, so you should check which is referenced in the question.

2. A   Print directionality refers to awareness that in English, we read starting at the left side of the page and moving to the right. We also go from top to bottom, meaning that the first sentence read is the first on the page. Choices B and C contain "directions," which can make them seem viable answers, but reading instructions and writing letters are more advanced skills than learners have at the stage of developing print directionality. Choice D is a good strategy for developing print awareness and modeling print directionality, but it is not the definition.

3. D   Choices A, B, and C target book handling skills that involve knowing how to properly hold a book by looking at the cover rather than the back, knowing that the story begins on the first page, and understanding that the story progresses by turning the page. Choice D is the only one not targeting book handling skills. It addresses print awareness, which includes an understanding that words convey thoughts, letters are made up of words, and words have spaces between them.

4. C   As choices A, B, and D explain, environmental print refers to print that surrounds children daily in the house and in public. Because of this frequent exposure, children often demonstrate emergent reading by pretending to read signs or words they often see and know have a meaning,

even if they cannot read the individual words. Although we know that environmental print contributes to print awareness, or the understanding that print carries meaning, choice C is correct because researchers have not determined that environmental print correlates to weak reading abilities later in life. In other words, the classroom is particularly important because even children who do not grow up in "print-rich" environments can master reading with the help of teachers.

5. **B** In choice A, Claire knows that books can be read, and she can identify the cover, but she has not yet developed understanding that the story is read from the pages following the cover, which is part of good book handling skills. The same can be said for choice D; the child has not mastered identifying the cover and back besides the idea that the story begins on the first page. Choice C shows that Henry has print awareness, because he pretends to read, but again, he turns to a random page because he does not understand that the story begins at the beginning.

6. **A** To promote understanding that print carries meaning, choice a, labeling objects in a classroom, can be a great place to start. Choices B and C involve phonological awareness skills; choice B targets segmenting, whereas choice C is for substituting skills. Choice D asks students to spell their names, which is too advanced for children at a level where they are developing print awareness.

7. **B** By writing scribbles under a picture, the child demonstrates an understanding that print has a separate function from pictures. Such behavior does not necessarily indicate that he understands that speech can be encoded (A), or that English words are made of separate sounds (phonemes) that can be written as in symbols (graphemes) (C). Choice D is a rewording of Choice C: the alphabetic principle states that in English, there is a relationship between speech and written letters.

8. **C** Is it not possible to determine whether this child has mastered phonics or phonological awareness, which eliminates choices A and B, because there is no indication about the child's ability to manipulate spoken language and distinguish phonemes. However, the child shows some print awareness by understanding that print in a book tells a story and carries meaning. Choice D is incorrect because the child, turning to the last page, has not mastered book handling skills.

9. A   Tracking print in connected text involves understanding that we read from left to right and top to bottom. It also includes one-to-one correspondence. Showing a student how to use your finger to follow along the sentence from left to right and then having the student do the same, choice A, is the best strategy. In choice B, the teacher promotes book handling skills. In choice C, the teacher's actions promote print awareness more than print directionality. Choice D involves phonological awareness and segmenting skills because it deals with spoken language and syllables.

10. A   This child demonstrates her awareness that print in her everyday life has meaning. Choices B and C require the child to show some ability to manipulate spoken language. This scenario involves print. This child has not shown book handling skills, choice D, because there is no mention of holding a book the correct way, understanding print directionality, and so on.

2.2 Alphabetic Principle & Letters

Alphabetic Principle and Letter Knowledge

The alphabetic principle tells us that there are specific relationships between written letters and spoken sounds. Teachers can use various explicit and implicit strategies to promote understanding of the alphabetic principle. The alphabetic principle states that there is a relationship between written letters and the spoken sounds of English. Many children begin school with a concept of the alphabetic principle. A lack of knowledge of letter names, shapes, and sounds hinders a student's ability to learn to read.

Effective reading instruction includes:
- ⊙ Explicit instruction
- ⊙ Sufficient practice and review
- ⊙ Appropriate opportunities to read words with the letters learned
- ⊙ Informal play with letter manipulatives and books

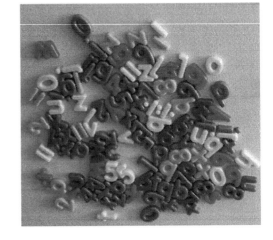

Knowledge of the alphabetic principle is evidenced in a student's ability to:
- ⊙ Identify letters (Which letter is a b?)
- ⊙ Name letters (What letter is this?)
- ⊙ Identify sounds (Which letter makes the sound /m/?)
- ⊙ Form letter sounds (What sound does *m* make?)
- ⊙ Write letters

Letter names

Research indicates that a child's ability to identify and name letters strongly indicates a child's future success in reading. Letter naming requires a student to distinguish between letters and to correspond the letter shape with the letter name. It also involves distinguishing between uppercase and lowercase letters.

Strategies

Explicit strategies that involve multisensory activities are effective for teaching letter names. For example, a teacher points to a letter and says the letter's name while students draw it on paper. Songs and rhymes are also effective for teaching letter names.

Some examples of implicit activities include:
- Letter stamps
- Flashcards
- Alphabet books
- Alphabet songs
- Forming letters out of clay

Teaching students letter names supports their learning of letter sounds. Once a basic knowledge of letter names is developed, students can progress to letter sounds and spellings.

Letter formation

Knowledge of letter shapes reinforces student understanding of the alphabetic principle. The skills of recognizing the shape of the uppercase and lowercase letters and writing the letters provide additional reinforcement of a student's knowledge of the alphabet to read successfully.

Strategies

- Matching activities with uppercase and lowercase letters
- Letter formation in sand, rice, flour

Letter-sound correspondence

To read fluently, the student must master the 44 phonemes (the basic units of sound in a language) connected to graphemes, or written letters that represent the phonemes. In professional circles, letter-sound relationships are sometimes referred to as grapho-phonemic patterns and the letters or groups of letters that represent the sounds are called phonograms.

Reading programs suggest various instructional plans. Common to the plans is that letter sounds are introduced in isolation at a rate that students can digest. High-frequency consonants (**m**, **n**, **r**, **s**, **f**) are commonly introduced first. To avoid confusion, it is best not to introduce two similar letter-sounds at the same time. Here are a few examples of similar letter-sounds that should be taught separately:

"b" and "v"
"b" and "d"
"b" and "p"
"e" and "i"
"m" and "n"

Introducing one or two short vowels (such as the "i" sound in "into" or "insect") with a few select consonants allows students to start reading words.

Explicit, teacher-directed instruction demonstrates to children that the relationship between letters and sounds is methodical and predictable. There is no need to wait until students know all letter names and sounds to begin to read words. Instruction in blending sounds into words can begin when students know several consonants and a vowel.

In addition to using letter-sound correspondence to read, students can also use the knowledge to write. Students can "write the room" in which they look for words in the room that begin with a particular letter or sound. Students can also write stories, lists, and notes by "stretching" words and writing the sounds that they hear.

Strategies

- Print a large letter on paper; students glue pictures of items beginning with that letter-sound on or around the letter.
- Display a letter and familiar objects that begin with that letter. Name an object and point to the letter. Invite students to participate.

- Oddity activities: display the letter f. Show pictures of a fan, a farm, and a vest. Which picture does not begin with f?
- Sorting activities: display the letters m, s, and r. Display pictures of a man, a mask, the sun, a sock, a robot, and rain. Students sort pictures to match initial letter sound.

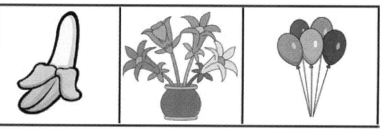

Which picture does not begin with b?

Individual students

Early intervention is critical for students who do not understand the alphabetic principle. At-risk students benefit from low teacher/student ratios and from increased instruction time. An accurate assessment can be conducted as early as kindergarten to identify students who need intervention.

Teachers can assess a student's understanding of the alphabetic principle by showing a student each uppercase and lowercase letter and asking the letter's name. In the next stage, letter cards are shown, and the student is asked the sound. Following assessment, continued monitoring keeps a teacher informed of each student's progress.

ALPHABETIC PRINCIPLE & LETTERS PRACTICE

1. Which of the following best defines the alphabetic principle?
   A. Letters and phonemes are loosely related.
   B. Letters and sounds correspond systematically and predictably.
   C. Print moves from left to right and from top to bottom on the page.
   D. Phonemes can be identified and manipulated.

2. Which statement accurately represents the alphabetic principle?
   A. Knowing letter names is a significant indicator of a child's future success in reading.
   B. Because of confusion that can arise, students should master letter sounds before being introduced to letter names.

C. Students enjoy rhymes before they develop the ability to generate rhymes.

D. An environment rich in print provides adequate support for at-risk students.

3. **Which strategy promotes internalizing the alphabetic principle?**
   A. Reading a big book and following along with one's finger
   B. Reading nursery rhymes
   C. Placing a child's picture under the letter of the alphabet that initiates the child's name
   D. Working with word families

4. **Systematically introducing isolated letters by displaying objects that begin with that letter is appropriate for which of the following?**
   A. Students who have recently mastered clapping syllables
   B. Students who have developed phonemic awareness and know most letter names
   C. Students who need explicit instruction on the formation of upper and lower case letters
   D. Students who automatically identify several high-frequency sight words

5. **Which question can be used to assess a student's knowledge of the alphabetic principle?**
   A. Do bee and tree rhyme?
   B. Which two words begin with the same sound: Cab, cod, sad?
   C. What letter makes the sound /b/?
   D. Can you show me where we start reading a book?

6. **Which sequence of letters is typical of the order in which letters are introduced?**
   A. a, e, i, o, u, b...
   B. b, d, v, f, l, r...
   C. b, bl, br, s, st, sh...
   D. m, f, n, s, r, a...

7. **Reading words by sounding out should begin**
   A. When students know a few consonants and a short vowel
   B. When students have mastered the 44 phonemes
   C. When students can identify letters by name
   D. When students can invent a sound for a letter symbol

8. **Which of the following activities should be used first to promote knowledge of the alphabetic principle in a four-year-old preschool classroom?**
   A. Read books aloud, identifying the beginning, middle and end of the story and discussing the main idea and details.
   B. As you call students one by one to line up at the door, have them clap the syllables in their name.
   C. Provide multiple opportunities for students to practice letter formation and identification such as tracing letters in shaving cream, matching uppercase and lowercase letters and identifying letters by name.
   D. Provide students with a wide range of reading materials that exposes them to a variety of genres.

9. **Which strategy best addresses the needs of first-grade students who do not understand the alphabetic principle?**
   A. Play in heterogeneous groups
   B. Student-initiated teaching moments
   C. Group recitation of nursery rhymes
   D. Small-group intensive instruction

10. **Students are shown the letter "g" and pictures of a goat, a game, a garden, a cow, and a car.**
    This activity is appropriate for which students?
    A. Language learners introduced to the letter "g"
    B. Kindergarteners who can generate rhymes
    C. First graders practicing alphabetic principle skills
    D. Kindergarteners who recognize print in their environment

1. B   The alphabetic principle states that the letters and sounds of English correspond systematically and predictably. Saying that they are "loosely" related (choice A) is incorrect. Print direction (choice C) is print awareness. Identification and manipulation of phonemes (choice D) is phonemic awareness.

2. A   Research shows that a student's ability to identify and name letters indicates future reading success. Knowing letter names supports a student in sequencing letters and forming sounds. Students typically learn letter names before sounds (choice B). Rhyme (choice C) is a phonological awareness skill. A print-rich environment is beneficial for developing print awareness (choice D), or the understanding that letters and text carry meaning, which must develop much before understanding letter-sound correspondence.

3. C   The alphabetic principle states that there is a relationship between letters and phonemes. Placing a child's picture under the initial letter of the child's name visually demonstrates that the sound of the name corresponds to a letter of the alphabet. Modeling reading by following print with the finger (choice a) promotes print awareness. Reading nursery rhymes (choice b) promotes phonological awareness. Work with word families (d) promotes phonological and phonemic awareness.

4. B   Many reading programs are designed to transition children from phonological and phonemic awareness to identifying letter names and then to identifying letter sounds. Clapping syllables (choice A) is an early phonological awareness skill and does not indicate a readiness to learn letter-sound correspondence. Letter formation (choice C) strengthens one's ability to identify letter sounds, but showing corresponding objects is not critical to learning letter formation. Instruction in letters and sounds typically precedes work with sight words (choice D).

5. C   The alphabetic principle encompasses letter names, sounds, shapes, and formation. Rhyming (choice a) and initial sounds (choice b) are phonological awareness skills. Demonstrating where to begin to read (choice d) demonstrates book handling skills.

6. D Most programs introduce high-utility consonants and a short vowel so students can read words early (man, fan, ran). Introduction of vowels first is unusual (choice A). Programs try to avoid introducing commonly confused letters (choice B). Isolated sounds are introduced before consonant blends (choice C).

7. A A goal of an effective reading program is to move students efficiently from letter sounds to reading words. Once students know a few high-utility letter sounds, they can begin to blend and to read words. Students need not wait until they have learned all 44 phonemes (choice b). Identifying letters by name (choice c) and inventing sounds (choice d) do not adequately equip a student for sounding out words.

8. C Alphabetic principle activities promote knowledge and practice of letter names, shapes, and sounds, making Choice C the best answer. Though reading books aloud and discussing the various parts of the story is a helpful exercise for students (Choice A), it does not directly promote an early awareness of the alphabetic principle. Asking students to clap the syllables in their name (Choice B) is an advanced way to chunk words. Though this is likewise a worthwhile activity, it may be too advanced for preschoolers just beginning to develop an understanding of the alphabetic principle. Finally, providing students with a wide range of reading materials is important (Choice D), however is helpful in exposing students to a variety of genres and maintaining their interest and motivation in reading. It also does not directly promote an early understanding of the alphabetic principle.

9. D Understanding of the alphabetic principle is critical to reading success. As early as kindergarten, students can be assessed and provided with instruction targeted at mastery of letter names, shapes, and forms. Although play (choice a), student initiative (choice b), and whole-group activities (choice c) are part of a balanced reading program, they are not the best strategies for at-risk students.

10. C Students learning alphabetic principle skills need sufficient review and practice. Picture sorts reinforce explicit instruction. Sorting "g" and "c" is inappropriate for an introduction of "g" for language learners, choice A, because voiced "g" and unvoiced "c" sounds are not distinguished in all languages. Generating rhymes (choice B) and recognizing environmental print (choice D) are more for phonemic and phonological awareness, rather than letter-print relationships.

2.3   Phonics & Decoding

Reading success depends on one's ability to break the code between the letters and the sounds of a word, as well as the ability to attach meaning to that word. Decoding is critical to a child's ability to read fluently and comprehend.

Definition

Phonics is a method of teaching reading that promotes understanding of the relationship between phonemes (the spoken sounds) and graphemes (the written letters). *Decoding* is the ability to use sound-letter correspondence to decipher words by sounding them out. Decoding may be done silently or aloud.

Teaching Phonics

Research indicates that children benefit from explicit, skillful, systematic instruction in phonics and decoding. Reading programs that teach children to blend sounds to decode words are more effective than programs that focus on letter-sound relationships in isolation, programs that depend on students to "figure out" the code independently, or whole-to-part (whole language) programs without phonics. Systematic phonics instruction, which can be entertaining and lively, is designed to equip students with accurate decoding skills that facilitate fluency and comprehension. Though some educators have promoted the idea of delaying instruction, research indicates that explicit instruction in letter-sound relationships leading to decoding is beneficial to students as early as kindergarten and first grade. Blending sounds into decoded words can start as soon as a child has learned a few consonants and a short vowel.

Decodable Readers

Decodable readers are books which learners can decipher using the phonics skills they have been taught. Decodables often come in many levels so that as more phonics rules are mastered, more text can be read. Although high-frequency words and predictable text books are part of a balanced literacy program and help students increase their fluency, they provide only limited practice in decoding.

Explicit instruction

Word Family Sort: Give a child flashcards with words that form various word families. Instruct the child to sort the cards by family. Noticing the letters is a prerequisite to sorting the cards accurately.

Show the child how to look for a familiar rime in an unfamiliar word. If the child knows the word king, he can use the rime *-ing* to decode *spring*.

at	ig	op
mat	big	pop
bat	dig	mop
cat	pig	drop
hat	twig	stop
flat	fig	hop
pat	wig	shop

Implicit instruction

Make a list of words from the environment. In this activity, students may make the connection between the sounds and letters.

Attention can be drawn to letter combinations imbedded in children's literature.

Interrelationship between Decoding, Comprehension, and Fluency

Decoding must be developed to the point of automaticity so that cognitive attention can be devoted to understanding the text instead of deciphering the text. Decoding and comprehension do not develop independently. Readers who struggle to decode frequently have difficulties comprehending text; when all effort is invested in decoding individual words, reading slows, and it is difficult to recall what each sentence is about and what the text means. Likewise, as decoding skills improve, less effort is required, and reading becomes more automatic. As a result, comprehension often becomes easier. After applying the rules of decoding to pronounce a word, the reader can analyze how the word connects with the sentence. If the word does not make sense, he can check for a misread and make a second attempt. Readers can also use context to confirm a word's meaning and pronunciation. While beginning and unskilled readers may rely heavily on context and pictures for clues for decoding, skilled readers rely on phonics. Syntactic and semantic clues are necessary to pronounce some homographs (bow/bow) and other words; however, good readers limit dependence on context, pictures, and guessing from beginning letters.

Decoding has limits. Students with wider, more varied oral vocabularies tend to decode more easily. Decoding does not require a large vocabulary; however, making sense of a decoded word is possible only for familiar words. Finding meaning from decoded words is only effective when the word is already in the child's oral vocabulary. Decoding activities such as reading words in a word family enhance decoding skills but do not efficiently increase vocabulary. Vocabulary development does not depend on decoding skills.

Prosody refers to the expression used in oral reading. It includes the timing, phrasing, emphasis, rhythm, intonation, and pitch that give meaning to oral language. Researchers have found a strong tie between prosody and comprehension. Young readers who lack prosody read word-by-word, skip over punctuation, and speak with a monotone or unnatural intonation. Skilled readers comprehend the text and demonstrate their comprehension through adult-sounding intonation and expression.

Sight words are high-frequency words which early readers are encouraged to memorize to automaticity as a whole by sight so that these words can be recognized without using decoding strategies. While words such as all, *good, are*, and *that* are decodable, these high-frequency words appear in many early reading books before students have studied the sound-spelling patterns used in these words. Memorizing sight words allows students to progress with less frustration.

Hierarchy

Most reading programs follow a logical order of instruction: CVC, CCVC, CVCC, CVCe. (CVC=consonant, vowel, consonant as in *rat*; CCVC=consonant, consonant, vowel, consonant as in *brat*; CVCe=consonant, vowel, consonant, e as in *rate*.) For example, students learn to read words in the following order: rat, brat, raft, rate.

A consonant blend is a sequence of two or more consonants in a word, each voicing a separate phoneme. Examples are *cl, br, sp*. Consonant blends differ from diphthongs (a vowel sound that begins with one sound

digraphs	diphthongs
sh	ou
ch	oi
wh	au
th	oy
ph	ew

and changes to another: for example, *ou*), digraphs (two consonants that produce a single phoneme: for example, *sh*), vowel teams (for example, *ay*), and r-controlled vowels (for example, *ar*).

By second grade, many students have learned to read a wide variety of one-syllable words. Because most multisyllable words follow the same patterns as one-syllable words, instruction can focus on recognizing syllables and applying prior knowledge to longer words. Although most students begin by decoding letter by letter, they cannot develop fluency in reading longer words letter by letter; they must apply phonics patterns to longer words.

PHONICS & DECODING PRACTICE

1. **Decoding is the best strategy for reading which words?**
   A. Where/were
   B. Run/running
   C. Sow/sew
   D. Mr./Mrs.

2. **Which word pair is the best example of onset/rime for decoding?**
   A. Said/bed
   B. String/strange
   C. Flap/trap
   D. Bear/bare

3. **Which of the following miscues is a diphthong error?**
   A. Reading *barn* for *born*
   B. Reading *short* for *shout*
   C. Reading *string* for *spring*
   D. Reading *tiger* for *tigers*

4. **Which of the following assessments can be used to monitor decoding skills?**
   A. Reading a list of words that follow predictable, systematic phonics rules
   B. Reading an age-appropriate passage with 10% new vocabulary
   C. Answering multiple-choice comprehension questions about text
   D. Observing where a student begins to read an unfamiliar book

5. **What is the relationship between oral vocabulary and decoding?**
   A. A student must have a word in his oral vocabulary to decode it.
   B. A student must decode a word first, and then draw from his oral vocabulary to determine meaning.
   C. A student can increase oral vocabulary efficiently by decoding.
   D. There is no relationship between oral vocabulary and decoding.

6. **Which statement accurately describes a decoding teaching strategy that is typically successful?**
   A. Teach phonics systematically and explicitly in first grade.
   B. Provide abundant environmental print so first graders can draw conclusions about letter-sound relationships.
   C. Replace phonics with a whole-to-part methodology for an end-of-year second grader who cannot decode unfamiliar multi-syllable words.
   D. Encourage mastery of all letter sounds before blending.

7. **Which reading skill does not depend on phonics knowledge?**
   A. Fluency
   B. Automaticity in word recognition
   C. Comprehension
   D. Letter recognition

8. **What is decoding?**
   A. Using surrounding words to correct pronunciation of a homophone
   B. Using automatic word recognition to read high-frequency words with fluency
   C. Using knowledge of letter-sound relationship to decipher words
   D. Using graphics as clues to sound out words

9. **Which of the following is typical of the order in which decoding is taught?**
   A. rip, rift, ripe, grip
   B. ripe, rift, grip, rip
   C. grip, rift, rip, ripe
   D. rip, grip, rift, ripe

10. **What role can syntactic or semantic clues play in decoding?**
   A. Pictures provide support for a student to learn to "guess" accurately.
   B. Application of letter-sound relationship allows a student to decipher a list of words accurately.
   C. Knowledge of word endings supports a student's efforts to correctly pronounce a decoded word in a sentence.
   D. Good readers can decode accurately without using context clues.

PHONICS & DECODING EXPLANATIONS

1. **B** Run and running are words that can be read using decoding skills. Choice a, where/were, has high-frequency words that can be memorized to automaticity. Choice c, sow/sew, depends on context for meaning, and Choice d, Mr./Mrs., includes abbreviations, which cannot be decoded.

2. **C** Choice C is the best answer as flap and trap use the same rime (–ap) plus common consonant blends. Although Choice a, said and bed, includes rhyming words, they do not use an onset/rime pattern. Choice b, string/strange, shares the same onset, and though -ing is a common rime, -ange is not. Choice d, bear and bare, has homophones that do not share the same rime.

3. **B** A diphthong is a combination of two vowels, such as *ou* or *oi*, in which pronunciation begins with one vowel and changes to the other. Choice a, *barn* and *born*, contain r-controlled vowels; *string* for *spring*(Choice c) is a substitution phoneme error; *tiger* for *tigers* (Choice d) is an omission phoneme error.

4. **A** Decoding skills can be assessed by having a student read decodable words isolated from context clues. Having a student read a passage, as suggested in Choice b, might allow him or her to depend on context for support. Although comprehension often depends on a student's ability to decode text, it does not provide accurate information about decoding abilities (Choice c). Finally, book handling skills (Choice d) are different skills that, likewise, do not demonstrate decoding skills.

5. **B** When reading, a student must first decode a word. If that word is part of his oral vocabulary, he can make sense of the word. Oral vocabulary is

not a prerequisite for decoding, as suggested in Choice a, as students can decode nonsense words. Choice c, which suggests a student can increase oral vocabulary through decoding, is not an efficient way of acquiring new vocabulary. Reading cat, bat, fat, hat, rat in a list without context does little to help students gain or understand new vocabulary. Finally, as explained correctly in Choice b, there is a relationship between oral vocabulary and decoding, making Choice d incorrect.

6. **A**   English is a systematically phonetic language. Explicitly teaching phonics in early grades helps students learn to read. Although awareness of environmental print (Choice b) is valuable, few students can draw conclusions accurately enough to become fluent readers. A second grader who is not accurately decoding words needs intervention through specific phonics instruction, not with whole-to-part reading instruction suggested in Choice c. Finally, Choice d is incorrect, as students can begin to blend letters when they have learned a few consonants and a vowel; delaying blending is not an effective teaching strategy.

7. **D**   Letter recognition precedes phonics knowledge. Fluency (a) (the ability to read with accuracy, an appropriate rate, and prosody), automaticity in word recognition (b) (the skill of recognizing words with little effort), and comprehension (c) depend on phonics skills.

8. **C**   Decoding is defined as applying knowledge of letter-sound relationships to correctly pronounce words. Surrounding words and graphics, as suggested in Choice A and Choice D, use context clues. Many high-frequency words, such as the, said, where, what, and so on, are not decodable, as they don't follow the typical letter-sound rules, and using automatic word recognition to read high-frequency words (Choice B) is not decoding, but rapid recognition.

9. **D**   Reading programs typically advance CVC, CCVC, CVCC, CVCe, CVVC, then additional phonics patterns.

10. **C**   Knowledge of typical word endings such as –*tion* for nouns, -*ous* for adjectives, -*ed* for verbs, and–*ly* for adverbs (syntax) supports a reader's efforts to pronounce words correctly. Using pictures to guess (Choice a) is counterproductive. Reading words from a list, as suggested in Choice b, does not use syntactic or semantic clues. Finally, some words, such as homophones, abbreviations, and foreign expressions, cannot be decoded (Choice d).

2.4 Chapter Review

1. **When a kindergarten teacher models good reading habits while reading a big book, which skill is not likely the focus of the activity?**
   A. book handling
   B. print directionality
   C. segmenting
   D. return sweep

2. **The assessment question "What sound does *m* make?" would assess what aptitude?**
   A. environmental print awareness
   B. alphabetic principle
   C. decoding
   D. print directionality

3. **Which statement best reflects proper explicit instruction in letter sound relationships?**
   A. Letters should be introduced in isolation at a rate students can learn; decoding words should begin as soon as students have knowledge of a few letter sounds.
   B. High-frequency, high interest words should be used to allow students to explore letter-sound relationships and draw conclusions about letters and sounds.
   C. Environmental print provides the basis for students to learn reading without intensive instruction in phonics.
   D. Students should progress from reading whole words on flashcards to sounds to letters until a complete knowledge of the alphabet and phonemes is acquired.

4. **Which child is demonstrating print awareness?**
   A. Duncan enjoys listening to and reciting nursery rhymes.
   B. MacKenzie picks up books, holds them correctly, and points to favorite pictures.
   C. Cooper draws squiggly lines under stick figures, points to the line, and tells what it says.
   D. All students demonstrate print awareness.

5. **Which of the following is environmental print that contributes to emergent reading?**
   A. art work displayed in the home
   B. fast food signs
   C. mother/child bonding through conversations
   D. movement activities to classical music

6. **Early childhood students create and "read" a predictable text book about themselves. "This is my nose. This is my mouth. These are my eyes. These are my ears." Which of the following is the activity <u>not</u> intended to promote?**
   A. Awareness of word boundaries.
   B. Awareness that words carry a message.
   C. Decoding skills
   D. Print directionality

7. **A kindergarten student picks up a book and flips through it and responds to the pictures. He seems unaware of the print. Which activity is most appropriate for the next step?**
   A. Provide unstructured play time in the classroom library.
   B. Provide intensive instruction in phonological awareness activities such as segmenting words.
   C. Structure small group activities focused on clapping syllables of student names.
   D. Model reading a big book, including moving a finger along the line of print.

8. **A student is invited to change words to form new words. Given the words** *cap*, *tap*, **and** *not*; **the student creates the words** *cape*, *tape*, **and** *note*. **Which concept is being introduced?**
   A. print directionality
   B. silent letters
   C. reading automaticity
   D. CVC words

9. **Which activity is likely to promote understanding of the alphabetic principle?**
   A. Wrap-up circle time in which a teacher scribes student responses to a question such as "What is your favorite color?"
   B. Singing repetitive songs such as "Where is Thumper?"
   C. Learning popular nursery rhymes such as "Hey, Diddle, Diddle"
   D. Purposefully selected dress-up costumes such as a policeman and a cape.

10. **A teacher will use an activity in which she says the name of a letter and a student practices air writing and tracing the letter on a sandpaper stencil. For which child is the activity designed?**
    A. Child practicing book handling skills
    B. Child learning letter shape and formation
    C. Child developing awareness of environmental print
    D. Child beginning to decode CVC words

11. **Which of the following is <u>not</u> commonly used to demonstrate print directionality and 1:1 correspondence of spoken and written English words?**
    A. Matching upper and lower case letter magnets
    B. Finger reading a big book
    C. Ordering a familiar poem in a pocket chart
    D. Using a pointer to follow lyrics of a song

12. **What is the role of writing in the early childhood classroom?**
    A. Students should master letter sounds before beginning to write.
    B. Students will naturally begin to write the sounds they hear and typically will not need explicit instruction in writing.
    C. Students benefit from structured activities that require them to apply knowledge of letter-sound relationships.
    D. Listening to children's literature read aloud enhances oral vocabulary.

13. **How does phonics instruction help students develop automatic word recognition?**
    A. It helps students understand that all spoken language can be broken down into smaller sound units.
    B. It helps students recognize common letter-sound correspondences and patterns that can be applied to decode words.
    C. It helps students develop strong reading comprehension skills.
    D. It helps students master high-frequency sight words

14. **Which of the following supports a child in learning where to begin reading a book?**
    A. pointing to words in a pocket chart
    B. labeling common objects in the classroom
    C. a classroom library with a wide range of genres and levels
    D. explicit instruction on book cover and backs

15. **Which of the following activities is not a benefit of decoding?**
    A. vocabulary acquisition
    B. fluency
    C. comprehension
    D. reading multi-syllable words

16. **Which answer provides the best definition of decoding and the best example of decodable words?**
    A. The ability to apply knowledge of letter-sound relationships to correctly write words: stop, try, bench, shout

B. The ability to apply knowledge of letter-sound relationships to correctly pronounce words: cap, capture, drive, driveway

C. The ability to read fluently with conversational speed and intonation: sow, sew, their, there, they're

D. The ability to predict the next step of a predictable text book: what, where, were, was

17. **After reading the text, "The boy's clothes are by the door," a student summarizes with "The boy closes the door." What steps should the teacher take?**

A. Increase read alouds to build up oral vocabulary

B. Preteach unfamiliar vocabulary

C. Check for cognates for language learners

D. Provide explicit instruction in letter-sound rules for decoding

18. **A student reads with the following miscue:** *The pie was eated by Bob.* **The instructor provides the following sentences for practice:** *Bob ate the pie. The pie was eaten by Bob.* **What is this practice designed to promote?**

A. use of semantic clues

B. use of syntactic clues

C. analysis of compound words

D. accuracy in reading diphthongs

19. **A second grader reads grade level material with labored word-by-word effort. What areas of reading development are impacted by this type of reading?**

A. only fluency; comprehension is not impacted by automaticity

B. only comprehension; fluency is not impacted by automaticity

C. both fluency and comprehension

D. only reading rate; accuracy and prosody are not impacted

20. **Which of the following is a miscue of a consonant digraph?**

A. reading *trick* for *thick*

B. reading *ring* for *rang*

C. reading *ring* for *rant*

D. reading *string* for *spring*

1. C   Segmenting is breaking a syllable into sounds or breaking a word into syllables. Since a big book is read with a natural tone and intonation, segmenting would be out of place. By contrast, book handling (A) (knowledge of front, back, where to begin, etc.), print directionality (B) (top to bottom, left to right), and return sweep (D) (tracking from the end of one line back to the beginning of the next) could all be modeled.

2. B   Alphabetic principle states that in English as an alphabetic language, the letters represent the phonemes of the spoken language. The letter *m* represents the sound /m/. The question does not involve environmental print (a) (the print of everyday life), decoding (c) (sounding out words), or print directionality (d).

3. A   Students benefit from explicit, systematic instruction in letters and sounds. Letters are typically introduced in isolation at a manageable rate. As soon as students know a few consonants and a short vowel, they can begin decoding. Effective, explicit instruction is not based in student exploration (B). While environmental print (C) does promote print awareness, it is not an example of explicit instruction in letters and sounds. Effective instruction transitions from letters to words, not from whole word back to letters (D).

4. C   This child's addition of the squiggly lines under a picture indicate that he is aware that print carries a message in addition to and separate from the pictures. Enjoyment of nursery rhymes (a) demonstrates phonological awareness. MacKenzie demonstrates some book handling skills (b), but her skills are not yet connected to print.

5. B   While all four are found in the child's environment and may contribute to emergent reading, only the signs (B) contain print. Art (a) is visual but does not necessary contain print; conversation (c) and music (d) are auditory and do not contain print.

6. C   A predictable text book is useful for promoting print awareness including word boundaries (A), awareness that print conveys a message (B), and print directionality (D). However, the words in this text are not easily decodable. They are high-frequency words that require memorization for reading with automaticity.

7. D This student needs explicit (not unstructured A) instruction in print awareness. Oral activities such as segmenting (B) and syllabication (c) are not a priority in instruction on print awareness.

8. B A student who is adding a silent e to create long vowel sound words has already mastered print directionality (A) and CVC words (D). Introduction of a new concept will require practice to become automatic (c). This activity is intended to introduce silent e.

9. A When students observe a teacher scribe spoken language into print, it promotes understanding of the alphabetic principle. Singing (B) and nursery rhymes (C) can promote oral vocabulary and phonological awareness. Pretend play (D) benefits in acquisition of content-specific oral vocabulary.

10. B Hearing the name of a letter spoken and tracing the letter promotes learning letter name, shape, and formation. This activity is unrelated to book handling (a). Writing air letters or tracing is not an example of environmental text, which is the text of everyday life (c). A student would likely have a familiarity with letter names, shapes, and formation before decoding CVC words (d)

11. A Matching upper and lower case letters can be done without print directionality and does not include words. Using a finger or pointer to follow text (b, d) and putting words of a familiar poem in order all are useful in instructing students in print directionality and 1:1 correspondence.

12. C Students can begin writing as soon as they have learned their first letter. Writing can facilitate mastery and should not be delayed (a). Students will not naturally begin to write (b). Reading aloud and oral vocabulary (d) do not address the role of writing.

13. B Phonics teaches letter and sound correspondences that students can use to decode words while reading. Choice A refers to phonological awareness skills, or the ability to manipulate spoken language. This question deals with print. Choice C goes a step beyond decoding print; phonics deals with knowing how to decode a word based on knowledge of how similar words are pronounced. Phonics knowledge is connected to strong reading comprehension skills, but this question deals specifically with automatic word recognition. Choice D, high-frequency sight words (i.e. said, some) are not dependent on phonics for decoding and automaticity.

14. D Providing explicit instruction on book covers and backs helps students to develop the book handling skill of knowing where to begin reading. A pocket chart (a), labels (b), and the library (c) do not specifically guide students in book handling skills.

15. A Students can practice decoding words that are not part of their everyday vocabulary. The act of decoding does not add the word to the vocabulary. Decoding does support fluency (a), comprehension (c), and reading multi-syllable words (D).

16. B Decoding is converting writing to speech using the rules of letter-sound relationships. It does not include writing (a); using letter-sound relationships for spelling is encoding. There is a strong tie between decoding and fluency (c); reading with conversational speed and intonation is a result of skilled decoding. The words *sow, sew, their, there,* and *there* are homophones; after decoding, the reader can derive meaning from context. Predictable text books (d) such as *Ten Little Monkeys* or *The Very Hungry Caterpillar* are helpful for emergent readers because they can build vocabulary and knowledge of syntax and semantics. These books often contain words that are not readily decodable. The words *what, where, were,* and *was* are high-frequency words that can be learned to automaticity without decoding.

17. D This student's decoding errors are interfering with comprehension. It is likely that all of the words are already in the child's oral vocabulary so vocabulary instruction (a,b) is not the need. Similarly while cognates support comprehension (c), the error in this situation is accuracy in reading.

18. B Syntax is the rules used to join words into meaningful sentences. Giving students sentences that are rearranged syntactically can promote knowledge of syntax and improve accuracy in reading for students who are already decoding at or near grade level. Semantic clues (B) are clues about the meaning that are derived from other words in the sentence. Compound words (C) are words made of two smaller words (*rainbow, popcorn*). Diphthongs are sounds made by a combination of vowels (*loud, coin*) in which the sound begins with one sound and moves to the other.

19. C Decoding, fluency, and comprehension are all interrelated. Decoding is a prerequisite to fluency. Fluency supports comprehension. A student who lacks automatic word recognition must use cognitive energy to decode.

The poor decoding skills then impact the student's ability to comprehend the text. Labored reading impacts all aspects of fluency: rate, accuracy, and prosody. (D)

20.A A consonant digraph is two letters that represent one phoneme. Examples of digraphs are ph, th, sh, and ch. Saying trick for the word thick would be a miscue of /th/. Saying ring for rang is a vowel error (B). Saying ring for rant is a final consonant error (C). Saying string for spring is a consonant blend miscue (D).

Chapter 3:
Word Analysis

Lessons

3.1   Word Analysis Introduction

Word analysis is using a word's structure (the relationship between spelling and pronunciation) to decode and attach meaning to an unfamiliar word. Word analysis includes base words, roots, affixes, inflections, and syllables. Word analysis skills are important to reading because they allow the reader to decipher morphemic words in a text and then acquire new vocabulary by applying the principles to additional words with the same morphemes.

Importance of Word Analysis Skills

Word analysis, fluency, and comprehension are interrelated:

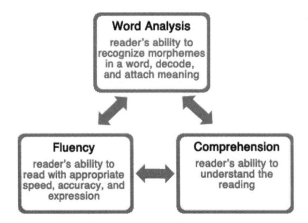

Although some fluency problems can be resolved through practice, the primary cause of fluency problems is weak decoding skills. Readers with higher fluency rates typically have higher comprehension levels. Understandably, because fluent readers can read many words with automaticity, they can focus on comprehension. Alternatively, readers who struggle to read fluently often put forth so much effort to decode, they are unable to efficiently and effectively process the information they are reading.

Chunking

Chunking is breaking a word into manageable parts. Beginning readers might chunk onset and rime. More advanced readers chunk by syllables. The ability to break a word into chunks or syllables helps a reader decode. The ability to break a word into syllables is a prerequisite of fluency. Below are several examples of chunking:

Onset/rime:

r at

th at

Syllabication:

con test

nap kin

Base word plus affixes:

sing er

sing ing

Syllabication

Teaching students the rules of syllabication often helps them to better able chunk words and thus read them accurately. For example:

- Every syllable has a sounded vowel. The vowel might be the only sound, or it might be combined with consonants.
  Example: *a-wake*: the syllable *a* is only the vowel; *wake* contains vowels and consonants
- Open syllables end with a vowel sound. That vowel sound is typically long.
  Examples: The long *e* in *believe*: *be*-lieve
  The long *a* in *table*: *ta*-ble
- Closed syllables end with a consonant sound.
  Examples: *pump*-kin, com-pu-ter
- Some words divide into syllables by roots and affixes.
  Example: *un-seem-ly*
- Some words divide into syllables by VC/CV.
  Example: *cos-met-ic*
- Some words divide into syllables by V/CV.
  Example: *pa-per*

Good readers use what they know about decoding single-syllable words to decode multisyllabic words. These readers can compare a new word's parts with a familiar word's syllables. They can apply their prior knowledge to the task of reading a new word. These readers are no longer reading phoneme by phoneme. They chunk and syllabicate to read fluently.

WORD ANALYSIS INTRODUCTION PRACTICE

1. **The word unbuttoned is found in a second grade text. What is the best strategy to encourage for reading unbuttoned?**
   A. Preteach unbuttoned using a schema map.
   B. Break unbuttoned down by each phoneme and then blend.
   C. Analyze the prefix, base word, and suffix of unbuttoned.
   D. Use flashcards to practice unbuttoned to automaticity.

2. **Which list of words demonstrates how a student can use morphemes to attach meaning to an unfamiliar word?**
   A. Transformer, transportation, portable, transformation
   B. Teach, beach, bleach, reach
   C. Climate, precipitation, temperature, weather
   D. "Brown Bear, Brown Bear, What Do You See?" (Carle, Eric. Brown Bear, Brown Bear)

3. **Which of the following syllabication rules should be explicitly taught to help a student read bacon?**
   A. Every syllable has a sounded vowel. Some words divide between roots and affixes.
   B. Closed syllables end in a consonant. The vowel is typically short.
   C. Syllables can divide VC/CV. A vowel might be the only sound in a syllable.
   D. Open syllables end in a vowel. Every syllable has a sounded vowel.

4. **Explicit instruction in breaking black into onset/rime and infection into syllables is an example of which word analysis strategy?**
   A. Using context clues
   B. Blending
   C. Chunking
   D. Developing automaticity

5. **Which of the following would demonstrate that a student has developed advanced word analysis skills?**
   A. A student decodes the word "school" by separating it into "sch" and "ool."
   B. A student decodes the word "fun" by separating it into "f" and "un."
   C. A student decodes the word "preview" by breaking it up into "pre" and "view."
   D. A student decodes the word "streak" by breaking it up into "str" and "eak."

6. **Which of the following best states the relationship among word analysis, fluency, and comprehension?**
   A. An ability to use word analysis skills facilitates a student's fluency. Fluent readers often have better comprehension.
   B. Comprehension precedes word analysis - only through comprehension can a reader skillfully predict the words in the text. With comprehension and word analysis in place, fluency follows naturally.
   C. Although fluent readers often enjoy reading more, comprehension functions independent of fluency and word analysis.
   D. Comprehension is the goal of all reading. With proper instruction, strong comprehension can be achieved even without strong word analysis or fluency skills.

7. **Which of the following is an example of a word that can be decoded and understood by analyzing a word's morphemic structure?**
   A. impossible
   B. colonel
   C. shoe
   D. through

8. **A first-grade student is able to decode the word "cheek" by first reading "ch" and then saying "eek." Which of the following is an explanation for why this student would be considered to be in the beginning stages of word analysis skills?**
   A. The beginning level of word analysis means that a student can decode words by looking at syllables.
   B. Students beginning to develop word analysis skills identify and segment phonemes.
   C. The early stages of word analysis skills involve decoding by automatically recognizing high-frequency words.
   D. The beginning level of word analysis involves decoding by onset and rime.

9. **A teacher wants to plan instruction for introducing chunking and syllabication. Which of the following would be an appropriate introduction activity?**

    A. Teach students that closed syllables end in a consonant, like in the word "din-ner."

    B. Review with students that words can be broken into onset and rime like in the word "ch" and "air."

    C. Teach students that some syllables are made up of only one vowel, like in the word "asleep."

    D. Teach students that some words' syllables follow a VC/CV pattern, like the word "basket."

10. **Which of the following does not represent decoding by using word analysis skills?**

    A. A student looks at morphemic structure to decode.

    B. A student looks at roots and affixes to decode.

    C. A student decodes by applying prior knowledge of familiar words to new words.

    D. A student decodes by looking at contextual cues.

WORD ANALYSIS INTRODUCTION EXPLANATIONS

1. **C**   By analyzing the prefix, base word, and suffix, readers can decode the word and likely recognize the base word *button*. Using their word analysis skills, students can then build on their current knowledge by considering how adding *un-* and *–ed* to *button* changes it's meaning (i.e. undone and in the past). The word *unbuttoned* is likely already in a student's oral vocabulary, and therefore, a schema map (Choice A) is unnecessary. Analyzing *unbuttoned* by phoneme, as suggested in Choice B, is simply inefficient given the number of sounds. Choice D is also incorrect - at this level, students should be taught to find syllables or chunks. Because *unbuttoned* is easily decodable, flashcard practice is not the best strategy.

2. **A**   The words listed in Choice A best demonstrate how morphemes can be used to attach meaning to unfamiliar words. The list includes various morphemes, including *trans-, form, -er, port, -tion,* and *-able*. With just some word analysis knowledge, a student can make sense of these words,

using the meanings of the individual morphemes to derive meaning. While rhyming words, such as those in Choice B, often share a rime, they do not necessarily share the same morphemes from which students can derive meaning. And, although subject-specific vocabulary often shares common morphemes, the list of words in Choice C does not. Finally, *Brown Bear, Brown Bear, What Do You See?*, is predictable text that does not depend on common morphemes.

3. D The word *bacon* demonstrates how open syllables end in a vowel (as the "*ba*" in *bacon*); Ba-*con* divides CV- and both syllables have a sounded vowel (the "*a*" in *ba* and the "*o*" in *con*). Choice A is incorrect as *bacon* does not have roots and affixes. Choice B is also incorrect – *bacon* does not have a closed syllable. Finally, *bacon* does not have a syllable made up of only a vowel as suggested in Choice C.

4. C Beginning readers chunk words by onset/rime. More advanced readers chunk by syllables. Both examples demonstrate that words can be broken into more manageable parts to both decode and understand. Because words in isolation do not have a context, Choice A does not apply. Choice B is incorrect as the question inquires about breaking words apart - blending refers to joining sounds. Finally, developing automaticity, as suggested in Choice D, does not break words into smaller parts.

5. C An advanced student can work with syllables like in the word "preview." The other examples are ways of looking at onset and rime, which is more typical of beginning students. Onset and rime entails breaking up a word into the initial consonant(s) before the vowel (like the "f" in "fun") and into the vowel and following sounds (like "un" in "fun").

6. A Word analysis skills allow readers to use a word's structure to decode with accuracy and automaticity. Reading fluently, or with appropriate accuracy, rate, and expression, allows students to better comprehend as their attention can be focused on meaning rather than decoding. Comprehension does not necessarily precede word analysis skills (Choice B) – students may be able to read fluently, but continue to have difficulties comprehending and vice versa, students who have high comprehension abilities may still struggle with decoding. Choice C is also incorrect – comprehension does not function independently from fluency and word analysis. The various components work together to create well-rounded, successful readers. Finally, though comprehension is often the goal of reading, word analysis and fluency skills are required to understand text in an efficient and effective manner.

7. A   Morphemic structure involves looking at the parts of a word in order to decode and attach meaning. Only choice A presents a word that can be broken up in order to pronounce and understand it—"impossible" can be broken into "im" and "poss" "ible." The other choices cannot be broken down into manageable parts in a way that helps decoding. The word colonel (B) is not decodable. Dividing shoe (C) into "sh" and "oe" do not make it easier to decipher or understand. "Through" (D) is not decodable and does not break down by morphemic structure.

8. D   At the beginning stage, onset and rime are a common way to chunk smaller parts of a word in order to decode and understand it. Beginning students first work with onset and rime whereas more advanced students work with syllables, choice A. Choice B involves phonemes, which are spoken language units, not print words. Choice C deals with automaticity, which means automatically recognizing common words, not using word analysis skills for unfamiliar words.

9. B   To introduce syllabication, a teacher would logically begin with onset and rime, choice B, since this tends to be the first way that students learn how to decode words using word analysis skills. The other activities are more advanced; choices A, C and D all involve syllables, which are more advanced than chunking in onset and rime.

10. D   Word analysis skills involve looking at parts of a word such as morphemic structure, choice A, which includes roots and affixes, choice B. By breaking words into manageable parts, students can apply prior knowledge to new words for decoding, choice C. Choice D is not word analysis because it involves looking at the context in which a word is used or at the words around the unfamiliar word rather than looking strictly at a word's morphemic structure.

3.2   Word Analysis Skills

Readers of all ages encounter unfamiliar words and use a variety of strategies to both decode and derive meaning. Because many English words are based on the Greek and Latin languages and share common roots, prefixes, and suffixes, word analysis skills are frequently needed. When readers have experience using these skills, they have a solid strategy in which to independently acquire new vocabulary.

It is important to explicitly teach students structural analysis skills, especially as they begin to read more difficult text. By using familiar word parts (such as familiar prefixes and suffixes) to determine the meaning of unknown words, students grow to be more skilled, independent readers.

Often, a student may be able to read and even appropriately pronounce a word but may still struggle to understand it's meaning independently or within text. By teaching and providing students opportunities to use context clues and their knowledge of roots and affixes, they will be more equipped to face difficult text.

Morphemes

As you may recall from previous sections, a phoneme is the most basic unit of speech sound and a morpheme is a meaningful part or unit of a word that cannot be divided into a smaller unit. Morphemic analysis is a strategy for determining the meaning of a word by using meaningful parts of the word or morphemes. With an understanding of morphemes, teachers can provide more effective instruction.

Classification of Morphemes

⊙ Free morphemes can stand alone or be combined with other morphemes. Example: *play* can be a single word, or it can be combined with *ground*: *playground*

⊙ Bound morphemes must be linked to a word. Example: *re-* and *un-* lend meaning when linked to a word

⊙ Derivational morphemes are added to a word to change the part of speech or meaning.

Examples: *sad* (adjective) becomes *sadness* (noun)
happy becomes *unhappy*

⊙ Inflectional morphemes change a verb tense or number.
Examples: *walk* becomes *walking*
peach becomes *peaches*

Roots and Affixes

Students begin to encounter Latin and Greek roots, prefixes, and suffixes early in their reading development. Teachers can explicitly point out examples and patterns and further student's word analysis ability.

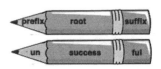

As the name suggests, a **root** is the basic word to which a **prefix** (affix that goes before the root) and/or a **suffix** (affix that follows the root) is added. Prefixes and suffixes are called **affixes** because they attach to or they are fixed to a root for meaning. Roots, prefixes, and suffixes do not usually stand alone. They combine to form words. The ability to recognize word parts and their meanings is a word analysis skill.

Here are two examples:
⊙ **Autograph:** *auto-* is a prefix meaning *self*, and *-graph* is a Greek root meaning writing.
⊙ **Homonym:** two roots are combined. *Homo-* is a Greek root for *same*, and *-nym* is a root for *name*.

Implicit and explicit instruction helps students learn to identify common roots and affixes which can significantly help children when they come across an unknown word.

See www.prepforward.com/assets/roots_prefixes_suffixes.pdf for common Greek and Latin roots.

Prefixes

Prefixes attach to the front of roots and words and relate important information. The four most common prefixes are

- ⊙ **un-** meaning not—undisclosed, unapologetic
- ⊙ **ir-** meaning not—irrelevant, irresponsible
- ⊙ **dis-** meaning the opposite of—disagree, discord
- ⊙ **re-** meaning again—reverse, repeat

Suffixes

Suffixes are added to the end of words or roots, and they convey grammatical information such as part of speech, number, or verb tense.
The four most common suffixes are

- ⊙ *-ly* meaning *characteristic of*—**humanly, systematically**
- ⊙ *-ing* denoting a verb form (present participle)—*reading, inventing*
- ⊙ *-ed* meaning past-tense verbs—*invented, gathered*
- ⊙ *-s* or *-es* meaning *more than one*—*books, wishes*

See www.prepforward.com/assets/roots_prefixes_suffixes.pdf for common prefixes and suffixes.

Although prefixes and suffixes provide a pattern for decoding a new word, the spelling of a suffix can vary depending on its root word. For example, *-able* in *durable, profitable,* and *unthinkable* becomes *-ible* in *indestructible, visible,* and *permissible.* Students can learn that patterns can be found in spelling variations as well.
Similarly, an affix can differ in the ways it is pronounced. This is especially common with the *-ed* suffix that indicates verb tense: *mapped /t/, merged /d/, unwanted /id/.* The same principle applies to prefixes: *reverse, renovate,* and *relocate.* Although spelling varies, it is more stable than pronunciation is.

Compound Words

Compound words are words formed from two words. It is important to teach students how to recognize, read and write compound words. Though at times it may be difficult to determine if a word is compound, it is helpful to remember that the two new words form a single word with a new meaning.

When reading or writing compound words, it is often helpful to break the word down into the two smaller words. This often makes decoding or spelling easier for students.

Examples: rainbow, mailbox, football

WORD ANALYSIS SKILLS PRACTICE

1. **A teacher works with small reading groups throughout the day to practice each of the following activities. Which activity requires the use of word analysis skills?**

    A. Students practice combining individual sounds to form words. They begin by forming simple CVC words such as /c/ /a/ /t/ to read cat and /m/ /o/ /p/ to read *mop*.

    B. Students play several games to work on identifying the beginning sounds of words.

    C. While reading, students use strategies to decode and derive meaning of unfamiliar words such as *unthinkable, misrepresentation* and *illiterate*.

    D. While reading, students come across unfamiliar terms such as, "lion's share", and work to derive meaning.

2. **After explicitly teaching and working with students to consider words that sound the same but have different meanings during the previous day's lesson, a teacher uses brainteasers such as the following for a warm-up activity for her fourth grade class.**

    Question - "What is the scariest lake?"
    Answer - "Lake Erie (eerie)"

    This activity is an example of which of the following?

A. Explicit instruction on morphemes
B. Implicit instruction on homophones
C. Explicit instruction on homographs
D. Implicit instruction on comparative adjectives

3. **Which of the following types of students would benefit from developing structural analysis skills?**
    A. Students who read below grade-level.
    B. All students benefit from structural analysis instruction.
    C. Students who read above grade-level.
    D. Students who have advanced phonics knowledge but struggle decoding multi-syllable words.

4. **A teacher wants to provide students with additional structural analysis practice. Specifically, she has noticed students struggling to make sense of unfamiliar words with varied prefixes and suffixes within their reading. Which list of words would be most helpful for addressing this particular need?**
    A. *cat, hat, bat*
    B. *jumped, jumps, jumping*
    C. *reface, preface, facing*
    D. *two, too, to*

5. **Which of the following is a reason to teach students the meanings of prefixes such as *im-* in *immaculate* within the following text?**

    > The young girl worked hard to clean the house. When she was finished, the house was immaculate.

    A. *Maculata*, the root word in *immaculate*, is Latin. Learning prefixes such as *im-* will help students to become proficient in Latin.
    B. Teaching prefixes will help students to become better decoders and equip them with skills that will help them determine the meaning of unknown words within text.
    C. Prefixes are not necessary to teach – students will simply learn them implicitly as they begin to read more difficult text.
    D. Prefixes teach students there can be multiple syllables within one word.

6. **A teacher notices that one of her students is having difficulties analyzing the following words within a passage:** *autobiography, telegraph,* **and** *prescribe.* **Which of the following skills should the teacher first assess to address the student's difficulties?**
    A. student's ability to segment words into syllables
    B. student's oral vocabulary of words containing roots and affixes
    C. student's ability to identify and blend two consonants
    D. student's ability to isolate phonemes

7. **Which of the following is <u>not</u> a true statement?**
    A. A morpheme is the basic part of a word and carries meaning.
    B. Free morphemes can stand alone, or they can be joined to other morphemes.
    C. Prefixes, suffixes, and roots are found alone as often as joined to other parts.
    D. A suffix is a type of morpheme.

8. **When suffixes are added to words, what is one possible consequence?**
    A. The spelling can sometimes change more than the pronunciation.
    B. Suffixes change the spelling of the root, but they always have the same pronunciation.
    C. Suffixes do not affect the spelling of the root word, and they always have the same spelling.
    D. The spelling can differ, but not as often as pronunciation.

9. **If a student encountered the word** *circumspect* **and wanted to use word analysis skills to understand what it means, what would roots, suffixes, or prefixes reveal as the meaning?**
    A. Looking glass
    B. Round
    C. Cautious
    D. Hostile

10. Yesterday, I _____(1)_____ to undertake the _____(2)_____ goal of running a marathon, which has always been _____ (3)_____ by my athletic trainer.

In the above sentence, a word with the suffix *-ous* would best fit in which blank?

A. 1

B. 2

C. 3

D. There are no appropriate spaces for a word containing the suffix -ous.

WORD ANALYSIS SKILLS EXPLANATIONS

1. **C**   Word analysis skills refer to a student's ability to decode and derive meaning from unfamiliar words, such as the scenario described in Choice C. The other possible choices do not require word analysis, but rather different types of reading skills: Choice A requires students to use blending skills, choice B allows students to practice identifying beginning sounds, and choice D provides an opportunity for students to explore idioms.

2. **B**   Because brainteasers are a form of implicit instruction (i.e. students draw their own conclusions and are not explicitly taught how to answer), Choices A and C are incorrect. Choice A is also incorrect as it refers to instruction regarding morphemes, which are the most basic unit of speech sound and not something addressed in the lesson. Choice C is also incorrect as homographs are words that have the same spelling with different pronunciation and meanings – Erie/eerie are spelled differently. While the sentence has a comparative adjective (scariest), it is not the activity's point, making Choice D incorrect as well. Choice B is therefore the best answer – the teacher is using implicit instruction to provide opportunities for students to practice homophones, which are words that sound the same but have different meanings - they may be spelled the same or differently.

3. **B**   It is important for teachers to teach structural analysis to all readers. Structural analysis provides students with the knowledge necessary to determine the meaning of unfamiliar words within text. Regardless

of a student's reading level, they will come across unfamiliar words at some point. Structural analysis, or the ability to break words down into smaller morphemic units, assists students in their abilities to decode and define words they don't already know.

4. C Prefixes and suffixes are types of affixes – they attach to a root word or are fixed to a root for meaning. Prefixes come before the root and suffixes after. Choice C provides the best list for addressing affixes – *reface* and *preface* include the prefixes *re* and *pre* and facing contains the suffix – *ing*. Choice A demonstrates rhyming words, Choice B only provides root words with suffixes (*-ed, -s,* and *–ing*) and Choice D contains homonyms.

5. B Teaching students prefixes allow them to be both better decoders and more able to derive meaning from unfamiliar words within text. By understanding *im-* means "in" or "not", students can then use context clues to determine that *immaculate* means perfect, clean, or pure. While it is often useful for students to learn foreign languages and knowing other languages may help students know the meanings of many prefixes, suffixes and root words, simply learning about Latin suffixes will not make a person proficient in Latin (Choice A). Choice C is also incorrect – it is important for students to be explicitly taught prefixes. By helping students to become comfortable with word analysis, they will become more fluent readers with better comprehension skills. Finally, prefixes are not typically used to teach younger students about how words break into syllables – syllables are often taught early in a child's reading education and word analysis skills are usually not taught until students have become more mature readers.

6. B If a student's oral vocabulary does not contain many words with roots and affixes, it is understandable they are not able to use roots and affixes to analyze unfamiliar words – they likely do not have the knowledge from which to draw upon, making Choice B the best answer. In such cases, students need to be explicitly taught the meaning of common roots and affixes. Then, they will be able to use the information to analyze unknown words and expand their oral vocabularies. Because many prefixes and suffixes resemble one another, grouping them by meaning can be a helpful strategy to promote automatic recognition. Students with a broad vocabulary base can add words more efficiently because of their ability to apply previous knowledge to a new situation. A student analyzing multi-syllabic words would already have mastered segmenting syllables (Choice A), consonant blends (Choice C), and isolating phonemes (Choice D).

7. C Choices A, B and D are all correct statements. Choice C, however, is not – prefixes and suffixes are seldom found alone and are typically joined to roots.

8. D When affixes are added to a root, the spelling can sometimes vary (*-able* and *-ible* both mean "characteristic of"). However, the pronunciation of prefixes and suffixes can vary even more. Both Choices B and C are thus incorrect. Choice A is also incorrect because spelling can vary, but it is more stable than the number of ways to pronounce a particular prefix or suffix.

9. C Because the prefix *circum-* means "around," and the root *spect* means "to look," you can think of a person looking around, as if being cautious. Choices A and B are meant as tricks because they contain words that sound similar to *circum-* and *spect*. Beware of answers that look too easy when figuring out the meaning of a vocabulary word. Choice D is too far from the meaning and has no relevance to the prefix or root to be accurate.

10. B When a question asks you how an affix is used in a sentence, the best strategy is to choose one or two words you know to analyze. This question asks about the suffix *-ous*, which is an ending for an adjective. You might think about *righteous* and *callous*. Both words are adjectives. The next step is to substitute words you think make sense. For example, you could fill in the sentences like this:

> Yesterday, I **decided** (1) to undertake the **monstrous** (2) goal of running a marathon, which has always been **encouraged** (3) by my athletic trainer.

Because you are looking for an adjective, the only possible place would be in space 2 (Choice B) as the other blanks require a verb.

3.3 Strategies for Words in Context

Text often provides information that further explains unfamiliar words. When students come across an unknown word, using surrounding words is often an excellent strategy independent readers incorporate. This is also known as contextual analysis. *Contextual analysis* may provide readers with information regarding a word's meaning, structure, pronunciation, and use.

Why is context important?

After students use decoding skills to read an unknown word, they must further determine the correct pronunciation and meaning through context. Often, prior knowledge and oral vocabulary provide a basis from which to draw meaning. A student with familiarity about a topic and specific vocabulary related to that topic can use context cues to anticipate and help decipher an unfamiliar word. Context allows a child to self-correct when he has misread a word, listen to it within context, and make necessary adjustments.

As valuable as context is to the reading process, it does not substitute for systematic instruction in alphabetic/phonetic code or the explicit teaching of vocabulary. Skilled readers should not depend solely on pictures and surrounding words for decoding—they likewise use phonics and the alphabetic code. Choosing on-level reading material that does not promote guessing is therefore important. Although true for all students, the importance of reinforcing phonics for decoding is compounded for children with learning disabilities and for language learners.

Homonyms, homographs, and homophones

Context is especially important as words may have more than one meaning.

- A homonym means two words that have the same spelling but have different meanings.
- A homophone means two words with the same pronunciation but different spellings and different meanings.
- A homograph means two words that have the same spelling but have different pronunciations and different meanings.

For example, if a student reads about cacti and lizards, context must be used to determine the correct pronunciation of *desert* – is the text referring to the eco-system or the verb "to abandon"?

Homonyms	Homophones	Homographs
tire on car	scene/seen	close the doors
tire after long day		he is sitting close
	mail/male	
the price is fair		the desert is hot
go to the fair	blue/blew	desert a friend in need
	ate/eight	
weigh on the scale		take a bow
scale the wall	fair/fare	tie a bow on box

Semantic cues

Semantic cues use the meaning of surrounding words to logically help determine the meaning of an unfamiliar word. The following are some common semantic cues with examples based on the word *telegraph*.

1. **Roots and Affixes:** *tele-* (distance) + *graph* (writing)
2. **Contrast and Antonyms:** The telegraph could be delivered promptly, *unlike* the letter carried by a stagecoach, which required months for delivery.
3. **Logic:** The telegraph conveyed messages electronically across the United States.
4. **Definition:** The telegraph was a system of communication that electronically transmitted a textual message across a distance.
5. **Example:** Telegraphs were common forms of communication, like the Pony Express.
6. **Cause and Effect:** The transcontinental telegraph was completed in 1861; *consequently*, the Pony Express was terminated.

the meaning of an unfamiliar word. The following are some common semantic

Syntactic Cues

Syntactic cues use grammar to help a student better understand an unfamiliar word.

⊙ **Word order:** position of the word reveals if it is a noun, subject, adjective, object, and so on. Common word orders include

SUBJECT + VERB + OBJECT ("Scientists are studying the solar eclipse.")

ADJECTIVE + NOUN ("solar eclipse")

ARTICLE + NOUN ("the eclipse")

⊙ **Word endings:** endings can also reveal part of speech:

-*tion* and -*ness* -- nouns (nation, happiness)

-*ous* and -*able* -- adjectives (cautious, lovable)

-*ed* and -*ing* -- verb (walked, talking)

-*ly* -- adverb (sadly, brightly)

Modeling with read-alouds

Reading high-quality children's literature aloud serves as an excellent model for students to demonstrate how to use context to derive meaning.

For example, a teacher may read a passage and then stop to ask, "Hmm…I wonder what precocious means. The sentence says…" The teacher is then able to model his/her thought process to determine the meaning of *precocious* based on surrounding text.

Dictionaries

For words undecipherable through context cues or structural analysis, a dictionary may be useful. This support also promotes the use of reference materials and encourages students to become more familiar with such processes.

Readers should be taught when to stop and look up a word and when to depend on context and/or maintain the flow of the passage. For example, dictionaries may be disruptive when students are reading longer sentences containing numerous details. Students may instead choose to underline the word or use a sticky note to later remind them look up the word. This way, the student's fluency is not interrupted and they may gain a better understanding through context clues as they continue. If not, they can simply go back and look up the unfamiliar word once they've reached a natural stopping place.

Students can work on their paraphrasing skills by looking up words and putting definitions in their own words. Dictionary use can also assist students in creating word maps such as the following:

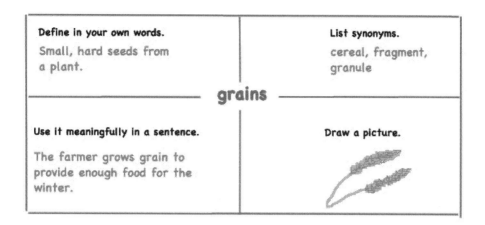

Define in your own words.	List synonyms.
Small, hard seeds from a plant.	cereal, fragment, granule

grains

Use it meaningfully in a sentence.	Draw a picture.
The farmer grows grain to provide enough food for the winter.	

Illustrations

Unfamiliar words can be figured out by looking at any visuals on the page. Charts, graphs, and pictures, as well as surrounding text, often provide helpful context for deciphering words.

For example: "The number of magazines our company sold grew exponentially in May."

Students might not comprehend "exponentially," but they can use illustrations as a context clue.

In some cases, such as with idioms and foreign expressions, using context can be important. However, explicitly teaching common idioms and foreign expressions so they are automatically recognized can help with reading fluency, which in turn, can increase reading comprehension.

Idioms

Both explicit and imbedded instruction in English idioms is beneficial. Because idioms have a meaning beyond the literal, expressions such as "bought a lemon" cannot be comprehended by looking up *bought* and *lemon* in the dictionary. Books such as the *Amelia Bedelia* series that contain jokes and pictures of the literal words can promote students' familiarity of common idioms.

Common Idioms
It's raining cats and dogs.
Every cloud has a silver lining.
A penny for your thoughts.
Beat around the bush.

It is important to note that English Language Learners may especially struggle with idioms as they are unfamiliar and often make no sense when first heard. It is therefore very important to either pre-teach such expressions or provide direct instruction to explain their meaning.

Foreign words

When words from other languages are embedded within text, students may or may not be able to simply look the word up in the dictionary. While common terms such as déjà vu may be easily found, looking up the words bona and fide in a dictionary will not lead a student to understand bona fide.
Therefore, some of the more frequently used foreign words that are grade and age appropriate should be taught in prereading activities or explicitly addressed while reading.
On the right are some common foreign expressions.

Alma mater - **school that one attended**
Carte blanche - **full discretionary power**
Deja vu - **feeling you already experienced something**
Du jour - **made for a particular day**
E. Pluribus unum - **one out of many**
Prima donna - **main female singer in an opera**
Status quo - **current situation**

Abbreviations

Students might recognize such abbreviations as "FBI" without a complete understanding of what the letters represent. By contrast, they might understand doctor, but not MD. Practice working with both the meaning of abbreviations and the abbreviations of common groups of words is effective for promoting automatic recognition.

BC - **Before Christ**
e.g. - **example given**
FYI - **for your information**
Mr. - **mister**
PS - **post script**
vs. - **versus**

STRATEGIES FOR WORDS IN CONTEXT PRACTICE

1. A fourth grader struggles to read the following list of words:
statues
gigantic
cuneiform
fountain

However, the student can accurately pronounce them when reading the following sentence,

> Gigantic statues stood in front of walls carved with cuneiform and fountains flowing with water.

What conclusion can be drawn?

A. The student has a limited oral vocabulary.

B. The student can use the dictionary to support comprehension.

C. The student uses syntactic and semantic clues to derive meaning but has difficulty decoding words in isolation.

D. The student has mastered morphologically complex words, but not fluency.

2. **During a read-aloud, a teacher reads a sentence using the expression "to cost an arm and a leg." What strategy should be followed to determine the meaning of the expression?**

A. Clap the syllables.

B. Look up the words *cost*, *arm*, and *leg* in the dictionary.

C. Model structural analysis.

D. Give examples of other situations in which the words "to cost an arm and a leg" are used.

3. **Which statement is <u>not</u> true about using a dictionary?**

A. Breaking from reading to enter words and definitions into a journal benefits comprehension.

B. Paraphrasing a dictionary definition of an unfamiliar word benefits comprehension.

C. When context is inconclusive, a dictionary definition might be the best option.

D. Skill in structural analysis of words helps limit the necessity for using the dictionary.

4. **The following sentence demonstrates which of the following concepts?**
    "With the well dug in the backyard, they could live well."
    A. Roots and affixes are useful context clues.
    B. Two words can be pronounced the same but have different meanings.
    C. English words have predictable suffixes that can be used to determine part of speech.
    D. Dictionaries do not help to understand the meaning of idioms.

5. **Which of the following activities would require students to use context cues to derive meaning?**
    A. Find alliteration in the sentence: "Three gray geese in the green grass grazing."
    B. Read a list of words in isolation.
    C. Read the italicized word with comprehension: "The athlete was asked, 'Which *attribute* has most helped you to succeed?'"
    D. Read the italicized word with comprehension: "The spirit was *malevolent*."

6. **Which sentence can be used to model the use of context cues to determine information about the italicized word?**
    A. The *turquoise* boxes were loaded into the van first.
    B. The van was *in* the driveway all day.
    C. Mechanics arrived promptly to repair the *stalled* van.
    D. The van was equipped with *radials*.

7. **What is the instructional need for a student who looks at a picture of a laptop and misreads the sentence "The *computer* is on the desk" as "The *laptop* is on the desk"?**
    A. Help build oral vocabulary
    B. Provide practice for automatic recognition of high-frequency words
    C. Remind the student to use illustrations to support decoding
    D. Instruct alphabetic code and phonics explicitly

8. **A student reads the sentence, "The ambitious flight attendant offered to store the luggage in the captain's closet." When a student attempts to comprehend the word** *ambitious* **by analyzing the word's location before a noun and analyzing the suffix** *–ous,* **that student is using what strategy?**
   A. Semantic cues
   B. Syntactic cues
   C. Alphabetic code
   D. Knowledge of synonyms

9. **In the following sentence, which type of cues would provide students information on the meaning of the italicized word?**

   "The teacher gave praise to the well-behaving student but *reprimanded* the unruly one."

   A. Semantic cues based on logic
   B. Syntactic cues based on word order
   C. Semantic cues based on contrasts
   D. Syntactic cues based on word endings

10. **An ELL student reads aloud, "The young boy wanted to improve his musical abilities" as "The young boy wants to improve his musical ability." Which of the following should a teacher first do to support the student's development of decoding skills?**
    A. Provide explicit instruction on how to use syntactic cues to decode unfamiliar words.
    B. Provide explicit instruction on how inflectional morphemes reflect verb tenses and singular/plurals.
    C. Provide implicit instruction on how affixes change the meaning of common roots.
    D. Provide implicit instruction on how derivational morphemes can be used to make a noun an adjective.

1. C Choice C is the best answer, as we know the student derives meaning from the context to support decoding by correctly reading them within a sentence. The student does not, however, have the ability to decode the same words when read in isolation, indicating a reliance on context cues to support fluency. Oral vocabulary, choice A, is important to reading comprehension, but the student certainly does not lack oral vocabulary when reading an advanced word aloud in context. The use of a dictionary to read this sentence, Choice B, would break the reader's flow; it would be preferable for the reader to derive meaning from the context in this example. Finally, this activity would not prove the student has mastered morphologically complex words as he or she is unable to decode words in isolation (Choice D).

2. D The expression "to cost an arm and a leg" is an idiom, which is an expression that does not make sense when read literally word-for-word. Idioms are best analyzed by considering other situations in which they are used, making Choice D the best answer. Though stopping to clap syllables during a read-aloud as suggested in Choice A, does help increase phonological awareness, it would not help to decipher the meaning of the expression. Similarly, looking up individual words (Choice B), would not help find an idiom's meaning beyond the literal. Choice C is also incorrect because *cost*, *arm*, and *leg* cannot be analyzed using structural analysis--there is no common affix (a prefix or suffix).

3. A Choice A is not true - it is often preferable to allow students to continue reading fluently and not interrupt their flow while reading to look up words in the dictionary. Though the dictionary can be an excellent reference tool, if a student were to stop every few sentences to look up a word, their fluency would likely decrease and further meaning would therefore be lost. However, there are certainly situations in which dictionary use is warranted such as when context is inconclusive (Choice C). Structural analysis, Choice D, often serves as a helpful alternative to using the dictionary. In choice B, paraphrasing the definition by putting it into one's own words is beneficial to reading skills and comprehension as it prompts students to put things into their own words, making it simpler to recall the meaning in the future.

4. B The word well, although pronounced the same in the sentence, has two *different* meanings. The first *well* refers to a water source and the second *well* means *good* or *positive*. The sentence does not contain roots and affixes, as suggested in Choices A and C, which would promote decoding. This sentence also does not contain an idiom as choice D suggests. An idiom would be an expression that cannot be understood because it contains nonliteral meanings; the words in this particular sentence could be looked up in the dictionary.

5. C Choice C would require students to use context cues as the sentence contains a homograph (*attribute* can be a noun referring to a characteristic of something or a verb referring to explaining by indicating a cause). Homographs require context in order to determine their pronunciation and meaning. Alliteration, Choice A, deals with common onsets and phonemic awareness, not comprehension. Choice B requires students to read words in isolation – this is simply a sight word and/or decoding activity; students do not need to understand the words to be successful. Finally, the sentence in Choice D does not provide any context clues from which to draw meaning. However, the word *malevolent* does include common roots and affixes so structural analysis could be used to help decode and possibly derive meaning.

6. C Choice C provides the best sentence to model the use of context cues to determine information about the italicized word. With this sentence, a skilled reader can support comprehension by considering the surrounding words, such as *mechanics* and repair which form context cues and help a reader make sense of the word *stalled*. By contrast, in Choices A and D, the context does not clarify the meaning. There is no word that clarifies turquoise in Choice A, and *radials* cannot be clarified in Choice D. Finally, the word *in* in choice B should be taught for automatic word recognition in order to be read independently of context cues.

7. D Although increasing oral vocabulary (as suggested in Choice A) and improving a student's automatic word recognition (Choice B), are both strategies to strengthen a student's reading skills, neither would necessarily help the student in this situation. Because the student is relying too heavily on pictures to support his reading, reminding him to use illustrations to support decoding will likewise provide insufficient help (Choice C). Rather, the student needs explicit instruction in letter-sound relations to help in decoding words rather than guessing based on illustrations as suggested in Choice D.

8. B   Choice B is the best answer - syntax cues use grammar to help students understand unfamiliar words. By analyzing the order of words (i.e. adjective (ambitious) + noun (flight attendant)) and relating the rules for word order and word endings (i.e. *–ous* in *ambitious*), readers can further derive meaning from words within text. Semantic cues, as suggested in Choice A, use the meaning of surrounding words to determine the meaning of unfamiliar terms. The alphabetic code, Choice C, involves letters and does not assist with determining meaning for unfamiliar words. Synonyms, choice D, are words with similar meanings and while they can be an excellent resource from which to pull, no synonyms for the word *ambitious* are mentioned in the sentence.

9. C   In this example, semantic cues, or cues that surface from looking at the meaning of the words surrounding the unfamiliar word, can be used to provide information. The use of the word "but" provides a contrast between "gave praise" for the behaving student and "reprimanded" for the unruly student. Students can thus figure out that reprimanded must be negative and deal with criticizing. Choice A also cites semantic cues, but logic does not provide information on reprimanded as much as the contrast does; without the contrast, logic may not be enough to figure out the meaning of reprimanded. Similarly, the word order, choice B, and word ending, choice D, do not reveal as much information as noticing the contrast would.

10. B   In this case, the student inaccurately reads the verb "wants" and the noun "abilities," which changes the tense and quantity. ELL students can benefit from explicit instruction on how inflectional morphemes are important to meaning, such as how the letter and sound "s" mark a plural. In this case, choice A, syntactic cues or looking at word order or part of speech would not correct this error. Roots and affixes, choice C, also would not explain the difference between verb tenses and quantities. The student does not present issues with derivational morphemes, choice D.

3.4   Teaching Vocabulary

As with most areas of reading, vocabulary demonstrates the Matthew effect. In terms of vocabulary, this means that students who begin a unit of study with a strong prior knowledge of vocabulary typically acquire additional vocabulary faster than students who enter with a weak vocabulary. As a result, the knowledge gap between students can widen rather than narrow. Despite where children begin, however, explicit vocabulary instruction can help all students acquire new words and build upon existing knowledge.

Definition

In its broadest definition, vocabulary is all the words that make a language. More restricted definitions refer to words related to a subject, words needed to communicate, knowledge of words and their meanings.

Vocabulary can be receptive (listening and reading) or expressive (speaking and reading). In other terms, a student's receptive language serves as the "input" (how a child understands vocabulary, for example), while expressive language serves as the "output" (or the vocabulary a child is able to use while talking or writing). Though receptive and expressive language skills go beyond vocabulary and can include how children interpret and use gestures, process information and level of grammatical understanding, vocabulary also contributes a great deal to language. It should be noted some students are stronger in one area of vocabulary than another and that oral language typically precedes development of written vocabulary.

- ⊙ Receptive Vocabulary - A student's receptive vocabulary is all of the words they are able to recognize and understand either while reading or listening to someone else talk.
- ⊙ Expressive Vocabulary - A student's expressive vocabulary includes all of the words he/she is able to appropriately use when writing or while speaking.

It is important students are provided with quality vocabulary instruction – both receptive and expressive – as this dictates what they will and will not understand and what they are able and not able to express. Providing children with varied reading experiences is the best way to improve upon both receptive and expressive vocabularies.

Vocabulary is considered a reliable indicator for reading comprehension – understandably, when students struggle with the meanings of words within text, their comprehension is compromised.

Instructional Strategies

There are many ways to teach vocabulary. While each of the following are valuable strategies, a combination of the various approaches should be used to meet the needs of diverse learners.

It is important to keep in mind that there are several ways in which children acquire new vocabulary – through both organic, implicit experiences as well as explicit lessons focused on teaching new terms and their meanings.

Read Alouds

Children's literature includes complex, specialized vocabulary. By listening to books read aloud, listeners gain access to words they may not otherwise hear or read themselves. For instance, the classic *Mike Mulligan and His Steam Shovel* contains the words *canals, cellar, town constable,* and *town hall*. Although basal readers are useful resources for teaching reading skills, they are not as valuable a source for teaching vocabulary as authentic text. Basals are not intended to build vocabulary, but rather restrict words to those likely found in a child's oral vocabulary. Authentic literature, however, contains broader vocabulary and is thus a better source for vocabulary development.

Teach Select Words

Vocabulary can be broken into several categories:
- High-frequency words (for example, *water*)
- Sight Words (for example: *is, to, the*)
- Words common to a specialized context (for example, *aquarium*)
- Low-frequency words related to subject-specific content (for example, *aqueduct*)

When considering words to teach, selection should focus on the latter two groups.

Vocabulary words can be contextual or noncontextual. Contextual words come from a text or unit of study. Noncontextual words are not related to a content area. Selecting and grouping noncontextual vocabulary by morpheme (prefix, root, suffix) is highly effective. Because more mature readers will learn to apply word analysis skills automatically, vocabulary selection for mature readers can focus on words not easily analyzed.

Preteach Vocabulary

Teachers may choose to preteach selected vocabulary to activate prior knowledge and provide background knowledge to set students up for success in their independent or group reading. This strategy also helps level the playing field as everyone is provided with an understanding of key vocabulary prior to reading new text.

Link to Prior Knowledge

Students can more efficiently acquire vocabulary when they are able to link it to prior knowledge. For example, when a student can read *quarter*, that knowledge can also be used to read and understand vocabulary such as *quart, quartet,* and *quarterly.*

Provide Definitions and Examples

Definitions and explanations should contain words students already understand. Conceptually difficult words should be taught explicitly using visuals and common examples that allow students to activate prior knowledge and make connections, making words more memorable. For example: if teaching the word axle, students could be provided with a simple definition, as well as a picture of a truck, bicycle, and car to illustrate and make connections about how axles are used and seen in our everyday activities.

Vocabulary Word: axle

Definition: bar that passes through a wheel

Transfer Vocabulary to New Contexts

After students understand contextual vocabulary in a unit, the next step is to transfer the word to a different context. For example, in "The Brave Tin Soldier" students are introduced to the word *shouldered*.

> "They shouldered arms and looked straight before them, and wore a splendid uniform, red and blue."

Once students understand *shouldered*, they may be asked to use the word in a context such as a batboy *shouldering* the bag of bats to the game. And, when they come across the same term in another text, they'll begin to recognize the word and understand it within the new context.

Use Familiar Synonyms and Antonyms

For some vocabulary, students can clearly understand an unfamiliar word through synonyms or antonyms. Having students generate their own list of synonyms and/or antonyms is also a good way to help them make connections and recall meaning.

Pronounce Words/Provide Auditory Exposure

Pronouncing a word enough times and leading the student to repeat helps secure the word in the student's oral vocabulary. Whereas some students are able to recall a new vocabulary word and meaning after hearing it just a few times, others require the auditory reminder ten or twenty times.
Students need to hear a clear pronunciation of unfamiliar words with several syllables (for example, *proboscis*) several times. Also, if students are confusing words with similar sounds (for example, *sell/sale*), clearly distinguish the sounds and take time to compare the individual sounds and syllables.
Specific attention should be given to language learners who might not know all English phonemes needed to distinguish words.

Look at the Spelling

Drawing attention to spelling can support students in reading vocabulary words (for example, *assistants/assistance*). Providing reminders for students to attend to word endings (*-ing, -ed, -s*) helps support both reading and comprehension.

Repeat/Review/Provide Sufficient Exposure

Teachers need to structure reviews so students are repeatedly exposed to vocabulary in varied contexts. Repetition is necessary for new vocabulary to be secured in the learner's mind, and it can be accomplished through word games and activities as well as through more organic experiences, such as noticing words in text and using them in content-specific manners.

Provide Semantic Maps (Graphic Organizers)

Visual representations help many students recall vocabulary. Semantic maps might include a dictionary definition or surrounding words from the text that give clues, synonyms, antonyms, pictures, phrases, or idioms.

These maps can be both provided for students to reference and may also be produced by the students – working with the term and developing their own definition, synonyms, and/or antonyms is often helpful.

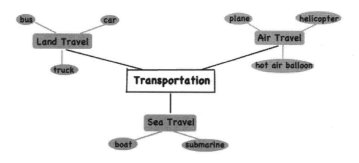

Group Words Conceptually

Grouping new sets of words conceptually can help make new vocabulary more meaningful. By organizing words into categories, students begin to connect among concepts, and are then often better able to recall word meanings. For example, after brainstorming a list of words associated with weather to introduce a science unit, the following could be created with teacher support:

Moderate Weather Conditions	Severe Weather Conditions
cold front	hurricane
warm front	blizzard
temperature	tornado
humidity	earthquake

Use Teacher Modeling

With consideration, a teacher can model sophisticated vocabulary. For example, a teacher might request her class line up in an *orderly* manner and progress *swiftly*. The teacher can commend a student's *exemplary work*. Students of all language levels need to hear sophisticated language used frequently and accurately. Teachers who strategically interject selected vocabulary into classroom conversations provide opportunities for students to appropriately hear otherwise unfamiliar vocabulary in natural and meaningful ways.

Use Cross-Domain/Cross-Disciplinary Examples

Connecting vocabulary across disciplines does not happen naturally. When a teacher can connect English vocabulary words to history or science, the teacher increases the possibility that the student will recognize that vocabulary in varied contexts.

For example, students who learn *terri*tory and Medi*terra*nean in social studies, *terra*rium in science, and extra*terre*strial in literature have more opportunities to hear the vocabulary in context and learn to automatically associate *terr* with land and earth.

Or, while studying the American Revolution in social studies, students who also read about the period during reading groups become more familiar and comfortable with key terms.

Teaching cross-curricularly often helps students acquire new vocabulary as well as understand other content related concepts – because students become immersed in the subject area there are more opportunities for them to make connections and process new ideas.

English Language Learners

Cognates

Cognates are words that share etymological origins with words in the same or different language (for example, the English word *celebrate* and Spanish word *celebrar*). Recognizing cognates helps English language learners simplify learning vocabulary by connecting English words to terms in the students' native language and/or connecting English words together.

Although English shares few cognates with Asian languages, it shares up to 40 percent of its words with Spanish.

Prior Knowledge

It is important to recognize English language learners might have extensive knowledge of content subjects in their native language. Determining if this is the case is often important; teaching the word *gravity* to a learner who already understands the concept is easier than explaining both the concept of gravity *and* teaching the vocabulary. Attaching the word to the learner's prior knowledge and experience can make the lessons significantly easier for students.

TEACHING VOCABULARY PRACTICE

1. **A fourth-grade class is reading a passage that starts out with the following line:**

   "Alfred Nobel, the Swede who invented dynamite in 1866, established the Nobel Peace Prize to help make amends for his destructive creation"
   (National Geographic Picture Atlas of Our World, 1990).

   Which of the following criteria should the teacher use to plan how to teach new vocabulary?
   A. Pre-teach high-frequency words to ensure fluency in reading.
   B. Pre-teach conceptually difficult words to ensure comprehension.
   C. Pre-teach words that can be deciphered through word analysis skills.
   D. Allow students to select vocabulary as they discover unfamiliar words.

2. **What is a benefit of reading literature aloud to children that leveled reading groups do not provide?**
   A. Exposure to specialized vocabulary, which leads to increased oral vocabulary
   B. Practice with decoding high-frequency words to automaticity
   C. Opportunities to increase fluency
   D. Support for students identifying word families

3. **Which statement accurately explains how most students acquire vocabulary?**
   A. Oral language typically precedes development of written vocabulary.
   B. Written vocabulary typically precedes development of oral language.

C. Written vocabulary and oral vocabulary are developed simultaneously.

D. Oral language has no effect on the development of written vocabulary.

4. **A fourth-grade class is beginning a unit on simple machines. Which activity would best prepare them to learn about the subject?**

A. Read a passage aloud that contains key specialized vocabulary.

B. Present pictures or objects of a bicycle, a ramp, and a hand-crank can opener.

C. Provide dictionary definitions of selected vocabulary.

D. Provide a Venn diagram to compare inclined planes and screws.

5. **After studying the Qing Dynasty, a fifth-grade class completes their first independent reading about the subject. Students were provided with books on their independent levels. A comprehension check reveals many comprehension levels in the group. What action should the teacher consider to improve reading comprehension for all students?**

A. Provide additional decoding instruction.

B. Listen to a recording of common Chinese sounds and words to facilitate fluency in pronunciation.

C. Determine the extent to which vocabulary limited student's comprehension. Select and teach vocabulary.

D. Show a documentary about the Qing Dynasty so all students have the same understanding and background knowledge.

6. **The English word** *carrot* **(a root vegetable) and the Vietnamese word** *ca rot* **(a root vegetable) are examples of which of the following?**

A. Words with multiple meanings

B. Homophones

C. Schema

D. Cognates

7. **A fifth-grade teacher selected the following words for a vocabulary lesson:** *evident, video, vision.* **What strategy does this selection demonstrate?**
   A. Grouping words by word family
   B. Grouping words by word structure
   C. Grouping words by content area
   D. Grouping words by intial sound

8. **A fourth-grade science teacher selected conceptually challenging words connected to a unit of study on insects and provided dictionary definitions for the words. The students were instructed to illustrate each word and use it in a sentence. What strategy is demonstrated?**
   A. Teach vocabulary across disciplines.
   B. Visualize and provide multiple opportunities for exposure.
   C. Transfer the content to a different setting.
   D. Link words to prior knowledge.

9. **A class brainstorms to develop a list of words about space. Which of the following would be the best follow-up activity?**
   A. Group words conceptually.
   B. Define unfamiliar words.
   C. Practice pronunciation to fluency.
   D. Set the brainstorming list aside and introduce words that will be part of the unit.

10. **A fourth-grade class is starting a unit on American writers. In pairs, the students talk about their favorite book. They then report back to the class about what their partners said. How does this activity promote vocabulary development?**
    A. Students are working on their receptive vocabulary by talking about their favorite book.
    B. Students are working on their expressive vocabulary by listening to others talk about their favorite book.

C. Students are working on their receptive vocabulary by listening to their partner and their expressive vocabulary by talking about their favorite book and sharing with the class.

D. Students are working on their receptive vocabulary by reporting to the class what their partners said.

TEACHING VOCABULARY EXPLANATIONS

1. B   By fourth grade, students should be reading high-frequency words with automaticity and understanding, as suggested in choice A. Although the passage has several words composed of common word parts (*dynamite, destructive, creation*), as suggested in choice C, it is best to select conceptually difficult words to introduce a passage or new unit of study, so that students use word analysis skills on their own while reading. Although choice D is a good idea, by pre-teaching selected vocabulary, everyone is provided with necessary background knowledge and is better prepared to understand the reading. It is appropriate to select words from the passage and, particularly, conceptually difficult words (for example, *amends*), which will promote understanding of the expression "make *amends*." Therefore, B is the best choice.

2. A   Reading literature aloud to students exposes them to vocabulary that might not otherwise be part of their everyday lives or are not yet part of their oral vocabulary. While leveled reading groups do often offer books with simple structures and high readability to promote decoding, fluency, and help students identify word families (as suggested in Choices B, C, and D), they do not necessarily provide exposure to rich vocabulary, making Choice A the best answer.

3. A   Students typically listen to and use new vocabulary orally before they incorporate the same words into their reading and writing. Therefore, Choice A is the best choice—oral language (listening and speaking) precedes development of written vocabulary (reading and writing). In contrast to what is suggested in Choice D, oral language does play an important role in a student's written vocabulary – if a child is not orally exposed to rich vocabulary, they are unable to use such words.

4. B   Providing students with examples of a subject by allowing them to see pictures or objects activates prior knowledge and provides a context in which to learn new information. Reading a passage (Choice A), finding dictionary definitions (Choice C), and completing a graphic organizer (Choice D) would be more meaningful activities once the student has acquired necessary background information.

5. C   Because unfamiliar vocabulary is a common cause of poor comprehension, it would be beneficial for the teacher to assess the level to which vocabulary is causing students' difficulties. If it is determined that students are struggling with vocabulary, additional instruction in this area could significantly increase their understanding of the material. Because students are already reading text at their independent levels, they should already be able to fluently read their assigned books. Therefore, additional decoding instruction is unlikely to increase their comprehension, as suggested in Choice A. Because the text is in English, providing exposure to common Chinese sounds will also do little to increase comprehension (Choice B). This activity, however, would provide students with pertinent background knowledge and help facilitate their ability to correctly pronounce new vocabulary words. Finally, showing students a documentary on the subject (Choice D) would be an excellent preteaching activity to ensure everyone begins the unit with the necessary background knowledge, however, it will not necessarily help students further comprehend their independent reading books.

6. D   Words that share similar pronunciation and meaning in the same language or across different languages are called cognates. Recognizing cognates is a helpful strategy in language learning. The words do not necessarily have multiple meanings (Choice A), the same sound (Choice B), or the schema or plan (Choice C). Cognates are especially important for English Language Learners – explicitly pointing out the language similarities often helps students make connections between their native language and English.

7. B   *Evident, video,* and *vision* come from the Latin root video. The words do not come from the same word family (Choice A) such as *can, fan,* and *man.* They also are not from the same content area or unit of study (Choice C), and the initial sounds are not the same among all three words (Choice D) as one begins with /e/ and two with /v/. The words are, however, similar in their structure as they all come from the root word *video,* making Choice B the best answer.

8. B Pictures and sentences support reinforcement for students when acquiring new vocabulary – by providing multiple opportunities to hear, see and use the words, the teacher is helping to make the words more meaningful and familiar. Choice A, teaching vocabulary across the disciplines, is done when words are connected among literature, science, and social studies. This unit is specific to science. The assignment to draw pictures and write sentences does not require students to put the words in different settings, as suggested by Choice C and the students will likely use the words in the science setting in which they were taught. Finally, the assignment does not link the words to student's prior knowledge (Choice D).

9. A When words are grouped conceptually, students can see a connection among words and master them with greater efficiency. Defining unfamiliar words (Choice B) and pronouncing words (Choice C) are easier once the student is able to connect them to other, already familiar, words. The words the class came up with while brainstorming, even if not comprehensive of the unit, can still be used and will provide students with some ownership of their learning, making Choice D invalid.

10. C Though receptive and expressive vocabulary are related, different activities may target one or the other. Choice C is the best answer as the activity described in the question involves both receptive and expressive vocabulary. While listening to their partner students are using receptive vocabulary; while telling their partner about their favorite book and reporting back to the class, they are using expressive vocabulary. Because receptive vocabulary involves listening and reading, Choices A and D are incorrect. Finally, because expressive vocabulary involves speaking or writing, Choice B is also incorrect.

3.5 Chapter Review

1. **Which list includes words that are decipherable through structural analysis?**
   A. Grapes, banana, oranges, guava
   B. Reaction, actor, deactivate, hyperactive
   C. Run, fun, sun, bun
   D. Mr., Mrs., Dr., Jr.

2. **An ability to analyze morphologically complex words supports a student's ability to read which sentence?**
   A. His impenetrable courage and unstoppable will energized his fellow soldiers.
   B. The cat sat in the tan van.
   C. Though the young bear cubs enjoyed the cold, the zookeeper could not bear to be outside very long.
   D. Her little brother had taken the lion's share of the pizza before she returned.

3. **While working one-on-one with a second grader, a teacher notices the student frequently leaves off word endings. For example, when reading the following sentence, the student said** *plate* **instead of** *plates*.
   His mother told him to take out plates for everyone.
   Which of the following is the most appropriate way for the teacher to address this type of error?
   A. Take a running record using a passage at the student's instructional level to determine fluency and accuracy rates.
   B. When the student finishes reading the passage, explicitly point out all of the errors that were made.
   C. Each time the student makes an error, stop him and have him decode the mispronounced word and add it to a list of words that should be practiced independently at home.
   D. Verify the student understands how endings change the meaning of words – for example, *plate* refers to one plate and *plates* refers to multiple plates.

4. Providing students with instruction in word analysis will likely increase all of the following except?

A. Comprehension

B. Decoding

C. Understand meaning of unfamiliar multisyllabic words

D. Literary analysis

5. A teacher writes this list of words on the board:

> *paper*
> *later*
> *maker*
> *gator*

Which of the following syllabication rules is demonstrated by this list of words?

A. Some words divide into syllables by roots and affixes.

B. Open syllables end with a vowel sound.

C. Some words divide by VC/CV

D. This list of words does not demonstrate any rules of syllabication.

6. A teacher has her students read these sentences aloud:

> While at the zoo, we got to see a *bear*.
> The kitchen cupboard was *bare*.

The italicized words are examples of which of the following?

A. Homophones

B. Homographs

C. Word Analysis

D. Phonemes

7. Read the following sentence:

> Chefs frequently use ____(1)____ when ____(2)____ with bland ____(3)____ to make the flavors more ____(4)____ .

A word with the suffix –ing would fit best in which of the above blanks?

A. 1
B. 2
C. 3
D. 4

8. Why might dictionaries not be the best resource to use when students come across an unfamiliar word within a long text?

A. Words often have multiple meanings and the meaning may change due to word endings, making it easy for a student to read the wrong definition.

B. Dictionaries should always be consulted when students come across an unfamiliar word – they promote the use of reference materials.

C. Dictionaries may become disruptive when students are reading longer, more complex sentences.

D. Students who have weak alphabetizing skills may find dictionaries difficult to use.

9. A third grader reads the following sentence aloud:

> "Please stop beating around the bush and tell me what happened," Angel's mother said.

How can the teacher best help her students understand the above idiomatic expression?

A. Have students use the dictionary to look up individual words within the phrase, "beating around the bush".

B. Have students come up with synonyms for beating.

C. Provide other examples that use the same expression in context for students.

D. Discuss other spellings and uses of the word beating.

10. **Using a literacy-based vocabulary strategy, teachers are encouraged to select vocabulary words from chapters of books used in guided reading. Which of the following vocabulary lists from The Velveteen Rabbit demonstrates conceptual grouping?**

   A. *shape, sharp, shabby*

   B. *rustling, mechanical, insignificant* (from chapter 1)

   C. *burrows, garden, bracken*

   D. "When you are *Real* you don't mind being hurt."

11. **After studying different climate patterns, a teacher leads students in creating a semantic map of words associated with climate. This type of activity likely helps to improve student's vocabulary through which of the following?**

   A. Structural analysis is a helpful tool for deciphering unknown words.

   B. Coming up with synonyms helps students to better understand unknown words.

   C. Working with students to group similar vocabulary words helps them to understand and recall the meaning of words.

   D. It helps students to compare and contrast different words using a semantic map like a Venn diagram.

12. **Why is it important to read aloud to students?**

   A. If students are fluent readers, they do not need to be read aloud to; instead, they should be encouraged to be independent readers.

   B. Reading aloud allows students to spend less time decoding unfamiliar words.

   C. Reading aloud allows students to be exposed to vocabulary they may not otherwise come across through reading at their independent and instructional levels.

   D. It allows all students to read the same story even if they are at different levels.

13. **Which of the following is not a primary reason for teaching vocabulary words across the curriculum?**

A. Teaching cross-curricular vocabulary allows students additional and more frequent exposure to similar root words and words that are related to each other contextually.

B. It allows students to make connections between various lessons, making it easier to recall vocabulary words.

C. Connecting vocabulary across disciplines increases chances students will recognize words in different contexts.

D. Teaching cross-curricular vocabulary improves skill in using text features of informational texts.

14. **Words that share the same etymological origins with words in the same or another language are known as which of the following?**
    A. Synonyms
    B. Homonyms
    C. Homophones
    D. Cognates

15. **Which of the following is important to do when promoting vocabulary acquisition with English language learners?**
    A. Attach vocabulary words to the learner's prior knowledge.
    B. Provide instruction in the learner's native language.
    C. Provide students with below grade-level vocabulary to make lessons simpler to understand.
    D. Avoid teaching cross curricular words.

16. **Which of the following strategies is an effective way for teachers to implicitly teach sophisticated vocabulary that students may not otherwise hear?**
    A. Provide students with a random list of vocabulary words each week.
    B. Teachers should do their best to speak using simple language so that students do not become confused by directions and requests.
    C. Strategically interject mature vocabulary into classroom conversation in meaningful ways.
    D. Have students write on a sticky note unknown words they come across in their independent reading.

17. **A fourth-grade class is instructed to use structural analysis skills in order to attach meaning to an unfamiliar word. Which of the following would demonstrate this skill?**
    A. comprehending a word by looking at its place in the sentence
    B. comprehending a word by using words around it to make a guess
    C. comprehending a word by looking for prefixes, suffixes and roots
    D. comprehending a word by chunking it

18. **Student vocabulary is considered a reliable indicator for**
    A. Reading comprehension abilities
    B. Future academic success
    C. Understanding of syllables
    D. Phonemic awareness skills

19. **Short words have been written on each half of a plastic egg. Students match two words to create one new word: butter + fly, pan + cake, mail + box. What concept does this activity promote?**
    A. compound words
    B. contractions
    C. expanded oral vocabulary
    D. homophones

20. **Second graders work in pairs to join two puzzle pieces with words written on them to form one word (for example, *cup* and *cake* become *cupcake* and *fire* and *fly* become *firefly*). Next, students draw a picture and write a sentence using the word. The teacher is most likely using this activity to promote which of the following?**
    A. how to use context clues to determine the meaning of an unknown word
    B. a strategy to decode multisyllabic words
    C. develop an understanding of compound words
    D. a strategy to help spell multisyllabic words

1. B Structural analysis is the process of breaking down a word into smaller parts to make it simpler to decode or understand. It could be used for words such as those listed in Choice B as they all have the root word "*act.*" Therefore, if you know "act" means "to move or to do," you can determine the meanings of the listed words using their prefixes (attached to the beginning of words) and/or suffixes (attached to the end of words):

Prefix	Meaning
re-	again
de-	opposite
hyper-	over, extra

Suffix	Meaning
-tion	action
-ive	inclined to

Based on the meanings of prefixes and suffixes:

- *reaction* means *to act again*
- *deactivate* means the opposite of *activate* or to *unactivate*
- *hyperactive* means *over* or *extra active*

Though Choice A contains words that are similar in topic that would provide context cues, structural analysis could not be used. Choice C lists words that share the same rime, which helps in pronunciation but not comprehension and would not be decipherable through the use of structural analysis. Finally, Choice D presents abbreviations that would need to be looked up or automatically recognized.

2. A The words in choice A - *impenetrable, unstoppable,* and *energized* - are examples of morphologically complex words, or words made up of parts (whether a compound word or a root with an affix, etc.). Choice B includes words that are beneficial for recognizing onset and rime (for words such as *cat/sat* and *tan/van*). Choice C would require a look at context in order to determine the homographs' pronunciation and meaning, and Choice D targets knowledge of idioms, or expressions made up of words that have nonliteral meanings (i.e. *a lion's share*).

3. D Verifying the student understands how word endings often alter meaning and/or providing explicit instruction to teach how various endings impact meaning would be the most appropriate strategy. By doing this, students are provided with the tools necessary to independently begin to recognize when they misread a word. Choice A would provide information regarding how fluently the student reads, not help the student to attend to word endings. While their lack of ability to recognize endings may impact their overall accuracy rating, this strategy will not help the issue at hand. Pointing out each error at the end of the passage is also not an effective strategy. Unless individual sentences are analyzed and there is a discussion about why the words in question have their respective endings, this is unlikely to encourage the student to attend to endings in the future. Having the student stop and make corrections while reading, as suggested in Choice C, could potentially further decrease comprehension by slowing down the student's fluency and making it difficult to understand the text. Furthermore, having the student independently practice a word list at home (also suggested in choice C) will not provide any context or feedback - the words would also likely be practiced incorrectly.

4. D By providing students with the tools necessary to use word analysis, their comprehension, decoding and understanding of multisyllabic words is likely to improve. Because word analysis allows students to break words into smaller parts, students can use their prior knowledge of root words, prefixes and suffixes to decode and understand individual words more easily, also improving their overall text comprehension. Word analysis is not directly related to literary analysis which includes review, criticism, or response to a literary work.

5. B The list of words demonstrates that open syllables (i.e. syllables in which nothing comes after the vowel) end with a vowel sound (the vowel sound is typically long – as in each of the listed words), making Choice B the best answer. The words in the list do not have roots and affixes (Choice A), or divide by VC/CV (Choice C). Because Choice B is correct, Choice D is void.

6. A *Bear* and *bare* are examples of homophones (Choice A). Homophones are words that are pronounced the same, but may have different spellings and meanings. Choice B, homographs, refers to words that have the same spelling but different pronunciation and meaning (i.e. I *read* a book yesterday, Did you *read* the newspaper today?). *Bear* and *bare* do not contain root words, prefixes or suffixes, so word analysis can not be used (Choice C) and phonemes are the most basic unit of speech sounds, not print, making Choice D incorrect.

7. B Syntactic cues use grammar to help students better understand unknown words. Because word position reveals if it is a noun, verb, adjective, etc. and word endings often reveal parts of speech, Choice B is the best answer since Blank #2 is most likely to contain a verb and therefore, a word ending with –*ing*. The easiest way to check this answer is to fill in the spaces with possible word choices - for example:

> *Chefs frequently use (1)spices* when *(2)cooking* with bland *(3)foods* to make the flavors more *(4)tasty.*

By filling in the spaces it becomes clear that Choice B, or space number 2, is the best place to include a vowel with the –*ing* ending.

8. C If students must constantly pause their reading to look up every unfamiliar word in the dictionary, their fluency is often interrupted which in turn, may compromise their comprehension, especially when reading more complex text, making Choice B incorrect (there are appropriate times when dictionaries should not be consulted) and Choice C correct. Instead, at times students may want to use context clues or word analysis to help them determine word meaning. Dictionaries often help to clarify the meaning of homonyms, words with multiple meanings, making Choice A incorrect. Finally, students with weak alphabetizing skills can still use dictionaries, and they may be used as an activity to practice ABC order (Choice D).

9. C By providing examples of how the same expression can be used in other contexts, students can better understand how to use the idiomatic expression, making Choice C the best answer. Having students look up individual words used in the phrase (i.e. *beating, bush*) (Choice A) asking them to generate a list of synonyms for one of the words (Choice B), or discussing other spellings or uses for one of the words within the phrase, will not provide them with an accurate understanding of the phrase's meaning.

10. **C** *Burrows, garden,*and *bracken* are all words that explain the outside environment where the Rabbit played. They can be taught together conceptually. *Shape, sharp,* and *shabby* are alliterated (Choice A); alliteration is not typically a consideration when choosing vocabulary. The words in Choice B are from the same chapter. For the sake of convenience, vocabulary words are often chosen chapter by chapter, rather than by a shared concept. The word *Real* is a use of figurative language (Choice D) rather than conceptual grouping.

11. **C** Creating semantic maps allows students to group vocabulary words into categories, thus making it easier to recall new words and their meanings. Semantic maps are not used to practice structural analysis skills (Choice A) or determine synonyms (Choice B). Choice D is incorrect because a Venn diagram is not a semantic map, and the point is to make associations rather than to compare and contrast two words.

12. **C** Reading aloud to students allows them to be exposed to vocabulary they may not otherwise hear or read in text at their independent or instructional levels, regardless of how fluently they read (making Choice C correct and Choice A incorrect). In fact, when reading aloud, teachers may also demonstrate how to use context cues to understand the meaning of unknown words, further teaching students how to be independent readers. Because students do not practice decoding unfamiliar words while being read aloud to, Choice B is also incorrect. Choice D is incorrect because a read aloud is not necessarily beneficial for keeping all students interested. For students to all know the same story is not necessarily a requirement since differentiated instruction is more effective for meeting the needs of all students.

13. **D** Teaching across the curriculum allows students additional and more frequent exposure to vocabulary words because they have more opportunities to hear and use the words (Choice A). It also provides ways for students to make connections between lessons so vocabulary becomes more memorable (Choice B), and allows vocabulary across subject areas to be connected so students will be more likely to recognize those words in varied contexts (Choice C). There is not a close tie between cross-curricular vocabulary and skill in text features such as table of contents, index, headings, and glossary.

14. D Cognates are words that share etymological origins with words in the same or different language. Explicitly showing students cognates helps them to recognize, learn and recall vocabulary words - especially for English Language Learners. Synonyms (choice A) are words that mean the same thing, homonyms (choice B) are words that sound alike but have different meanings, and homophones (choice C) are types of homonyms in which the words are spelled differently.

15. A By attaching vocabulary words to the learner's prior knowledge, English language learners are more easily able to learn and recall new words. For example, if a student has already learned about gravity in their native language, they only need to learn the English word, not also the meaning. This is much simpler than teaching them both the word and its meaning. Creating experiences for ELL in which to pull from will also help to make vocabulary words and their meanings more concrete. Only providing instruction in the learner's native language will not help students to use and recall English, as suggested in Choice B, and only providing them with below grade-level vocabulary will not expose them to new words or help them maintain pace with their peers. Instead, visuals, hands-on experiences and explicit instruction should be used to help ELL to learn and recall new vocabulary. Teaching across the subjects can support memory and proper usage (Choice D).

16. C By strategically using mature vocabulary words throughout the day, teachers are able to demonstrate how to use vocabulary words students may not otherwise hear - for example, a teacher might ask students to *"Please line up in an orderly manner."* Giving students a weekly list of vocabulary words will not provide any context and should present low-frequency but practical vocabulary (Choice A), and only using simple language will not create opportunities for students to hear new words (Choice B). Finally, while having students write unknown words they come across in their reading on sticky notes can be an excellent strategy when teachers follow up with it at a later time, it does not frequently expose all students to new words in contexts they can easily understand.

17. C Structural analysis involves looking at parts of a word like the prefix to determine its meaning. Choice A would be a syntactic cue, while choice B is a semantic cue. Choice D may help with decoding but not necessarily comprehending it.

18. A Student vocabulary is considered a reliable indicator for their reading comprehension abilities, making Choice A the best answer. Students who have larger vocabularies tend to have higher reading comprehension as they simply understand and can more easily recognize words within text. Student's vocabulary skills, or lack thereof, do not necessarily predict their future academic success (Choice B) as vocabulary skills can be improved through implicit and explicit instruction. Also, a student's vocabulary knowledge does not indicate their understanding of syllables (Choice C) or phonemic awareness skills (Choice D).

19. A Compound words are two short words joined to form one word. Examples include butterfly, pancake, and mailbox. Contractions (Choice B) are shortened forms of a word/words. Examples include I'm, he's, let's, o'clock. The activity may expand oral vocabulary, but it is intended to promote knowledge of compound words (Choice C). Homophones are words that sound the same but have different spellings and meanings. Examples include their, they're, there; to, two, too.

20. C This activity is most likely being used to help students develop an understanding of compound words, or words that are formed using two separate words, making Choice C the best answer. Because the words are given and created in isolation (i.e. they are not presented in a sentence or paragraph), students cannot use context clues to determine their meaning (Choice A). While dividing words by syllables is often a useful decoding or spelling strategy (Choices B and D), because the teacher is having the students go through the motion of linking two words together to form a new word, the purpose of the lesson is more likely targeting compound words.

Chapter 4:
Reading Comprehension Concepts and Strategies

Lessons

4.1   Identifying the Basics

Whether skimming an article from the newspaper, reading a friend's note, or analyzing a legal contract to be signed, reading and comprehension are important skills needed in our personal and professional lives.

When educators think of reading, they are referring to the complex skill of deriving meaning from a written text. There are multiple facets to a complete reading diet in schools today, including each of the following:

- ⊙ Phonemic Awareness/Phonics
- ⊙ Decoding
- ⊙ Fluency
- ⊙ Vocabulary
- ⊙ Comprehension

Within comprehension, there exist several levels. These levels are typically identified as literal, inferential, and evaluative.

Literal

The literal level is the ability to understand information conveyed within text. Literal comprehension is fact-based and responses come directly from the text. Words used in questions often come directly from the text. For example, literal questions about the fictional book, *Charlotte's Web*, may read as follows:

- ⊙ What is the spider's name?
- ⊙ What word did Templeton find for Charlotte?
- ⊙ Where did Wilbur put Charlotte's egg sac?

Questions from non-fiction text are likewise direct and answers are fact-based. They may look like the following:

- ⊙ Who was the governor of Jamestown?
- ⊙ What are the three parts of an insect?

Inferential

This level refers to an individual's ability to make inferences about text. This level is important as readers often need to logically guess or draw conclusions based on information and implied concepts. Whereas the literal level targets what is explicitly said, the inferential level of reading entails what is *not* said. Often involving what the author is implicitly communicating, the writer's style, genre, and text's purpose all affect the level to which a student must make inferences. For example, an abstract poem can involve more inferential understanding than a newspaper article that aims to provide readers with facts.

As inferential statements are what the author has hinted at, and not necessarily said, inferential questions may read as follows:

- ⊙ *What can we infer* about the relationships among characters?
- ⊙ *What can we guess* will likely occur next?
- ⊙ What will characters *most likely* do next?

Evaluative

Evaluative reading is the most complex level of reading. Whereas early readers tend to read for meaning, more mature readers evaluate, analyze, and critique while reading.

Consider class assignments you may have had in high school or college. Perhaps you were asked to write a paper on your opinion of a book. You may have explored whether the author's style, topic, or overall writing captured your interest (or failed to do so). In completing such an assignment, you read on an evaluative level by assessing the book and the author's strategies.

Evaluative skills are crucial because they allow for more critical and informed reading that assesses the validity and credibility of the author's sources and claims. Additionally, students who can evaluate others' writing inevitably improve their own writing skills by learning to identify varied and effective writing strategies.

In summary, evaluative reading allows us to do the following:

Learning from Reading

- ⊙ What have you learned from the reading? What new information did you learn about a place, event, group of people, etc.?
- ⊙ What conclusions can you make based on the writer's main points?
- ⊙ What is the overall message about society's or people's actions, values, practices, etc.?

Relating

- ⊙ How does the author's argument compare with readings on similar topics?
- ⊙ Is the author's main point different from similar texts? Does it contradict previous assumptions?

- How does the reading clarify what is known about a topic?
- How does the author's style and organization resemble or differ from other readings of the time?

Assessing and Making Judgments

- Is the passage organized coherently and logically?
- Does the author support his or her main argument?
- What can you say about the author's main point—is it his or her opinion, or is it fact-based on objective information?
- Does the author use supporting evidence you trust? Is it accurate?
- Why did the author write the passage? Does the author want to teach readers something? Does the author want to change readers' viewpoints? Is it a creative piece expressing something from the author's personal life?

Applying the Various Levels of Reading

To further illustrate how reading comprehension occurs on the various levels, consider the following passage:

"On a cold, snowy day, Clara's mother stood outside of their house in the cold for hours on end braving subzero temperatures, hoping to catch a glimpse of the American presidential candidate she would soon be voting for in just a matter of days."

Depending on a student's reading comprehension abilities and the level at which they are working, the following may be derived:

Literal	Inferential	Evaluative
Students who are able to cite any of the below or similar information are demonstrating able to glean text for important, straightforward information.	Students with this level of comprehension are able to derive additional information based on the facts provided and way in which the author describes situations.	When working on this level, perhaps the students begin with an understanding that the story takes place during the **1960**s and the presidential candidate is a proponent of civil rights.

Literal	Inferential	Evaluative
It is cold and snowing outside.	If Clara's mother is preparing to vote for a presidential candidate, it must be November.	Women, like Clara, were involved in the civil rights movement.
The temperature is close to or below zero.	She must be interested in politics because she likes a particular candidate enough to wait for hours.	Women and people in general saw voting as a way to voice the need for change.
Clara's mother is the main character.	If it is snowing close to Election Day, and the temperature is below zero, Clara's family must live in a cold climate, such as in Alaska, Vermont, Montana, Minnesota, etc.	Clara is growing up around a female figure with strong feelings about politics, which might influence her political involvement.
She wants to see a candidate whom she likes.		
The candidate is running for US President.		
She has been waiting.	She most likely does not live in Georgia, Texas, or a place with a warmer climate.	People feel strongly about politics, and they are willing to endure much to make contact with a candidate they like.
There is an upcoming election.	It must be after the 1920s because Clara's mother can vote.	Political candidates have much power in society.

Relating Text-to-Text, Text-to-Self and Text-to-World

Students on the evaluative level may have also read other passages, such as the following, regarding similar issues:

> "While woman got the right to vote in 1920, most women did not participate in the political domain until well into the 1970s, reflecting their overall apathy."

Reading on an evaluative level requires making connections between such texts. Had you read the second example above prior to reading the book about Clara's mother, you may have gleaned that women generally didn't care about voting. Upon reading about Clara's mother, however, you may have changed your mind if you believed the claim regarding women's lack of participation.

As we get older, our reading comprehension becomes more nuanced so we can relate various texts and our own opinions, taking meaning from multiple perspectives, rather than viewing only one as accurate.

1. When asked to tell about what she is reading, a second grader responds that the book talks about why rabbits love garden vegetables. She also states she is not sure she agrees with the author's claim that carrots are a healthy snack for rabbits because they contain a lot of sugar. Her response reflects reading on which level?

   A. Literal
   B. Inferential
   C. Evaluative
   D. Descriptive

2. Students read a biography about George Washington. The author states where Washington was born, the date he was born, his wife's name, and that he became President. The teacher then asks children to figure out Washington's birthplace, birthday and spouse's name. The children are asked to read on what level?

   A. Literal
   B. Inferential
   C. Evaluative
   D. All of the above

3. A magazine article discusses the health benefits of drinking water. Based on a recent study showing the relationship between higher attention spans and hydration levels in children under 15, the writer argues the government should require school children be given water breaks every fifteen minutes. If you were to read on an evaluative level, which statement would best assess the article?

   A. The writer says children under 15 need to rehydrate every fifteen minutes.
   B. The writer does not believe children over 15 need to be included in the mandate.

C. The writer bases his assumptions on one study. The writer's argument is unsubstantiated, but could be regarded more seriously were additional studies that supported his conclusions also presented.

D. The writer believes that hydration levels affect attention spans.

4. A sixth grader is provided the following passage:

"On hands and knees, she scrubbed the floors, never stopping to complain once. While most girls her age were out on dates, she spent her nights cleaning and helping her sick mother. She'd give the world to see her mother get better. For now, she'd clean houses to make enough to pay the rent."

The student writes the following response to the passage:

"The girl cleans houses. She scrubs floors. Her mom is sick. Other girls her age are on dates. The girl hates that she doesn't get to go out like her friends do."

Based on the above response, which of the following best assesses the student's level of reading comprehension?

A. The student can read on literal and inferential levels but has a difficult time evaluating the passage's structure.

B. The student shows a literal understanding of the girl's job and her mother's sickness but cannot make appropriate inferences based on what is implied by the text.

C. The student does not grasp literal details about the girl such as her job, age, physical description, personality, etc.

D. The student demonstrates an inferential level of understanding about the girl's relationship with her mother, but does not evaluate the passage or discuss the author's purpose.

5. After reading a passage, two students demonstrated their literary response skills below. Here are their responses:

Student A: "The story was good. It was about the importance of history. I think the author wanted us to know that we have to learn history so that we don't repeat it. The things in the past can't be undone, but we can learn from them."

Student B: "I found the story interesting. It talked about an old man who was a soldier in the Revolutionary War. Each night, he taught his grandson about the war and told him what he did. He said he wanted his grandson to remember the stories. He said that it was sad how many men died."

The difference between the two responses can best be described by which of the following statements?

A. Student B demonstrates inferential and evaluative understandings by talking about the author's purpose and concluding how or what people should do based on the reading.

B. Student A discusses literal aspects of the story such as the specific time and what the author mentions.

C. Both students brought different approaches to their literary responses. Student A focuses on larger inferential and evaluative readings, whereas Student B took a more literal approach.

D. The students demonstrated the same level of understanding by focusing on inferences they made, rather than literal aspects discussed in the text or further or evaluating the text.

The following is an excerpt from L. Frank Baum's short story, "The Box of Robbers" from the book, *Father Goose*.

No one intended to leave Martha alone that afternoon, but it happened that everyone was called away, for one reason or another. Mrs. McFarland was attending the weekly card party held by the Women's Anti-Gambling League. Sister Nell's young man had called quite unexpectedly to take her for a long drive. Papa was at the office, as usual. It was Mary Ann's day out. As for Emeline, she certainly should have stayed in the house and looked after the little girl; but Emeline had a restless nature.

"Would you mind, miss, if I just crossed the alley to speak a word to Mrs. Carleton's girl?" she asked Martha.

"'Course not," replied the child. "You'd better lock the back door, though, and take the key, for I shall be upstairs."

"Oh, I'll do that, of course, miss," said the delighted maid, and ran away to spend the afternoon with her friend, leaving Martha quite alone in the big house, and locked in, into the bargain.

The little girl read a few pages in her new book, sewed a few stitches in her embroidery and started to "play visiting" with her four favorite dolls. Then she remembered that in the attic was a doll's playhouse that hadn't been used for months...

6. **After reading the passage, the teacher asks students what they think Martha is about to do next. Which type of comprehension is the teacher promoting?**
   A. Literal
   B. Inferential
   C. Evaluative
   D. All of the above

The following is a 1799 poem by William Wordsworth entitled "I Travelled among Unknown Men":

I TRAVELLED among unknown men,
In lands beyond the sea;
Nor, England! did I know till then
What love I bore to thee.

'Tis past, that melancholy dream!
Nor will I quit thy shore
A second time; for still I seem
To love thee more and more.

Among thy mountains did I feel
The joy of my desire;
And she I cherished turned her wheel
Beside an English fire.

Thy mornings showed, thy nights concealed
The bowers where Lucy played;
And thine too is the last green field
That Lucy's eyes surveyed.

7. **Which response demonstrates an inferential understanding of the poem?**

   A. "The person in the poem is now back in England after leaving. The author suggests he is back in England because he mentions he won't leave the shores again and the melancholy is in the past, which means he must be back in England."

   B. "Lucy wrote the poem about how she loves England."

   C. "I don't like Wadsworth's poems that much. I think Wadsworth's values don't apply to today's times as people now are always moving and traveling. They like more than just the place they are from."

   D. "Poems of the eighteenth century focus on patriotism at a time in history when many people were at war."

8. **Read the following two student responses based on the poem by Wordsworth above:**

   Student #1: "Wadsworth talks about the shores, then the mountains, and the green fields."

   Student #2: "The poet misses England because that's the last place where someone dear to him named Lucy was."

   Based on the student responses, which of the following assessments are most accurate?

   A. Both students make literal and inferential references in their responses.

   B. Student #1 makes an evaluative statement about the themes in the poem.

C. Student #1 discusses literal references, whereas Student #2 makes more inferences.

D. Student #2 makes an evaluative statement about the themes in the poem.

9. **Following independent reading of a beginning imaginative fiction chapter book, students are asked to write a literary response to the task** "*Compare and contrast this detective with another detective you have read about.*"
Which comprehension strategy is demonstrated in this activity?
   A. making connections
   B. drawing inferences
   C. identifying characteristics of a genre
   D. summarizing

10. **Which of the following literary response questions can be used to teach students the strategy of making connections?**
   A. What advice would you give the character in this reading?
   B. What does this reading remind you of from real life?
   C. Which character do you most admire? Why?
   D. What does this story teach?

IDENTIFYING THE BASICS EXPLANATIONS

1. **C** When students read on the evaluative level they assess text, relate it to other readings and form opinions regarding the author's argument(s). In this case, the student understands the author's opinion, however doubts its validity based upon her prior knowledge of the subject. If she were reading on a literal level, (Choice A), she would state basic information such as, "Rabbits need fiber and carrots." Choice B, the inferential level, deals with understanding what the author implies or what is implicitly stated. In this case, the student might conclude, "The author argues that any vegetable is healthy for rabbits." Choice D (descriptive) is not a level of comprehension.

2. A The literal level, the most basic level of comprehension, refers to information explicitly stated in text. Because we know the information the teacher asked about is specifically stated in the reading, this is an example of students reading on a literal level (Choice A). Choice B, inferential, involves students making inferences based on the text, however this level is not required as the teacher asked fact based questions that were explicitly answered by the author. If children learned that Martha Washington often gave George Washington advice, they could infer she was an intelligent woman who had a role in Washington's decisions. Choice C, evaluative, involves assessing the biography's accuracy and structure, which is not something required of the students.

3. C The statements made in Choices A and D are literal, not evaluative, as they reiterate specific details mentioned in the article (i.e. the writer states the study is for children under 15 and that hydration is important to attention span for this age group). Choice B is a logical inference and reflective of the inferential level of comprehension; if the mandate is only for children under 15, those over 15 are not included in his argument. Choice C is the only answer that cannot be eliminated and also makes the most sense. An evaluative statement includes an assessment of the sources and the evidence the writer uses to support the argument. In this case, only one study is used to support a potential mandate.

4. B The student accurately discussed the girl's job, that her friends go out, and her mother's illness, which demonstrates a literal level of comprehension, eliminating Choice C. Choices A and D state the student makes inferences, but there are no appropriate inferences made in the student's response. Choice B is the best answer. It correctly explains that the student makes inaccurate inferences (i.e. that the girl resents staying home). The student most likely misinterprets the phrasings "never stopping to complain once" and "she'd give the world to see her mother get better," which provide a source for inferring that the girl does *not* feel resentful.

5. C Student B focuses predominately on literal details, just beginning to touch on inferential details in his statement referring to wanting the grandson to remember the stories. He does not demonstrate reading on an evaluative level, making Choice A incorrect. Choice B is also incorrect because Student A does not discuss literal details in his response. Finally, Choice D is incorrect as it states the students demonstrated the same level of understanding though their responses showed two different levels. Choice C is therefore the best answer – it correctly explains Student A makes inferential statements (i.e. "I think the author wanted us to know that we have to learn history so that we don't repeat it.") and evaluative statements (i.e. "The things in the past can't be undone, but we can learn from them") whereas Student B focuses on literal references (i.e. "It talked about an old man who was a soldier in the Revolutionary War. Each night, he taught his grandson about the war and told him what he did").

6. B   The teacher is promoting an inferential level of understanding (Choice B), which involves predicting a likely subsequent event based on information provided. We know Martha is alone, and the story ends with, "Then she remembered that in the attic was a doll's playhouse that hadn't been used for months…." A student would logically think Martha would look for the playhouse but because this information is not yet given, the student would be inferring this action. Choice A, a literal level of understanding, is not correct as the details regarding what comes next have not yet explicitly been stated. Choice C, an evaluative level of understanding is also not correct – students are not asked to evaluate the text based on their prior knowledge or make conclusions regarding it's accuracy.

7. A   Inferential reading involves generalizing about information hinted at, but not explicitly given, in the passage. Choice A is the only response that involves inferences; the student understood from the poem that the person is back in England. Choice B shows an overall lack of comprehension; the student understands that on a literal level, England and someone named Lucy are involved, but cannot infer the relationship between Lucy and the speaker. Choices C and D model evaluative responses. Choice C provides an example of a student relating the text to present day while Choice D demonstrates a response from a student who has likely read other poems from this time period and is able to interpret this particular poem using his prior knowledge about the time period and about larger historical issues.

8. C   Choices A and B can be eliminated as Student #1 gives only literal (not inferential or evaluative) references from the poem. Though Student #2 does appear to use a high level of comprehension, an example of an evaluative level of understanding could include, "Many poets use the symbol of a woman to represent a nation," or "Wadsworth's poem contains themes of patriotism and love that were important at the turn of the nineteenth century." Choice C is therefore the best answer – Student #1 focuses on literal inferences whereas Student #2 makes inferences based on the poem.

9. **A** Students are asked to make a text-to-text connection. Drawing inferences is a skill of figuring something out based on what is implied in a reading (Choice B). The comparison and contrast activity can be completed based on stated information such as detectives are same/different gender, age, etc. The task calls for students to make comparisons of character who are likely both found in imaginative literature, not different genres (Choice C). The comparison does not specify that students must use summarizing skills to select the most important information and ignore irrelevant information (Choice D).

10. **B** Making connections is a comprehension strategy that guides students to connect what may be unfamiliar in the text to relevant schema. In this prompt, students must make a text-to-world connection. Other common connections are text-to-self and text-to-text. Giving advice to a character (Choice A), recognizing admirable qualities (Choice C), and identifying a lesson (Choice C) are all higher-level comprehension questions; but they do not require students to connect individuals, events, settings, ideas, etc. to a specific individual, event, setting, idea, etc. outside the text.

4.2 General Strategies

General Strategies for Reading Comprehension

Teachers can introduce various strategies, such as pre-reading and post-reading activities, to interpret and analyze informational, expository, and literary texts.

The Importance of Pre-Reading Activities

Using pre-reading activities to introduce new books helps prepare students to further engage with text. The following three tasks can help students be more successful and promote a greater understanding of text in general:

1. Introduce key words, concepts and difficult vocabulary
2. Activate prior knowledge
3. Deepen current knowledge by connecting it to the text

It is also helpful, especially when working with beginning readers, to encourage students to reread text. Students are more likely to reread books they know and text that contains words they have heard and can identify. Therefore, pre-reading activities often serve to clarify unfamiliar words, connect prior knowledge and promote students' desire to reread.

Pre-Reading Activities and Strategies

Schema building

Schema building, or knowledge building, refers to activities that activate prior knowledge about a particular topic by encouraging students to recall, consider, and connect what they already know regarding text they are preparing to read. Pre-reading activities that target schema building can incorporate **visual aids** in conjunction with oral prompts to get students talking about main themes addressed within text. Visuals, such as pictures, video clips, objects, charts, etc. are beneficial for reasons such as the following:

- They grab students' attention, especially those who are visual learners, encouraging a more active reading experience.
- They help students visualize about what they will read, which furthers their overall understanding of the material.
- They introduce new words and concepts so they are familiar while reading.
- They promote comprehension for struggling readers and ELL students who may lack an advanced vocabulary.

For example, a class is preparing to read a story about a girl who sells fruit at a market in Senegal. The teacher might show the following images prior to reading:

In this example, the teacher primes students with an image of a market that allows them to visualize the setting of the story. The map provides a geographical marker to reinforce that Senegal is a country in Africa. Simultaneously, the teacher may ask, "What does a market make you think about?" or provide similar prompts to activate prior knowledge and capture students' interest.

Graphic Organizers

Graphic organizers, such as word maps and semantic maps, can also be used for schema building and as a pre-reading activity to promote comprehension.

Word Maps

A word map shows a word or concept written in the middle with several boxes surrounding that word. Students can look up the word in the dictionary and write a definition, synonyms, a sentence using the word, and a visual to help recall meaning. For example, a class preparing to talk about farms in the South might complete a word map for the word *agriculture*:

Definition	Image
The science or art concerned with cultivating land, raising crops, and feeding, breeding, and raising livestock.	

—————————— Agriculture ——————————

Synonyms	Sentence
cultivation, farming, horticulture	I am studying agriculture so one day I can successfully manage my family's dairy farm.

Semantic Maps

A semantic (meaning) map can be used to write and categorize words and concepts that students associate with a given topic, thus activating prior knowledge and introducing main themes. As with word maps, similar terms are grouped together to help students make connections. This is helpful as our memory works best when we are able to categorize and chunk information – sort of a filing system for our brains.

Prior to reading about the Civil War, a teacher may ask students what words or concepts come to mind and then record these words on the board. Writing the words on the board helps to visually organize different terms. Students then categorize the words on their semantic map in ways that make sense to them. In this example, the teacher might ask questions such as "Why do you associate slavery with the South?" to push students to further analyze relationships and concepts. Even when students complete a semantic map in small groups, it is important to ask why students associate certain concepts to encourage them to express their thoughts and examine what they know. Asking why they make such associations also strengthens students' expressive and receptive vocabularies.

Strategies for Comprehension While Reading

Metacognitive strategies are particularly important for beginning readers. Metacognition involves strategies for analyzing and reinterpreting information that has already been learned. The following are examples of questions students may ask themselves:

Predicting:

- ⊙ What will happen next based on what I just read?
- ⊙ What do the graphics on the page tell me about what will happen?
- ⊙ What can I guess will be the topic or argument based on what has been read?

Questioning:

- ⊙ What is this reading about?
- ⊙ What is the author's purpose?
- ⊙ Why is this character/event/topic important?
- ⊙ What do I already know or what I have I already read that relates to this?

Visualizing:

- ⊙ What does the story "look like"?
- ⊙ What images come to mind?
- ⊙ How would I envision the senses (smell, taste, sight, sound)?

Paraphrasing:

- ⊙ What are the main ideas?
- ⊙ What one word summarizes the topic?
- ⊙ What is the ultimate argument or purpose?

Monitoring:

- ⊙ Do I understand this correctly?
- ⊙ Do I need to reread that part?

Written Activities

Students can fill out **word maps, semantic maps, and other graphic organizers** during reading to promote comprehension or work on vocabulary. For unfamiliar words, students can make word maps using context clues instead of using reference materials. For example, a student encounters the word *gregarious* in the following sentence:

> "The **gregarious** young boy spent countless hours walking around his dad's shop, talking to every person who would converse with him."

Next, based on context clues, a word map for *gregarious* could be created. Graphic organizers can also play a key role in supporting student comprehension – not only do they make higher level thinking concepts (main idea/detail, cause/effect, etc.) more concrete, but they also allow text specific information to be visually organized in varied manners that may make more sense for some. For example, graphic organizers are often useful when students are learning to glean the following from text:

- Main Idea/Detail
- Compare/Contrast
- Cause and Effect
- Sequencing
- Problem and Solution
- Fact vs. Opinion

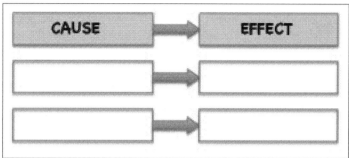

Teachers can use graphic organizers in various ways. Students can simply fill them out while reading to keep track or organize information learned from the text, they may be used as teacher-led activities providing students with guidance as they complete the organizer, or they may be given to students blank, partially filled out or completed. Likewise, graphic organizers may be used differently for different students. Whereas some students might benefit from completing them independently, others may require varied levels of support.

Post-Reading Activities

After reading a passage, students can also engage in several activities to further comprehension and analysis skills.

Retelling

Retelling is a common way to assess a student's comprehension of text. When students retell, or put the story in their own words, teachers can assess literal, inferential, and evaluative understanding to better grasp strengths and weaknesses. For example, two students have just read the story of Joan of Arc. Here are their retellings:

Student #1: "A girl pretends to be a guy because women can't join the military. She becomes a soldier and goes to war. She is burned at the stake."

Student #2: "The story suggests that Joan was a religious and unselfish person. They killed her, but her courage was so great we still talk about her."

These retellings demonstrate that both students understood the reading. Whereas Student #1 cites more details that are literal, Student #2 makes more inferences.

Post-Reading Discussions

Similar to how a person masters a subject by teaching it, retelling and discussing helps students make sense of text.

Prompts for discussions can target literal details, such as asking students to discuss the following:

⊙ What does the writer say about Joan of Arc?

⊙ How does he describe her?

⊙ Where does she live?

⊙ How old is she?

Questions can also encourage discussions about inferential details:

⊙ What does the writer suggest pushed Joan to join the military, apart from the reason he gives about the dream she has?

Because an evaluative level of understanding builds on prior knowledge by relating text to other works or to students' lives, prompts such as the following may be used:

⊙ Do you know anyone from our time that reminds you of Joan of Arc?

⊙ Do you agree with the writer that Joan of Arc is an image of a hero?

Potential writing activities will be discussed in the next few lessons.

GENERAL STRATEGIES PRACTICE

1. **Which of the following is an example of a metacognitive strategy students can use while reading?**
    A. A student writes a response to a reading.
    B. A student finds an unfamiliar word in a text and looks it up.
    C. A student uses a graphic organizer to sequence events in the text.
    D. A student predicts what will happen while reading.

2. **After reading about Ancient Greece during class, a teacher asks a student to retell the passage. Which of the following is likely one of the teacher's goals?**

   A. To get students thinking about what they already know about Ancient Greece.
   B. To have students compare Ancient Greece to the Roman Empire.
   C. To assess student's reading comprehension.
   D. To evaluate problems with phonemic awareness.

3. **A group of third graders prepares to read text about Egyptian hieroglyphics. Which of the following would be the most effective pre-reading activity for schema building?**

   A. The teacher asks students to write *hieroglyphics* in the middle of a word map and asks them to look it up in the dictionary to complete the word map.
   B. The teacher shows images of hieroglyphics and puts a timeline with the date 4000 BC on the board. She asks students, "What comes to mind when you think of Ancient Egypt?"
   C. The teacher has students write *hieroglyphics* in the middle of a word map and asks them to find the word in the reading and use context clues to complete the word map.
   D. The teacher asks students to write a response in their journal about what they learned from the reading.

4. **Students in a sixth-grade class are making semantic maps as a pre-reading activity for a fictional story they will read in class. After having them write down words they associate with the reading's topic, the teacher asks them to explain in small groups the reasons for those associations. Which of the following is the best explanation for the teacher's follow-up question?**

   A. A semantic map allows the associations to be categorized, which is better for long-term memory.
   B. It is important for students to explain why they associate certain words with others because it allows them to work on expressing and analyzing their thoughts, which builds on expressive and receptive vocabularies.

C. It is essential that students can explain their reasoning by citing specific evidence from the text to prove they have developed reading analysis skills.

D. Students can learn new vocabulary by looking at context clues and making logical guesses that can then be used to make a word map.

5. **A teacher wants to do a pre-reading activity with her third graders for a story about a girl who lives in Oklahoma during the Great Depression. Some students have difficulty with reading comprehension. Which of the following is likely the most effective activity to prepare students for this reading?**

A. In small groups, students discuss the Great Depression.

B. The teacher asks the students to do a word map with *Depression* in the center, using resource materials to help.

C. The teacher shows images of the Great Depression, writes "the 1920s" on the board, and asks students what they already know about this period.

D. The teacher asks students what they know about the Great Depression and after reading the passage, has them write a paragraph summarizing what they learned.

6. **A student demonstrates problems comprehending long passages. He says he has a difficult time keeping track of ideas presented while reading. Which of the following is an effective strategy to help the student?**

A. The teacher asks students to make a semantic map that categorizes the main ideas after reading the text.

B. The teacher provides a graphic organizer (designed to record main ideas and details) for the student to fill out while reading to help keep track of the main ideas presented throughout the passage.

C. The teacher assesses the student's understanding of the reading by asking the student to perform a retelling.

D. The teacher asks the students to discuss the main idea.

7. **A fourth-grade student who has difficulty with content-area texts reports having difficulty with comprehension. When the teacher asks the student what she does when she doesn't understand something while reading, the student replies, "I start off good and when I don't get it, I just keep going and hope that it makes sense by the end." This student could benefit most from which of the following:**

   A. Self-monitoring skills, such as adapting reading speed or rereading certain parts that seem difficult, should be explicitly taught to the student.

   B. The student could make a semantic map after reading to better understand the structure and layout.

   C. The teacher could ask students to write questions about the text that summarize the main points.

   D. The teacher could provide images beforehand to introduce the main theme and allow students to visualize an element of the story before reading.

8. **Students in a fifth-grade class take turns reading the book, *The Giver*, aloud. While reading, the teacher says, "I wonder where the Receiver is rushing off to. I bet he is going to talk to the Giver." This teacher is modeling which metacognitive strategy?**

   A. Summarizing

   B. Visualizing

   C. Predicting

   D. Retelling

9. **A student has difficulty comprehending literary texts. The teacher suggests the student take time every few pages to think about what has just been read to engage with the reading. Which of the following would be beneficial to promote development of these skills?**

   A. The teacher has the student do a pre-reading activity that promotes schema building by activating prior knowledge about the topic.

   B. The student completes a word map and uses reference materials to find a definition and synonym.

C. The student writes a response to the reading by summarizing the main events.

D. The teacher reads a passage with the student and frequently stops to ask what mental images come to mind and what the student predicts will occur.

10. **Why would a sixth-grade teacher most likely model and prompt her students to predict, question and visualize text while reading aloud when students already appear to be fluently reading and engaged in the lesson?**
    A. To encourage metacognitive strategies for comprehension
    B. To ensure students do not become bored during the lesson
    C. To encourage students to interpret the text on a literal level
    D. To demonstrate how to retell text

GENERAL STRATEGIES EXPLANATIONS

1. **D** Students use metacognitive strategies while reading to further engage and better comprehend by thinking about what has just been read. Choice A is a good written activity, however would be used as a post-reading exercise. Looking up unfamiliar words (Choice B) is often helpful for vocabulary building, but is not a way to question and reiterate one's understanding of a text while reading. Choice C, which suggests using a graphic organizer to sequence events, is an excellent way a visual student can further their understanding, however, is not an example of a metacognitive strategy. Choice D, predicting what will happen in the text, is done before or while reading. This is the best answer as it requires students to analyze what has been read/what will be read by making predictions, questioning and predicting what will happen next.

2. **C** Teachers often ask students to retell what happened in text to assess reading comprehension and analysis skills. Activating prior knowledge, as suggested in Choice A, is typically done as a pre-reading activity to prepare students for what they are about to read. Such activities help students make connections with text and put what they read into perspective. Choice B is more specific than a retelling – it asks students to compare and contrast which assumes students have also already read

text associated with the Roman Empire. If a student were to mention the Roman Empire in a retelling, it would demonstrate an evaluative level of understanding, though this is not likely the teacher's intention. Choice D involves phonemic awareness – not something that would be assessed through retelling. Choice C is therefore the best answer – the teacher has likely asked the student to retell the passage so he/she can gain a sense of the student's level of comprehension for the text at hand.

3. B Schema building refers to activities that activate students' schema (knowledge) of a certain topic and then builds upon that knowledge through connections to the text. Choices A and C involve word maps, an exercise better suited to increase vocabulary. Choice D entails a written response that is a post-reading activity rather than a pre-reading activity, making it incorrect. Choice B – showing students pictures of hieroglyphics and a timeline while prompting conversation – would be the best schema building activity. The pictures allow students a visual with which to make connections and the teacher's question regarding Ancient Egypt encourages conversation that will allow students to learn from each other and draw connections with other text, previous experiences and knowledge. Through such conversations, students are provided with key information and background knowledge so they are better able to engage and comprehend the text.

4. B Schema building activities that seek to activate students' prior knowledge work best when students not only list concepts and words they associate with a reading's theme, but also when they explain why they make such associations, making Choice B the best answer. Such conversations push students to further analyze what they already know and better connect with text. Choices A and D refer to graphic organizers that help with vocabulary development –they do not likely relate to the teacher's question about why students make certain associations. Although Choice C makes a valid point, citing evidence from the text would need to be done during or after reading, and the question explains that the teacher uses this activity as a pre-reading exercise.

5. C The use of visual images can greatly help engage students and provide them with essential knowledge (such as basic details about the setting or period). Choice A involves advanced analysis skills that would be better used after reading. Choice B looks more at the word's meaning but does little to prepare students to help them have a more solid understand-

ing of the time period being discussed and the context in which the word is used. Choice D touches on schema building, or activating students' knowledge about the Depression; however, it does little for those with limited background information. Additionally, though the follow-up writing activity could be useful, it will not help to prepare students prior to reading. Choice C is the best answer because it includes visuals and provides basic information to frame the text, which is especially helpful for readers struggling with comprehension.

6. B   Students who have difficulty with comprehension can use metacognitive strategies to think through what they read. This student most likely requires strategies to assist him in organizing and keeping track of information while reading. Although a semantic map (Choice A) promotes comprehension, having him complete the map after reading will likely be difficult because he requires assistance to organize information while reading. Choice C is based on a retelling, which would be a way to assess this student's comprehension, but again is not a strategy the student can use while reading. Similarly, Choice D requires a level of comprehension that would be difficult for the student without earlier supports. Choice B, however, provides the student with a strategy and support while reading. Depending on the assistance required, the teacher could provide the student with a blank, partially completed, or already completed graphic organizer to fill out, reference, or use as a guide while reading.

7. A   The student's comment about how she keeps reading even when she does not understand demonstrates she is not adapting her reading in times of difficulty. Fluidity is important, but for reading comprehension, adapting one's speed or rereading can be necessary to understand the text - making Choice A the best answer. Semantic maps can be helpful, but the student will likely find it difficult to complete if she does not comprehend what she reads. Similarly, Choice C involves student-generated questions that are good for further promoting comprehension and analysis, but such an activity is difficult if text is not understood. Choice D is an appropriate pre-reading activity, but this student's problem involves comprehending and processing text while reading and knowing when adapt her reading accordingly.

8. C   Choices A, B, and C are all metacognitive strategies, or ways of thinking about how we comprehend what we read. Choice D can be eliminated because a teacher would use this post-reading activity to assess a student's

comprehension levels. Choice A, summarizing, involves paraphrasing or briefly describing the main events. Visualizing, Choice B targets what the reading looks like and imagining the scenes in order to engage. Choice C best describes what the teacher is modeling; she is showing her students how to predict what will happen, basing her guess on previous events.

9. **D** This question asks about strategies that can be used during reading, which eliminates Choice A, a pre-reading activity, and Choice C, a post-reading activity. Choice B involves a word map – though it could be used as an activity during reading, it would be more appropriate for a student who required vocabulary support. Choice D is therefore the best answer – by reading the passage with the student, the teacher is able to frequently stop and assess comprehension. Through questions about what the student envisions while reading, the teacher can explicitly teach how such strategies can be used while reading to promote comprehension.

10. **A** Metacognitive strategies, or thinking about thinking, involve strategies for analyzing, interpreting and re-interpreting information that has just been learned, or read. Such strategies include predicting, questioning, visualizing, paraphrasing and self-monitoring. Therefore, the teacher is most likely modeling and prompting students in such ways to encourage metacognitive strategies, making Choice A the best answer. Choice B, ensuring students don't become bored, is not likely the teacher's motivation as the question states the students appear engaged. Because metacognitive strategies are often taught and done with readers who are already interpreting text on inferential and evaluative levels, Choice C is also incorrect. Finally, Choice D is likewise incorrect – retelling is a common way to assess comprehension; however the teacher is not reciting what occurred but rather leading students in considering and interpreting text as it is being read.

4.3   Informational/Expository Texts

Because informational and expository texts are inherently different from narratives (with which children are often more familiar), teachers need to explicitly teach students how to comprehend and analyze these types of literature. Though many people mistake information and expository texts as the same, they are actually quite different.

- ⊙ Informational Text: Provides readers with facts and the author does not share his or her opinion.
- ⊙ Expository Text: Author often takes on an authoritative tone while providing factual information.

In expository texts, the author is typically knowledgeable about the subject matter and they go beyond straightforward facts to provide additional details. As informational and expository texts are often non-fiction, they make up a great deal of what is read in classrooms. And, because they include features such as a table of contents, glossary, and index, it becomes critical students know how to read and navigate these texts.

Reading Analysis Skills

Specific reading analysis skills are needed to appropriately analyze and evaluate informational texts. These skills permit students to better understand on literal, inferential, and evaluative levels so they are able to make informed opinions about what they read.

Analyzing informational texts often includes looking at the text's purpose, author's position, support for the main points, relationship of this text to other information, text structure, text features, and graphic features.

Text Purpose

Nonfiction texts can be classified according to the author's purpose. Below are several types of common text types:

- ⊙ **Expository:** This type of text is written to explain – all content is factual.
- ⊙ **Argumentative:** Written to convince or persuade, persuasive writing is expository writing in which the writer takes a stand.

- **Technical:** Typically, technical writing is about technical or specialized topics.
- **Narrative:** Narratives are written to recount a particular time, situation or series of events.

Author's Position

Informational and argumentative texts often reflect an author's viewpoint of a topic. As students become more proficient and analytical readers, they start to look at the writer in addition to the words on the page. Emphasizing **point of view** and asking students, "Who is speaking?" helps call attention to how the writer's personal and professional beliefs and experiences have influenced the presentation of information.

Support for the Main Points and Arguments

A skilled reader can appropriately evaluate arguments made by authors. Supporting information may come in the form of reasons or examples, may be opinion- and experience-based, or fact-based.

Fact vs. Opinion

The ability to differentiate between fact and opinion is key to deciphering the validity of a text's argument and supporting evidence. Offering examples of opinion-based statements as opposed to fact-based statements can help model the vocabulary each uses. For example, phrases that typically announce opinions include:

- I think...
- I believe...
- It seems...
- It appears...

Faulty Logic

Forming a critical opinion of a text's claims requires identifying faulty logic that leads to false conclusions. Ways in which faulty logic might occur in a text include the following:

- **Generalization:** Does the claim make a broad statement unsupported by the evidence?

- ⊙ **Exaggeration:** Does the author use words such as *always*, *never*, *all*, or *none*?
- ⊙ **Improper Cause and Effect**: Is the relationship truly causal or merely a false assumption based on faulty logic? Is the relationship between the cause and effect accurately and clearly proved?

Here's an example of a claim containing faulty logic:

> People always build muscle when they take our unique blend of amino acids, vitamins, and minerals, which are also guaranteed to double the amount you can lift.

The claim seems suspicious given the use of "always," which marks a strong generalization and uses exaggeration.

Graphs, charts, and other illustrations can also be examined for false logic. Do the illustrations represent valid, relevant information? Do they support the author's argument? Providing examples of reliable and ambiguous illustrations can help students practice identifying faulty or one-sided claims.

Text-to-Self, Text-to-Text, Text-to-World

This analysis skill involves comparing text with the reader's personal experiences, prior knowledge about the subject at hand, other written works, or events in the world. Through these connections, readers can better understand text and determine the extent to which they agree or disagree with the author's position.

Text Structure (Organization)

The structure of a paragraph or piece of writing refers to the way the text is written and the type of information being conveyed. To help students determine text structure, they can be exposed to a list of keywords and/or signals that typically indicate the type of information being disclosed. By also providing students with a visual/graphic organizer such as those shown in the previous section, they become better able to pull important information from varied structures.

Graphic Features

Many graphic features exist to better describe concepts explained in text. These visuals may be provided in various ways, depending on the text's content, arguments being made and concepts being explained.

Common graphic features include the following:

- ⊙ Pictures
- ⊙ Captions
- ⊙ Inset photos
- ⊙ Labeled diagrams
- ⊙ Charts
- ⊙ Graphs
- ⊙ Maps

Text Features

Text features bring clarity and provide direction. They also exist to help readers find information efficiently, without necessarily requiring them to read a book or article in its entirety. Informational texts typically inlcude at least some of the following:

Title
Table of Contents
Preface
Marginal notes
Index
Glossary
Headings or subheadings
Sidebars

Reference Materials

Working with informational and expository texts also often involves understanding how to use reference materials, including a dictionary, atlas, almanac, and handbook.

Strategies for Reading Informational and Expository Text

Previewing

As discussed on the previous page, previewing text can be a good way to build schema. It also prepares students so they can focus on understanding text, rather than having to focus on deciphering the pronunciation and meaning of words.

Previewing also helps spark students' curiosity and makes them excited to read. Oral activities for previewing texts builds vocabulary, which helps students more coherently express their thoughts while reading and once finished. Additionally, students can be directed to look at the title, images, illustrations, and other basic information to gain information about text. They may skim through picture captions or charts. Other concepts students may consider while previewing include the following:

- What is the text structure - are paragraphs long or short?
- How is the text presented? Does it look like other stories you've seen?
- What type of information is relayed in the text, are facts such as dates or amounts included?

While Reading

Metacognitive Strategies

One of the most basic but crucial metacognitive strategies is **self-questioning**, or posing questions while reading. This is done to reiterate what is being explained and to anticipate what comes next. For beginning readers, this strategy can be used while the teacher reads a book aloud. Questions such as the following provide checkpoints for students along the way:

- What do you think the character will do next?
- Why do you think the character did that?
- What else might we need to know about the topic?

Rereading is also a useful strategy. When a passage is read aloud and then reread (often in smaller groups or silently), students can identify additional details. Exposing students to the same passage allows them to go beyond their initial, basic understanding of the text.

Students may also reread text to better comprehend difficult passages. By going back over the same material, they are more likely to gain a more solid understanding. Paraphrasing while reading likewise allows students to put new concepts into their words. This is often a helpful skill for teachers to model while reading.

Skimming and Scanning

Skimming and scanning are reading strategies students can use depending on the text and purpose.

Skimming is quick reading to look for general or main ideas. A skimming strategy is to read the first couple paragraphs of an informational text and then read only the first sentence of the following paragraphs. Skimming is a useful strategy when reading non-fiction about a familiar subject in a short amount of time. Scanning is quick reading to look for specific facts or information. Efficient scanning depends on recognizing the text structure as alphabetical, chronological, by category, etc. Scanning is a useful strategy to locate items in a dictionary, phone numbers in a phone book, or specific content such as the event that occurred on a particular date.

Graphic Organizers

Students learning to analyze text structure often benefit from using preselected graphic organizers that coordinate with the text. Given practice and instruction, students can complete the organizers while reading and eventually learn to choose appropriate organizers that complement a text's structure. Eventually, skilled readers will automatically analyze text's structures.

Timelines are also often effective graphics that provide student's with a visual to reinforce dates, events, or concepts that occur sequentially. These may be created by or provided to help students gain a better understanding of the order of events.

Post-Reading Strategies

Oral review

By reviewing text aloud, students are able to further analyze and better understand any concepts that were initially confusing. Simultaneously, teachers can monitor student comprehension. Smaller groups also allow individual questions to be answered and an environment in which students can further discuss, debate and share their thoughts about the text.

Summarizing

Summarizing, which can be done orally or as a written activity, can likewise be used to assess student comprehension. Summarizing allows main points to be reiterated and follows the text's structure. For example, after reading a comparison text, the summary should also take the form of a comparison.

Student-Generated Questions

Students may generate questions individually, in small groups or as a class. Such activities often establish ownership; having thought of the question, students are likely more motivated to find the answer.

Written Research Projects

When students complete research projects they use informational and expository texts. To teach students how to organize research projects and promote self-directed learning, K-W-L Charts, such as the one below, or other similar graphic organizers that promote written expression, schema building, and analysis skills, may be used.

What I Know	What I Want to Know	What I Learned
bears sleep for a long time they live in the forest they're big and scary	why bears hibernate	I learned that bears hibernate because they don't have much food in the winter, so they wake when it's spring.

INFORMATIONAL/EXPOSITORY TEXTS PRACTICE

1. **A teacher models an expository or argumentative text's pre-reading activities. Which activity listed below would be inappropriate for a previewing activity?**

   A. Read the first and last paragraphs, and draw conclusions about the characters.

   B. Look at the illustrations and activate students' prior knowledge.

   C. Introduce conceptually challenging vocabulary.

   D. Skim the text for information about paragraph length and level of difficulty.

2. A teacher wants to assess a sixth-grade student's comprehension of an informational text using a written activity. Which of the following would be most appropriate?

   A. Do a retelling of the text.
   B. Complete a K-W-L chart.
   C. Do an oral preview.
   D. Complete a summary.

The following two questions are based on the following expository reading:

Water is the foundation of all life forms. Every year, people pollute more and more, which causes our waters to become dirty and toxic. Companies refuse to take action too. Soon, all our water sources will be dried up and unable to be used. What would happen if our kids and grandkids have no water to play in, let alone drink? If we don't do something soon, we will face a horrendous situation.

3. During an oral review of the passage, students are asked whether the writer makes a solid argument and if they agree. Which of the following responses shows the best understanding of how to spot faulty logic?

   A. "The writer makes a good point that many people pollute, but she uses exaggeration by saying water will disappear 'soon.' It's also unlikely that her kids and grandkids would know a world without water. I agree water is important."
   B. "This writer makes a good point that we need to worry about water. I can't believe that my kids will not have water to drink. It shows us that we need to stock up on bottled water."
   C. "The writer exaggerates by saying our water will disappear. I don't believe that because we have too much water. Nothing she says is credible."
   D. "The writer wants her kids to have water to play in and drink. I agree. However, I am unsure she is realistic."

4. **Two students write passage summaries:**

> Student #1: "The writer feels really bad about the water. She wants her kids and grandkids to be able to play in it and drink it."
> Student #2: "The writer wants people to stop polluting, and she wants to start protecting water, because if we don't, we won't have any more water."

Which would be a proper assessment of the skills they use?

A. Neither student comprehends the writer's main argument.

B. The students' summaries show literal levels of comprehension by mentioning the writer's feelings toward water.

C. Student #1 makes no literal references, whereas Student #2 makes only literal references by talking about stopping pollution.

D. Student #1 shows a literal understanding, but he did not point out a main part of the reading, which was the need for preservation. Student #2 makes this inference.

5. **Students in a fifth-grade class are completing research projects. The teacher asks them to pick a topic and read relevant articles. She asks them to write a paragraph about what they learned. Which of the following could this teacher incorporate to promote self-directed learning?**

A. The teacher could ask students to compare and contrast the articles they read.

B. The teacher could ask students to complete a semantic map that charts the main points each article presents.

C. The teacher could ask students to fill out a K-W-L chart before, during, and after the project.

D. The teacher could ask students to complete word maps for difficult vocabulary they come across during their research.

6. **A teacher wants to prepare students prior to beginning an expository text about George Washington Carver's unrecognized accomplishments. Part of her pre-reading activity involves having student's preview the text and discuss what they think the reading will be about based on headings, subheadings, and illustrations.**

Which of the following is <u>not</u> an explanation for this preview?

A. The teacher wants to stimulate students' interest in the text to promote a more active, engaged read.

B. The teacher wants students to use metacognitive strategies to facilitate comprehension.

C. The teacher wants to get students talking about what comes to mind when they consider the time period, individuals involved, key terms embedded in the headings and illustrations to activate their prior knowledge.

D. The teacher wants to build students' receptive and expressive vocabularies through the class discussion.

7. **A teacher begins to introduce reading analysis skills for informational and expository text. Until now, her students have been exposed primarily to imaginative literature. Which skill should be taught while using expository texts that is not typically covered in imaginative literature?**

A. Using a graphic organizer to support comprehension

B. Evaluating the author's purpose

C. Demonstrating comprehension through retelling

D. Using text features such as the glossary and index

8. **Technology can certainly play a useful role in the classroom. However, if used inappropriately or in excess, student learning could suffer. For example, if we only teach children how to type on computers, they might not learn to write properly with proper spelling and grammar. If they don't learn to write, they might not have the skills necessary to land a job.**

Which graphic organizer would best facilitate comprehension of this passage?

A. Timeline

B. Word map for "type"

C. Graphic organizer showing cause and effect

D. Semantic map showing comparison

The following is an excerpt from *Bookbinding, and the Care of Books* (1910) by Douglas Cockerell:

The reasons for binding the leaves of a book are to keep them together in their proper order and to protect them. That bindings can be made that will adequately protect books can be seen from the large number of fifteenth and sixteenth century bindings now existing on books still in excellent condition. That bindings are made, that fail to protect books, may be seen by visiting any large library, when it will be found that many bindings have their boards loose and the leather crumbling to dust. Nearly all librarians complain, that they have to be continually rebinding books, and this not after four hundred, but after only five or ten years.

9. **After reading, two students are asked to retell the passage. Their responses are as follows:**

Student #1: The guy says that bindings on books can be weak or poor. There are some really old books from the fifteenth and sixteenth centuries, and they have good bindings. There are also a lot of books that don't have good bindings. You can see them in any library.

Student #2: The author is saying that if done right, binding can last a long time. He makes a good point, but he uses generalizations like "nearly all librarians," which seems unlikely.

Which would be the most accurate assessment of their retellings?

A. Both students make literal, inferential, and evaluative observations.
B. Student #1 makes more inferences, whereas student #2 cites literal references.

C. Student #1 cites literal and inferential details, whereas student #2 makes only an evaluative statement.

D. Student #1 cites literal references and infers information, but does not provide any evaluative statements. Student #2 demonstrates an evaluative level of comprehension, but does not cite literal details.

10. **Students need the ability to read quickly through a piece of informational text and locate specific information. Which skill will be useful for completing this task?**

A. skimming

B. self-questioning

C. scanning

D. note taking

INFORMATIONAL/EXPOSITORY TEXTS EXPLANATIONS

1. A Although reading an expository text's first and last paragraphs can be used as a previewing activity, it will not lead to drawing conclusions about characters. Also, characters are a feature of fictional narrative, not expository/argumentative text. For these reasons, Choice A would be the most inappropriate previewing activity. By contrast, looking at illustrations and activating prior knowledge (Choice B), introducing vocabulary (Choice C), and skimming for structure and difficulty (Choice D) are all appropriate previewing activities.

2. D A summary is like a retelling in that it presents a text's basic facts and main points. A retelling is always oral, however, which eliminates Choice A. A K-W-L chart (Choice B) is a graphic organizer that students can use to track their learning before, during and after reading. A student must comprehend the text to include it on the chart, but this question targets an assessment rather than a self-directed monitoring activity. An oral preview (Choice C) prepares students before reading; it does not assess them after reading and is a verbal activity. Choice D, having the student complete a written summary, would therefore be the best answer.

3. A Analysis includes looking at faulty logic and considering all elements when making a decision. Only Choice A presents examples of faulty logic while also considering parts of the passage that might be based on sound reasoning. Choice B fails to identify faulty logic used by the author. Choice C acknowledges the faulty logic, but doesn't point to any potential logical parts and doesn't say whether the person agrees. Choice D shows the student suspects faulty logic, but the response does not provide examples as in Choice A.

4. D As Choice D explains, Student #1 cites literal details by mentioning the writer's kids and grandkids and Student #2 infers the author's goal to persuade readers why they should protect water, making this the best answer. Choice A is incorrect because Student #2 states the main argument. Choices B and C are incorrect because Student #1 makes literal references, and Student #2 does not.

5. C Choice C, a K-W-L Chart, is the most appropriate activity to promote self-directed learning. K-W-L charts are divided into three columns: "What I **K**now," "What I **W**ant to Know," and "What I **L**earned." Incorporating these organizers allow students to activate schema and direct their learning from prior knowledge. Choices A and B help comprehension, but do not necessarily show students the progression between what they know, want to know and have learned as a result of their research. Choice D is incorrect - word maps are better used to increase student's vocabulary.

6. B As choices A, C, and D indicate, this type of pre-reading activity has many benefits. By engaging students and peaking their interest, prior knowledge will be activated and students will be more likely to actively engage in the reading and make connections with the text. Verbal discussions allow students to both practice and improve upon their expressive and receptive language skills, as well as help peer's to make associations and consider what others already know about the topic. Additionally, such activities allow teachers to ensure all students begin reading with necessary background information. Metacognitive strategies or thinking about what you're reading, certainly help comprehension *while* reading, however, are not used during this particular pre-reading activity, making Choice B an inappropriate explanation of this previewing activity.

7. D A distinguishing characteristic of informational and expository text is their use of text features such as a glossary, index, and headings, making Choice D the best answer. Skillful use of these features is an important part of instruction in reading these texts that is not part of reading imaginative text. Graphic organizers, author's purpose, and retelling (Choices A, B and C) are skills used in imaginative text as well.

8. C The above passage discusses pros and cons of using technology in the classroom, but also cautions against using it inappropriately, citing an example about what could happen if children learn to write *only* with technology. A graphic organizer showing cause and effect (Choice C) is the best answer as it provides a visual for students to understand the author's belief that a cause (focusing on typing) produces an effect (poor writing skills). A timeline (Choice A), should instead be used to visually present dates or sequential information and a word map (Choice B) is best used to reinforce vocabulary. And, in this particular case, a word map for "type" wouldn't reinforce the author's main point (that technology affects writing skills). A semantic map showing comparison (Choice D) wouldn't work either, as the author is not comparing typing and writing but rather presenting a cause/effect relationship.

9. D Student #1 cites literal details (old books with good bindings) and infers that bindings can be weak or poor; it is an inference because the author does not explicitly state this information. He does not relate this passage to others or analyze the form and argument, which would demonstrate an evaluative level of comprehension, making Choice A incorrect. Student #2 infers that "if done right, binding can last a long time." The author does not directly say that, but hints at it, makes Choice C incorrect. Student #2 does not cite literal details, but evaluates faulty logic by talking about the use of "nearly all librarians." This makes choice B incorrect – Choice D is therefore the best answer.

10. C Scanning is quick reading to look for specific facts or information. Efficient scanning depends on identifying text structure and locating important information while ignoring information irrelevant to the task. Skimming (Choice A) is quick reading to look for the general idea. Self-questioning is interaction with the text in which a reader actively processes the reading by self-checking, summarizing, reflecting, drawing inferences, etc (Choice B). Note taking (Choice D) is a comprehension strategy in which students summarize relevant points of a text. Neither self-questioning nor note taking are specifically quick reading techniques.

4.4 Imaginative/Literary Texts

Whether through fairy tales, children's literature, or traditional tales, most children are exposed to imaginative stories from an early age. Imaginative literature is distinguished from nonfiction in that imaginative text is from the author's mind. Although the setting, incidents, characters, conflict, and themes might originate in the real world, the story itself is invented. By contrast, a nonfiction book should be entirely factual and verifiable. From an early age, readers can appreciate an author's craft and style. The reader's analytical skills build through upper elementary and beyond.

Literary analysis skills

Explicit instruction on literary analysis can equip students with the skills needed to comprehend and analyze literary texts on literal, inferential, and evaluative levels. Beyond comprehension, through analysis, students learn to predict, interpret, draw conclusions, and support their ideas through citing the text. Literary analyses may consider the following factors:

Genre: type of literature

Genre is determined by the text's structure and contents. The most common genres of imaginative literature are the following:

Picture books and picture storybooks

Picture books have a picture on every page. Picture storybooks (chapter books) have some pictures, but not on every page; pictures and text tell the story. Although picture books have long been the world of early childhood, the genre has expanded into upper grades as writers have begun to use pictures alongside advanced themes.

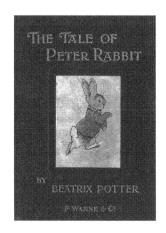

Traditional literature

Traditional literature includes folktales, fables, myths, legends, epics, religious stories, tall tales, and fairy tales.

Contemporary and historical fiction

In contemporary and historical fiction, the story places people in a specific time in our world. The reader's age and experience determine whether a story (for example, a refugee fleeing Cambodia under the Khmer Rouge) is contemporary or historical.

Fantasy fiction

Although all fiction is imaginative, fantasy fiction violates or goes beyond the laws of the universe. Spiders talk. Characters time travel. Toys have and demonstrate emotions. Fantasy fiction includes modern folktales, animal fantasy, and science fiction. In science fiction, the elements existing outside our universe are explainable with science, and an attempt is made to explain them. Other fantasy does not justify unrealistic events such as a swan playing a trumpet.

Realistic fiction

In realistic fiction, the laws of the universe are intact. The setting might be real Philadelphia or an imagined village, but within that setting, the sun still rises in the East, and food still provides the nourishment for life. In mystery books, a crime is solved or a secret is unraveled.

Drama

A type of fiction represented in performance. Dramas include classic drama, pantomime, reader's theater, storytelling, puppetry, skits, and theater. As a genre, drama is typically narrative, though scripts for content areas are available for educational purposes.

Poetry

Poetry includes Mother Goose, nursery rhymes, and lines containing rhythm or rhyme to communicate meaning that goes beyond prose.

Story elements

- ⊙ **Characters:** the people in the story. Authors develop characters through features such as the character's appearance, conversation, history, relationships, flaws, and ambitions. Development might be direct or indirect. Readers might be asked to infer details such as personality, social status, and even appearance, based on written features. Early in their reading experience, students can begin to identify static characters (staying the same through the conflict) and dynamic (changing during the story).

- ⊙ **Plot:** the plan or story line. Young readers can speak simply about the story's beginning, middle, and end. More advanced readers can analyze the rising action, climax, and resolution. They can trace the events directing the plot.

- ⊙ **Setting:** the time, place, and conditions.

- ⊙ **Conflict:** the struggle or opposition. Young readers can speak simply of the problem and solution. More mature readers can begin to recognize conflicts such as person vs. person, person vs. nature, person vs. himself, person vs. society, or person vs. a force greater than himself.

- ⊙ **Theme:** the main idea. The theme is generally separate from the story's events, and it applies to all people of all times. Common themes include love, death, imagination, and power.In a theme study, students read various books by various authors dealing with the same theme. For instance, readers studying a theme of crossing cultures might read books such as *How My Parents Learned to Eat, I Hate English, Grandfather's Journey, Allison,* and *One Green Apple.* Theme is rarely stated explicitly; instead, the reader must connect, consider supporting evidence, infer, and conclude about the theme.

Figurative language

Gifted writers of children's literature communicate through analogies, metaphors, similes, symbols, personification, and other figurative language.

- ⊙ **Analogy:** a comparison of two things based on their similarity. Similes, metaphors, and allegories are types of analogies.

- ⊙ **Metaphor:** a word or phrase expressed in terms of something else. Something unfamiliar or unclear is explained by something clear and familiar. "The young woman, *a star in the night sky,* was dressed in yellow."

- **Simile**: **a** metaphor that uses the words *like* or *as*. "The current caught her as a piece of paper thrown from a moving train is snatched away by the wind." (Knight, Eric. *Lassie Come Home*.)

- **Symbol:** a symbol stands for something else. Just as the United States has national symbols such as the Statue of Liberty and Mount Rushmore, literature has symbols such as a poisonous apple or a rabbit that comes of age.

- **Personification**: **giving** human characteristics to something that is not human. *"The trees whistled loudly as the wind rushed off."*

- **Allusion:** A literary allusion is a reference to someone or something from an outside source. In *Goodnight, Moon*, "Goodnight cow jumping over the moon" has significance to children who know "Hey, Diddle, Diddle."

Point of View

Point of view is the narrator's perspective, and it is revealed using pronouns. In first person, the narrator is a character in the story, and he tells the story from his perspective using first-person pronouns such as *I* and *we*. In second person, the narrator speaks to the reader as *you*. In third person, the narrator tells the story from outside the story with pronouns such as *he, she*, and *they*.

Instructional strategies

Analysis of story elements

Teachers can explicitly teach students to analyze literature. Teachers can model the thought processes of comprehending a story on many levels and for various purposes.

Passage for analysis: Excerpt from *Anne of Green Gables* by Lucy Maud Montgomery

[Anne speaking] "... It wouldn't be half so interesting if we know all about everything, would it? There'd be no scope for imagination then, would there? But am I talking too *much? People are always telling me I do. Would you rather I didn't talk? If you say so I'll stop. I can STOP when I make up my mind to it, although it's difficult."*

Matthew, much to his own surprise, was enjoying himself. Like most quiet folks he liked talkative people when they were willing to do the talking themselves and did not expect him to keep up his end of it. But he had never expected to enjoy the society of a little girl. Women were bad enough in all conscience, but little girls were worse. He detested the way they had of sidling past him timidly, with sidewise glances, as if they expected him to gobble them up at a mouthful if they ventured to say a word. That was the Avonlea type of well-bred little girl. But this freckled witch was very different, and although he found it rather difficult for his slower intelligence to keep up with her brisk mental processes he thought that he "kind of liked her chatter." So he said as shyly as usual:

"Oh, you can talk as much as you like. I don't mind."

- ⊙ **Genre:** coming-of-age novel; juvenile
- ⊙ **Story elements**:
  - *characters***:** Anne, Matthew, Marilla
  - *setting***:** Prince Edward Island, turn of the twentieth century
  - *conflict***:** Anne's imagination vs. strict expectations of small Canadian town
  - *themes***:** imagination/expectations, love, acceptance, friendship

- ⊙ **Character development**: Anne is the protagonist. She is an orphan adopted by Matthew and Marilla. She is highly imaginative, passionate, and intelligent. She desires to be good and fulfill expectations but struggles to adapt to the traditions and rules of Avonlea.

- ⊙ **Point of view:** third person narrator who has access to characters thoughts and emotions

Literary analysis considers how and why a selection was written. It gives close attention to the original text to defend and explain the reader's observations. Example: The theme of imagination vs. expectation is demonstrated from Anne's first meeting with Matthew when Anne's *"scope for imagination"* is contrasted to *"the Avonlea type of well-bred little girl."*

Analysis of Different Versions

Many classic stories have different versions from various times or cultures. For instance, *Little Red Riding Hood* has more than fifty versions, including the Brothers Grimm, *Lon Po Po* from China, beginning reader versions, and modern versions told from the wolf's perspective. Young students can appreciate the differences among the accounts and choose a favorite telling.

Author Study

In an author study, students study the author as a person, analyze his craft, and read a selection of his works. From their knowledge base, students can read, respond to, and practice critical thinking. For instance, young readers can see parallels among Leo Lionni's characters such as Alexander, Frederick, and Swimmy and make observations about the author's favorite themes.

Promoting reading comprehension while reading

As with informational and expository texts, students can use metacognitive strategies while reading to assess their comprehension and engage more in the text. Besides predicting, visualizing, self-questioning,and rereading, students should use **self-monitoring** skills. Self-monitoring means that a student gauges comprehension and, in difficulty, deals with the problem by choosing an effective strategy. For example, if a particular concept seems complex, the student can adapt his or her reading rate. Skimming is a good practice for getting the gist of the overall meaning before reading more closely. Skimming can also be helpful with longer passages in timed tests.

With literary texts, especially those using figurative language, close reading is beneficial. Close reading of a literary text involves rereading it and looking closely at all the possible meanings.

Post-reading: Literary responses and literary analysis skills

Post-reading graphic organizers

Graphic organizers can be used to promote comprehension and as literary analysis skills in post-reading activities, just as during reading. Children of any grade can also begin literary analysis skills by making story maps appropriate to the age and level.

Story maps are effective tools for promoting comprehension and basic analysis of a literary text. Young readers can create basic maps that show the character in the story setting engaged in a plot event. More mature readers can produce maps that analyze any element of the selection (that is, character development, plot, conflict, and so on). In small group work, students can exchange ideas. By comparing maps, they can add and amend information.

Look at an example of a story map for Cinderella:

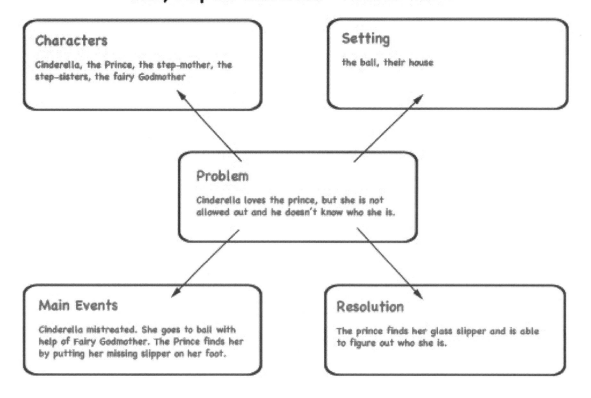

Story Map for Cinderella – Grades 1 & 2

Characters
Cinderella, the Prince, the step-mother, the step-sisters, the fairy Godmother

Setting
the ball, their house

Problem
Cinderella loves the prince, but she is not allowed out and he doesn't know who she is.

Main Events
Cinderella mistreated. She goes to ball with help of Fairy Godmother. The Prince finds her by putting her missing slipper on her foot.

Resolution
The prince finds her glass slipper and is able to figure out who she is.

Venn Diagrams work great for comparisons of two or more books, authors, genres, and so on. They are helpful for students to visualize the commonalities and the differences. They can also be used to compare two accounts so differences and similarities can be discerned. For example, students could be told to create a Venn diagram graphic of two books such as *The Very Busy Spider* and *The Very Hungry Caterpillar*.

Literary responses

Significant research suggests that written literary responses to literature are critical to developing analytical thinking skills. Talking about literature is helpful to ensure comprehension on different levels and stimulate discussion for analysis. However, a written component forces students to put their thoughts into coherent language, requiring a high level of thought.

Writing activities can be tailored to promote different skills at different levels. Prompts that target comprehension include:

- ⊙ What happened in the story?
- ⊙ Who are the characters in the story? What do they do?
- ⊙ Talk about the main events.

Prompts that promote analysis ask students **to relate texts to prior knowledge** (other books they have read or other discussions on the themes) or ask them **to evaluate the book, the author's style**, and so on. Some examples include:

- ⊙ Can we tell what the author thinks about the topic? How?
- ⊙ How does this book compare with another story we read?
- ⊙ What did you expect to read, and what happened that you did not expect?

Student and teacher shared journals

In classrooms where students read different texts, journals work to monitor and promote literary analysis. Students and teacher can collaborate. Students can practice citing evidence from the text to support their ideas.

Through regular written feedback on journals, teachers open a dialog with students, and they can assess their literary response skills, give feedback, and encourage critical thought. Journals establish ownership for students because the project's success depends on their engaging with the reading and committing to writing a thorough response.

Use the following passage from Lewis Carroll's Alice's Adventures in Wonderland for Questions 1 through 3:

"What a curious feeling!' said Alice; 'I must be shutting up like a telescope.' And so it was indeed: she was now only ten inches high, and her face brightened up at the thought that she was now the right size for going through the little door into that lovely garden. First, however, she waited for a few minutes to see if she was going to shrink any further: she felt a little nervous about this; 'for it might end, you know,' said Alice to herself, 'in my going out altogether, like a candle. I wonder what I should be like then.' And she tried to fancy what the flame of a candle is like after the candle is blown out, for she could not remember ever having seen such a thing."

1. **A fourth grade teacher asks students to read the passage and then write a journal entry about what they think it would be like to be only ten inches tall. This activity is most likely to promote which skill?**
   A. Literary analysis
   B. Structural analysis
   C. Reading analysis of expository texts
   D. Phonological awareness

2. **A second-grade teacher reads the passage aloud, stopping intermittently to say, "My goodness, I wonder what's going to happen next. Will she go into the little door?" Which of the following comprehension strategies is the teacher modeling?**
   A. The teacher models print directionality.
   B. The teacher models analysis of story elements.
   C. The teacher models predicting.
   D. The teacher models paraphrasing.

3. **After reading "I must be shutting up like a telescope," a student thinks Alice has literally closed like a telescope. This student could benefit from which of the following?**
   A. Author study
   B. Story map of character development
   C. Skills for comprehending figurative language
   D. Skills for analyzing genre

4. **A fifth-grade class is reading Jean Craighead George's novel, *My Side of the Mountain*. The book is about Sam, a boy who runs away to live on his grandparent's abandoned farm in the mountains. The story describes Sam's difficulties living independently during the winter, including finding food and shelter. Which of the following graphic organizers would be most beneficial to help students specifically analyze Sam's struggles and conflicts?**
   A. Problem/solution map
   B. Timeline
   C. Semantic map
   D. Venn diagram

5. **A teacher introduces the concept of self-monitoring and has students practice these skills using an unfamiliar literary text. Which of the following are the students most likely to do while reading?**
   A. They will create word maps.
   B. They will adjust their reading rate and reread when necessary.
   C. They will take notes.
   D. They will collaborate with peers.

6. **A second-grade class is listening to a teacher read a story about a family with a dragon. Afterwards, the teacher has the students complete a story map. Why is the teacher most likely having students engage in this particular activity?**
   A. A story map improves comprehension and literary analysis skills.
   B. A story map provides help when decoding unfamiliar words.
   C. A story map helps compare two or more works, people, themes, authors, and so on.
   D. A story map provides an opportunity for students to work in groups.

7. **A fourth grader is having a difficult time comprehending a particular literary passage. The student prefers to read the entire text without stopping and as a result, sometimes misses literal and inferential details. Which of the following should a teacher recommend to this student?**

A. The teacher could work on explicit phonics instruction.

B. The teacher could ask the student what associations come to mind.

C. The teacher could ask students to skim the text rather than slowing down.

D. The teacher could teach the student about the importance of close reading and rereading.

8. **The following question is based on an excerpt from Louisa May Alcott's** *Little Women***:**

> "'Christmas won't be Christmas without any presents,' grumbled Jo, lying on the rug.
> 'It's so dreadful to be poor!' sighed Meg, looking down at her old dress.
> 'I don't think it's fair for some girls to have plenty of pretty things, and other girls nothing at all,' added little Amy, with an injured sniff.
> 'We've got Father and Mother, and each other,' said Beth contentedly from her corner."

During a free-writing assignment a student writes the following:

> "It's clear that Jo, Meg, and Amy are sad about their life because they are poor, but Beth is the optimist and gets people to look on the bright side. They remind me of my sisters. Even though this is from a long time ago, families are still the same."

Which of the following most accurately assesses this student's response?

A. The student cites literal details.

B. The student cites literal and inferential details.

C. The student cites evaluative details.

D. The student cites literal, inferential, and evaluative details.

9. **Which of the following unit plans includes reading a variety of genres?**

   A. Sixth graders read selected modern adaptations of Homer's *The Iliad* and *The Odyssey*.

   B. Kindergarteners read nursery rhymes and write variations such as "Humpty Dumpty sat on a cow."

   C. In a *Fun With Pets* unit, students read an informational text about caring for pets, a realistic fiction about a child who finds a dog, and a fantasy fiction about a pet dragon.

   D. Students research background information about westward expansion in the 1800s before reading a chapter book on the subject.

10. **A kindergarten teacher has designed a unit in which students will listen to the following books read aloud:** *Jack and the Beanstalk* **by Joseph Jacobs,** *Jack and the Beanstalk* **by Steven Kellogg,** *Kate and the Beanstalk* **by Mary Pope Osbourne, and** *Trust Me, Jack's Beanstalk Stinks!: The Story of Jack and the Beanstalk Told by the Giant* **by Eric Braun and Cristian Bernardini.**
    These selections are well suited to explore which of the following objectives?

    A. treatment of similar topics in different genres

    B. comparing and contrasting different versions of a story

    C. comparing and contrasting different books by the same author

    D. analyzing multiple accounts of the same event

IMAGINATIVE/LITERARY TEXTS EXPLANATIONS

1. **A**   By writing about a passage and relating it to themselves, students must think about and analyze the text. This type of activity promotes comprehension and literary analysis skills, making Choice A the best answer. Choice B, structural analysis, involves looking at word parts to decipher unfamiliar words – not something addressed through this type of activity. Choice C is also incorrect as the referenced text is an imaginative or literary text, not expository. Finally, phonological awareness (Choice D) refers to an awareness that oral language is comprised of smaller units. Activities targeting identification and manipulation of sounds in words,

syllables and phonemes would be more appropriate for student's developing phonological awareness than the reading, analyzing and writing about text as described in the question.

2. C   In this scenario, the teacher is modeling a metacognitive strategy, or a way to think about what one has comprehended. Specifically, she is showing students how to predict as a way to engage in constructing meaning, making Choice C the best answer. Print directionality (Choice A) is incorrect – this involves understanding that text reads from left to right. Story elements (Choice B) are also not modeled – they are features such as characters, setting, plot, conflict, and theme. Finally, paraphrasing involves summarizing and putting the story into one's own words, also making Choice D incorrect.

3. C   The sentence referenced is a simile, which is a way to use nonliteral language to compare things using the word *'like'*. "I must be shutting up like a telescope" is an example of figurative language – the phrase is not meant to be interpreted in a literal manner. Providing the student with strategies to recognize and comprehend figurative language would be most beneficial, making Choice C the best answer. Author studies (Choice A), involve learning about a particular author and his craft and Character maps, (Choice B) promote an understanding of the character, making these choices incorrect. Choice D is also incorrect because a simile is a literary device, not part of the text's genre.

4. A   A problem/solution map is used to analyze the conflict, making Choice A the best answer. When using problem/solution maps, students are able to visually observe the problem/solution relationship and further analyze conflicts within text. Timelines (Choice B) are intended to display and help students meaningfully sequence a series of dates and/or events. For example, if the teacher wanted students to sequentially arrange events that occurred in *My Side of the Mountain*, a timeline would be most useful. Word maps (Choice C) target vocabulary and support students in their understanding of an unfamiliar or keyword in a passage. Finally, venn diagrams (Choice D) are used to compare and contrast two things.

5. B   Self-monitoring involves checking comprehension and slowing down one's reading rate as necessary, making Choice B the best answer. When learning such skills, students are also frequently taught to skim passages to capture the main idea, level of difficulty and overall structure of the text. By quickly gaining an idea for these text elements, students are better able to pace themselves. Students would be more likely to use a word map, Choice A, when working on expanding their vocabulary. Note taking (Choice C), though an excellent strategy to help learn difficult materials, may disrupt the flow of reading while working with literary text and is not something the student's will likely be practicing in this situation. Choice D is also incorrect; self-monitoring is done independent of others and does not involve peer collaboration.

6. A   A story map can be simple or complex depending on age and ability levels. Story maps are a type of graphic organizer that helps students to identify various story components including characters, setting, problems/solutions, etc. For example, in second grade, students might complete a story map detailing characters, setting, the beginning, middle, and end of the story, and the problem/solution within the story. This type of activity greatly enhances student's understanding and helps children further analyze text beyond what the author conveys on a literal level, making Choice A the best answer. Decoding (Choice B), refers to breaking down sounds and syllables when reading unfamiliar words, and is not addressed through story maps. Story maps are also not used to compare and contrast - were students to compare and contrast two characters, themes or authors, as suggested in Choice C, a Venn Diagram would be a better graphic organizer. Though story maps may be completed in groups, as suggested in Choice D, it is not likely this is why the teacher had her students engage in this activity.

7. D   For difficult literary texts, close reading and rereading difficult parts can significantly improve comprehension, making Choice D the best answer. Rereading allows students to gain a better overall understanding of literal, inferential and evaluative details, as well as the author's point and purpose. Choice A, explicit phonics instruction, would be appropriate when helping students understand letter-sound correspondences. Though likely not necessary for students reading at this level, stopping to deliver specific phonics instruction in the middle of a difficult literary passage would likely only serve to further slow comprehension as reading would become disjointed and choppy. Naming associations (Choice B) is helpful for schema building and prereading activities, but this particular student needs an effective strategy to use *while* reading. Choice C is also incorrect - skimming would not encourage a student to slow down and/or reread to further consider specific details or pieces of the text that are confusing.

8. D   The student cites literal details when mentioning the girls are poor (a detail which is explicitly stated). The student also demonstrates an inferential level of comprehension by explaining that Beth is optimistic and likes to look on the bright side of things. Finally, the student also provides evaluative details by comparing the family described in *Little Women* to their own family, building on prior knowledge, and making a larger statement on the importance of families in society. Choice D is therefore the best answer as the student effectively cites literal, inferential and evaluative details.

9. C   In Choice C, students read from three different genres: information, realistic fiction, and fantasy fiction. Reading from a variety of genres can expands student vocabulary, provide exposure to different text structures, and encourage a love of reading. In Choice A, students read only one genre: epic poetry. In Choice B, likewise, students read only a nursery rhyme. In Choice D, student research may include reading a variety of genres; however because a variety of genres is not specifically noted (Students could watch videos for background information.), choice C remains the best choice.

10. B   The teacher has selected the classic Joseph Jacobs's version as well as a variety of modern versions of a traditional story. This collection is well suited to explore different versions of a story. All of the selections tell or give clever twists to a traditional story. For this reason, they are not diverse enough to explore different genres (Choice A). The books all have different authors so cannot be used to analyze books by the same author (Choice C). "Multiple accounts of the same event" is an expression typically used for nonfiction text about historic events. A traditional tale would not be considered an account of an event (Choice D).

4.5 Chapter Review

1. **A fifth-grade class just finished reading two expository texts about the environment. Which of the following would be the most logical and effective way to promote comprehension and analysis skills of both texts?**
    A. Have the students complete a K-W-L chart.
    B. Have the students complete a Venn diagram.
    C. Have the students do a preview of the texts' titles.
    D. Have the students do a retelling of both texts.

Questions 2 and 3 are based on the following excerpt from *A Brief History of the United States* by Jon McMaster.

Long before Columbus was born, the people of Europe had been trading with the Far East. Spices, drugs, and precious stones, silks, and other articles of luxury were brought, partly by vessels and partly by camels, from India, the Spice Islands, and Cathay (China) by various routes to Constantinople and the cities in Egypt and along the eastern shore of the Mediterranean. There they were traded for the copper, tin, and lead, coral, and woolens of Europe, and then carried to Venice and Genoa, whence merchants spread them over all Europe. The merchants of Genoa traded chiefly with Constantinople, and those of Venice with Egypt.

2. **Which of the following activities would be most beneficial to promoting memorization of the different articles and regions mentioned in the passage?**
    A. Students write self-generated questions in small groups after reading.
    B. Students make a semantic map that categorizes the types of products according to the place.

C. After reading, students do a retelling of the passage.

D. Students work on a K-W-L chart before and after reading.

3. **As a pre-reading activity, a teacher asks students what comes to mind when they think of explorers. She writes down what they say and asks them to elaborate. Why does the teacher most likely have students engage in this discussion prior to reading the passage?**

   A. It is meant to activate students' schema.

   B. It is meant to introduce unfamiliar words.

   C. It is meant to give a preview of the reading.

   D. It is meant to aide students in structural analysis.

4. **A teacher wants to orally assess a student's ability to make inferences. Which of the following would be the best option?**

   A. The student completes a K-W-L chart.

   B. The student performs a re-telling.

   C. The student "free-writes" in a journal.

   D. The student engages in an oral preview.

The following is an excerpt from *The Usurper: An Episode in Japanese History* by Judith Gautier:

"Dawn trembled in the air, and the tree-tops were more plainly outlined against the sky, which grew bluer every moment. Soon a pale glimmer touched the highest branches, slipped between the boughs and their leaves, and filtered downward to the ground. Then, in the gardens of the Prince, alleys thick with brambles displayed their dim perspective; the grass resumed its emerald hue; a tuft of poppies renewed the splendor of its sumptuous flowers, and a snowy flight of steps was faintly visible through the mist, down a distant avenue."

5. **A sixth-grade teacher wants to promote comprehension of this passage. Which of the following would be most effective for use while reading?**
   A. retelling and noting literal and inferential details
   B. metacognition skills, including visualizing
   C. outlining
   D. structural analysis

6. **A student has a hard time understanding the personification and metaphors in the passage. Which of the following activities would be most beneficial to promoting comprehension of the figurative language?**
   A. Ask a student to make a graphic organizer that shows the basic events post-reading.
   B. During a pre-reading activity have students skim headings and subheadings.
   C. Have students draw pictures after reading this passage aloud in pairs.
   D. Have students complete a word map by using context clues to decode the meaning of the nonliteral language.

7. **A third-grade class is preparing to read** Charlie and the Chocolate Factory **by Ronald Dahl. Which of the following pre-reading activities would best promote comprehension?**
   A. Students read headings and look at illustrations.
   B. Students think about faulty logic.
   C. Students read the front and back covers.
   D. Students use a dictionary to look up a list of unfamiliar words provided by the teacher.

8. **A teacher asks students to work on a KWL chart in small groups before reading a chapter about the atmosphere. This activity is most likely to promote which of the following skills?**
   A. It will help students connect prior knowledge to the reading.
   B. It will help students memorize the main points in the text.
   C. It will help students synthesize information.
   D. It will promote metacognition.

9. **After reading a chapter in a tradebook, students create role-plays and perform them in front of the class. This activity is likely to promote which of the following?**

    A. The activity promotes literary response skills.
    B. The activity promotes literary analysis skills.
    C. The activity promotes synthesizing skills.
    D. The activity promotes decoding skills.

10. **Which of the following is <u>not</u> an example of how a teacher might model self-monitoring for comprehension while reading the following lines of a poem?**

    > "Come to the sunset tree,
    > The day is past and gone;
    > The woodman's ax lies free,
    > And the reaper's work is done;"

    A. The teacher says, "Hmm..I'm having some trouble with that last line. Let me read it again."
    B. The teacher says, "That word didn't make sense. Let me see if I read it correctly."
    C. The teacher analyzes, "Oh, I see. The author is giving a description.
    D. The teacher reads rapidly and smoothly,

    > "Come to the sunset tree,
    > The day is past and gone;
    > The woodman's ax lies free,
    > And the reaper's work is done;"

11. **A sixth-grade teacher asks students to pick one sentence from a high-interest short story that touched them the most and to discuss it with a partner. How does this activity promote reading development?**

    A. It encourages metacognition.
    B. The activity helps students understand the structure and organization of the text.
    C. It promotes personal interpretations of texts.
    D. It allows students to consider the main point.

12. **A teacher asks students to respond in a teacher-student dialog journal explaining the main idea of a high-interest literary text and to note any questions they have. Which of the following does this activity promote?**

    A. active construction of meaning within the text
    B. automatic word recognition and reading fluency
    C. understanding of genres
    D. consideration of author's point of view

13. **A sixth-grade class is reading about the endocrine system in a textbook. Which of the following would be a beneficial strategy or activity to promote comprehension?**

    A. retelling
    B. literary response
    C. outlining
    D. skimming

This question is based on the following excerpt from *The Velveteen Rabbit*.

"He was naturally shy, and being only made of velveteen, some of the more expensive toys quite snubbed him. The mechanical toys were very superior, and looked down upon everyone else; they were full of modern ideas, and pretended they were real. The model boat, who had lived through two seasons and lost most of his paint, caught the tone from them and never missed an opportunity of referring to his rigging in technical terms."

14. **Prior to reading the passage aloud to first graders, which of the following pre-reading strategies would be most beneficial?**

    A. Analyze story elements
    B. Model print directionality and finger sweep
    C. Consider the author's point of view
    D. Pre-teach unfamiliar vocabulary

15. **A student encounters an unfamiliar word while reading and despite using context clues, is unable to attach meaning. The teacher asks the student to look up the word in a dictionary and then rewrite the meaning in his own words. Besides determining the meaning of the word, which of the following is an added benefit to this activity?**

    A. It provides practice in metacognition.

    B. It promotes paraphrasing.

    C. It allows the student to practice predicting.

    D. The student is able to practice how to infer meaning.

16. **In a fifth-grade class, the teacher designs the following lesson plan:**

    Look at the headings and subheadings in Chapter 1.
    Discuss possible main ideas within the chapter.
    Have students skim the first section to identify
    unfamiliar words.
    Read the first page aloud. Have students read in pairs the
    rest of the first section.

    This type of lesson plan would work best with which of the following texts?

    A. an imaginative text

    B. a high-interest tradebook

    C. a poem

    D. a content-area textbook

Use the following excerpt from *Letters from a Cat* by Helen Jackson to answer questions 17, 18 and 19:

"I do not feel wholly sure that my cat wrote these letters herself. They always came inside the letters written to me by my mamma, or other friends, and I never caught cat writing at any time when I was at home; but the printing was pretty bad, and they were signed by cat's name; and my mamma always looked very mysterious when I asked about them, as if there were some very great secret about it all; so that until I grew to be a big girl, I never doubted but that cat printed them all alone by herself, after dark."

17. **A third-grade student, Jennifer, silently read the passage. The teacher then asked the student to do a retelling. Following is her response.**

"The girl gets letters from her cat. Her mom and her friends send her letters, too. She never sees the cat writing them. The cat must hide when it is writing letters."

Which of the following would be the most accurate assessment of this student's strengths and weaknesses in comprehension?

A. Jennifer demonstrates a need for help with literal information based on her comment that the cat must be hiding when writing letters. She would benefit from explicit instruction and possibly one-on-one help to understand literal details.

B. Jennifer demonstrates an evaluative level of understanding based on her comments about the cat hiding when writing letters. She clearly has an excellent grasp on the text.

C. Jennifer makes several excellent literal and inferential references in her re-telling by appropriately inferring cat must hide while writing. She demonstrates an understanding that the narrator receives letters from her mother and "cat," who clearly isn't sending letters. Her inference that the cat must hide demonstrates her awareness of how an author uses allusions and figurative language.

D. Jennifer shows she is able to understand a somewhat difficult text rather well in terms of literal details. She understands the girl receives letters from her mom and "cat." She also understands the cat is never seen writing letters. However, Jennifer does not demonstrate understanding on an inferential level. For example, she does not note the girl suspects her cat is writing the letters, but rather inappropriately infers the cat must have been hiding.

18. In addition to the *Letters From A Cat* **excerpt, a second-grade teacher reads aloud a full chapter. Which of the following would be the most appropriate and effective way to extend student understanding after the reading?**
   A. The students complete a KWL chart.
   B. The teacher has the students write an alternative ending.
   C. The students complete a story map.
   D. The students write student-generated questions.

19. **A student reads the passage silently and then reads it again aloud. The student then retells the passage by saying the following:**

   "The girl starts off saying she's not sure if her cat is really writing letters because the cat's letters come with the mom's. Then, I'm not really sure what happens. I don't remember the next part."

   This student could benefit most from which of the following to promote a better understanding of the passage?
   A. The student needs more explicit phonics instruction.
   B. The student needs practice with metacognition and self-monitoring.
   C. The student needs to read more varied texts that are rich in vocabulary.
   D. The student needs one-on-one instruction.

20. **A fourth grade teacher organizes a unit on Lewis and Clark in which students read excerpts from** *The Lewis & Clark Expedition* **(Neuberger, Richard L.),** *How We Crossed the West—The Adventures of Lewis and Clark* **(Schanzer, Rosalyn), and** *Lewis and Clark and Me: A Dog's Tale* **(Myers, Laurie). Individually and in small groups, students use text, index, and maps from the excerpts to complete comprehension activities. The whole group cooperates to create a timeline graphic to display in the classroom.**
   Which strategy for comprehension is not included in this plan?
   A. use of reference materials
   B. knowledge of text structure
   C. use of text and graphic features
   D. analysis of multiple accounts

1. B A Venn diagram is a helpful graphic organizer for comparing and contrasting two texts. Using two circles that overlap, Venn Diagrams allow students to visually portray similarities and differences between two texts, making Choice B the best answer. Choice A, a KWL chart (depicting what students *Already* **K***now,* **W***ant to Know, and* **L***earned* before, during and after reading), could be useful if used before, during and after reading, however the question states students already read the passages. A KWL chart would also not be the best organizer to use when comparing two texts. Choice C, a preview, is a pre-reading activity that allows students to look at the text's headings to get a feel for what the reading will be about – again, this would not be appropriate as a post-reading activity or to compare/contrast different texts. While Choice D, a retelling, would be a post-reading activity, it would not as obviously allow students to analyze similarities and differences between two texts.

2. B Graphic organizers often help to organize and understand nonfiction content area passages in which a lot of information is provided. Semantic maps, Choice B, would be the best organizer to use in this situation as they specifically help readers to categorize information and establish relationships that make memorizing information simpler. Having students write self-generated questions (Choice A) would promote comprehension, but would likely miss the targeted objective of memorizing specific content. Retelling, Choice C, is an oral strategy typically used to assess student comprehension. Though helpful, this strategy also fails to specifically help students efficiently memorize information. Finally, while KWL charts (Choice D) help with schema building and compare what students already know and what they want to know with what they learned, they likewise fail to help students with memorization. Therefore, semantic maps (Choice B) remain the only choice that will specifically address the teacher's full objective – by explicitly organizing the information, student's will be better able to memorize the articles and regions.

3. A By asking students what comes to mind when they think of explorers, the teacher is getting students to talk about their previous knowledge, also known as activating students' schema related to the topic. Schema building allows students to have an idea of what they will be reading and encourages them to deepen their current knowledge by relating previous information to new information, making Choice A the best answer. Choice B involves introducing unfamiliar vocabulary words, which is good for words that are idioms, foreign, or hard to decipher, but this discussion will not likely focus on unfamiliar words. Though previews (as suggested in Choice C) are excellent pre-reading activities, the teacher does not have the students look through the text or skim through headings and illustrations. Instead, she has encouraged students to engage in a discussion. Structural analysis, Choice D, is a strategy for decoding unfamiliar words by looking at their affixes (prefixes and suffixes) and base words. While students may likewise benefit from this type of activity, this is not why the teacher posed her question.

4. B A re-telling (Choice B), is an oral reaction or summary of a text. Through this activity students often demonstrate if they understand a text's literal meaning, inferences based on what is suggested, and their ability to evaluate and relate to the text, making Choice B the best answer. KWL charts (Choice A) and free-writing (Choice C) are written activities, not oral activities which the teacher prefers to use in this situation. Additionally, depending on what the student chooses to write about, these activities may or may not provide any indication of the student's ability to make inferences. While oral previews (Choice D) often promote comprehension and schema building which allow students to more easily make inferences, they are a pre-reading activity, not an assessment tool.

5. B Metacognition skills (Choice B) include use of mental strategies that encourage students to engage with and actively process text. With a passage like *The Usurper* that contains nonliteral language and many descriptive words, metacognitive skills such as visualizing greatly enhance reading, making this the best answer. Retelling (Choice A) is a more open-ended assessment tool that allows students to demonstrate their level of comprehension rather than promoting a better understanding of the text. Outlining (Choice C) is a beneficial tool for analysis of informational or expository text that contains main ideas and supporting details. For descriptive texts like this, an outline would be less beneficial. Structural analysis (Choice D), involves looking at parts of an unfamiliar word (such as the prefix and suffix) to decode its meaning – though this would likely help students better understand vocabulary within the passage, stopping to analyze words while reading may also decrease fluency and thus overall comprehension. Metacognitive strategies (Choice B) remain the best approach for this type of descriptive passage.

6. D   Choice A, which describes a timeline of sorts, would be better for event or chronologically-based text. Since this passage deals more with description and interpretation, the basic events are not what would most likely hinder comprehension. A previewing activity that looks at headings (Choice B) would be beneficial for comprehension of an informational or expository text, but would not likely help with understanding the author's use of figurative language in this particular passage. Pictures (Choice C) following paired reading could be beneficial, but as a tool to specifically address nonliteral language, a word map (Choice D), would be the best choice. Because word maps allow readers to focus on specific examples of nonliteral language and encourage the use of context in determining the meaning of metaphors, this would be the best choice of an activity to promote comprehension of figurative language.

7. C   When reading a tradebook such as *Charlie and the Chocolate Factory*, the book's covers can provide important background information that piques students' anticipation and interest, making Choice C the best answer. Having students review headings and illustrations (Choice A), would be an excellent pre-reading exercise for an expository or informational text such as a textbook or magazine article. A tradebook or literary work, however, may not necessarily have headings that correspond to the meaning of the book. Likewise, having students consider faulty logic (Choice B), would be appropriate before reading expository texts that present arguments and supporting evidence. Again, however, this is not likely to be the case in a book such as *Charlie and the Chocolate Factory*. Though looking up words in the dictionary (Choice D) may be beneficial, this process may actually slow the fluency rate down when reading a tradebook, thus decreasing comprehension.

8. A   A KWL chart allows students to write what they already know, what they want to know, and what they learned about a specific topic. It allows students to view reading as a process to construct meaning and make connections with other text and experiences. By comparing what they already knew to what they learned, students build on prior knowledge, making Choice A the best answer. Were the teacher to promote memorization (Choice B), synthesizing (Choice C) or metacognition (Choice D), other graphic organizers or strategies would likely be used instead of a KWL Chart. For example, to promote memorizing, a semantic map would be useful. When synthesizing information, students should be given strategies to find faulty logic and make informed decisions. And, when encouraging metacognition, tools that help students self-monitor, visualize and consider what has been read should be provided.

9. B   Activities like role-plays can help promote literary analysis by allowing students to show comprehension in a way that involves creative interpretation, making Choice B the best answer. Literary response skills (Choice A) involve written responses whereas the activity described (role-playing) is an oral activity. Synthesizing skills (Choice C), have students consider different accounts or arguments and analyze how they converge and diverge. Finally, decoding skills (Choice D), are required to read and understanding unfamiliar words, something role-plays don't likely address.

10. D   Self-monitoring implies that students are actively engaged with the text, stopping as necessary to reread a detailed or difficult part, to ensure the reading makes sense, or to consider the author's purpose. In Choice D the teacher simply reads fluently, failing to stop and show her students how to appropriately figure out words, phrases and meaning. The other choices (A, B and C) all demonstrate ways in which a person could self-monitor for comprehension, making Choice D the only non-example and the correct answer.

11. C   When students are encouraged to interpret text for themselves, they are better able to understand how meaning exists beyond literal information provided. Having students select the sentence most meaningful to them requires a general understanding of the passage as well as the ability to determine how one sentence relates to the text as a whole and to their own lives, making Choice C the best answer. Metacognition (Choice A) refers to strategies to promote comprehension and may involve visualizing or paraphrasing – though students may be using metacognitive strategies while completing the assignment, the activity was more likely designed to promote personal interpretation. Similarly, though students may consider the main idea (Choice D) when completing the activity, this is not likely why the exercise was assigned. Choice B – an activity to promote an understanding of the text's structure - would entail a more specific look at the organization of the text, not one sentence.

12. A   A teacher-student dialog journal allows students to engage with text or respond with comments or questions. This activity demonstrates how their understanding of text continually deepens. Additionally, it promotes self-directed learning and analytical skills by allowing students to build on their own thoughts and share ideas, making Choice A the best answer. This activity does not necessarily promote the skills referenced in Choices

B, C and D. Word recognition and fluency (Choice B) refer to sight word and decoding skills which are not demonstrated through written activities such as a teacher-student journals. Such skills would be better addressed through word work, fluency practice, running records, etc. Though a student may refer to the text's genres (Choice C) or author's point of view (Choice D) in their journal response, this is not the skill journals specifically target. Therefore, Choice A remains the best answer.

13. **C** For textbook readings that present concepts, names, and details, outlines (Choice C) can help students organize information, thus promoting comprehension and memorization. A retelling (Choice A), is an open-ended way for students to construct and demonstrate their understanding of text – it would be better used for fictional text and/or less complicated non-fiction works. Retellings allow teachers to determine how much a student comprehends. A literary response (Choice B), is likewise better suited for fictional works such as imaginative text. Finally, though skimming (Choice D) is a useful pre-reading activity that allows students to quickly understand the structure and level of difficulty within a passage, it does not scaffold students through overall text comprehension to the same degree as outlining.

14. **D** First graders are likely unfamiliar with words such as *velveteen* and *mechanical*. Because misunderstanding these words would interfere with comprehension, introducing unfamiliar vocabulary would be most beneficial. By doing this, students would be better able to focus on the text's meaning without getting caught up with difficult vocabulary. While analyzing story elements (Choice A) would be an excellent exercise for students during or after reading, it would not be appropriate for pre-reading activity. Choice B is somewhat unreasonable given that most first graders have already mastered directionality. Though Choice C, the author's point of view is a good concept to discuss before, during or after reading, this would likely take a backseat to the difficult vocabulary. Without the vocabulary knowledge, children won't understand the text on even the most basic level and will therefore be unable to effectively determine the author's point of view. Pre-teaching vocabulary, or Choice D, therefore remains the best answer.

15. **B** Dictionary work can be extremely beneficial for learning and practicing how to use reference materials. Additionally, it provides the student with the definition so they can better understand the word in context. By having the student also put the definition in his own words, the student

also practices paraphrasing, making Choice B the best answer. Paraphrasing allows students to consider and summarize the main idea which in turn helps them further process and gain a better understanding of the material. Choices A, C and D, however, are not addressed during this type of reference material activity. Choice A, metacognition, refers to how a reader thinks while reading. Choice C, predicting, uses one's knowledge of the reading to guess what will happen next. Finally, Choice D – inferences - requires students to consider what the author suggests rather than simply what is stated.

16. **D** Since the question specifically refers to chapters, headings and subheadings, the reading is most likely from a textbook and presents informational or expository text. The remaining answers, imaginative texts, tradebooks and poems (Choice A, B and C), are less likely to have headings and subheadings. Additionally, these choices do not lend themselves as well to skimming or previews as a whole. Rather, teachers may have students use the front and back cover or illustrations when previewing imaginative texts or tradebooks. Choice C, a poem, is also not the most likely scenario for a preview. As textbooks and other informational writings are typically organized with headings and present an argument or a main point, Choice D remains the best answer.

17. **D** Since the question asks for strengths and weaknesses, it's important to address both parts. Jennifer's comments demonstrate her strength of understanding of literal details (i.e. she appropriately understood the girl gets letters from her cat, mother and friend, she never sees the cat actually writing) and her difficulties making inferences (she incorrectly notes the cat must hide while writing the letters since she didn't see him writing). Choice A is incorrect as it states that Jennifer requires help with literal details. Choice B confuses Jennifer's incorrect comment about the cat hiding as a correct evaluative comment. Were Jennifer making evaluative statements, she would have connected the text to other passages or her own experiences and made correct inferences. Though Choice C is correct regarding Jennifer's accurate understanding on a literal level, it incorrectly states Jennifer makes solid inferential comments – Choice C is therefore wrong as well. Choice D explains that Jennifer makes good literal comments but does not demonstrate the ability to make inferences, making this the best choice.

18. C A story map (Choice C) is an excellent tool for second graders. Story maps help students focus on specific story elements such as characters, setting, or plot for fictional books, making this the best answer. A KWL chart (Choice A) has students note what they already know, want to learn and learned. Though KWL charts also promote comprehension, they are used before and after reading to promote self-directed learning and schema building, making this choice incorrect. Student-generated questions (Choice D), a rather advanced exercise for second-graders require students to develop their own comprehension questions by analyzing the main point and supporting evidence of a text. Generating an alternative ending involves a certain level of interpretation that may be inappropriate for second grade and is more of an analysis skill than comprehension strategy. As these questions are better suited for an informational or expository text, Choice D is also incorrect.

19. B Since the student is not having problems reading but rather comprehending, phonics instruction (Choice A) is incorrect. Explicit phonics instruction would involve letter/sound and decoding strategies which would not help in this situation. Though reading varied texts with rich vocabulary (Choice C) may help by providing additional exposure and improving comprehension skills, if the student lacks strategies to interpret text this might not be enough. Similarly, one-on-one instruction (Choice D) could help the student through this particular activity. But, without being taught appropriate strategies, comprehending other text will remain a challenge. This student requires help to know when to pause and think about what has just been read in order to keep track of the main points. Self-monitoring involves knowing when to re-read a sentence or go back and verify the meaning of a word or idea. Metacognition includes self-monitoring and other mental strategies that students can use while reading to better comprehend, including visualizing, self-questioning, and paraphrasing. Choice B is therefore the best answer.

20. A The unit study designed does not include reference materials such as a dictionary, encyclopedia, or atlas. The plan includes knowledge of text structure (e.g. chronological, comparison/contrast, cause/effect) to create the timeline (Choice B). It includes use of text features (e.g. index, glossary, maps) to complete comprehension activities (Choice C). It includes analysis of multiple accounts. (Choice D).

5. *Theories for Teaching Reading Skills*

Chapter 5:
Theories for Teaching Reading Skills

Lessons

5.1 Theories & Approaches

Theories and methods behind reading instruction can:

- ⊙ Help instructors understand learning processes
- ⊙ Provide research-based ideas for planning, organizing, managing, and differentiating reading instruction
- ⊙ Demonstrate which activities promote particular skills so leveled and targeted reading instruction can be provided

Schema theory

Schema theory states that our knowledge is organized and stored in units which are connected in the brain. Schema is prior knowledge. Throughout our lives, schema change in response to our environment and learning. The schema theory addresses two aspects of reading comprehension: building schema and activating schema.

Building Schema: Schema is built by experiencing new things and learning from those experiences. The more background knowledge a reader has about the text, whether that is knowledge of the topic, the genre, the vocabulary, etc., the better he is able to comprehend. It can be helpful and necessary to build schema through prereading activities. Our prior knowledge affects what we take away from a text. When a student confronts new content or language in a text, s/he can internalize the content or language more readily when it is connected to existing schema.

Activating Schema: Activating schema is using existing knowledge to build understanding of a text. Following this theory, students can be taught the strategy of connecting to prior knowledge while reading.

Scaffolding

Scaffolding is not part of one theory or method; rather it forms the backbone of several teaching practices across subject areas. Scaffolding is instruction that introduces new concepts by building off of previously learned concepts gradually and incrementally. As in construction, educational scaffolding provides instructional/expert support by setting up the reader with solid information and strategies during the learning process which will help the student achieve the goal. As the reader gains independence, scaffolding is removed.

The goal is to provide students with appropriate support before, during, and after reading. By explicitly activating and connecting to prior knowledge, teaching background information and unfamiliar words, and by promoting various comprehension strategies, instructors support students in the learning process. Instructors can do the following to scaffold:

- Introduce details such as the author or story elements (setting, theme, or the characters).
- Introduce unfamiliar words repeatedly used and difficult to decipher.
- Read aloud before asking students to read independently.
- Do paired readings after reading the text once.
- Complete graphic organizers such as word maps, cause-and-effect charts, or Venn diagrams.

Differentiation

Differentiation is the process teachers use to maximize instruction and assessment for every student. Teachers tailor their teaching for individuals or small group. The practice is based on the theory that instructional approaches can and should vary for individual students. To differentiate well, reading instruction needs to be based on ongoing assessment and appropriately leveled for individuals and/or reading groups.

Areas of differentiation

- Content
- Process
- Product

Some methods for differentiating include the following:

- Leveled reading groups
- Whole group instruction with varied text, activities, or accommodations provided for different levels.
- Book buddies
- Listening Centers
- Technology

Approaches to Instruction

Multiple approaches have been utilized for reading instruction. The most common are a phonics approach, language experience approach, and balanced literacy.

Phonics Approach

The phonics approach utilizes systematic, explicit, sequential instruction of grapheme phoneme (letter sound) associations. Students learn letter and letter combination sounds (i.e. *ck* in duck, *ay* in play, *wr* in wrinkle) to automaticity. As students learn each rule, they begin reading text that offers opportunities to practice applying the rules to sound out unfamiliar words. Reading books utilize a controlled vocabulary that aligns with the rules taught. Letter-sound associations are practiced through various activities such as highlighting silent *e* or circling *ight* in a list of words containing the rule.

Language Experience Approach

The language experience approach utilizes a student's oral vocabulary, children's literature, writing activities, and communication activities to teach recognition of whole words. Shared reading and writing allow teachers to model skills and to involve students in language activities. Students come to recognize that ideas can be conveyed in print which can be read. Students are encouraged to use invented spelling in their writing. Reading activities focus on familiar topics and vocabulary.

Balanced Literacy

Most reading classrooms utilized a balanced approach to reading instruction. Systematic instruction in phonics is taught alongside whole language activities such as shared writing. Children's literature is seen as a vital and enjoyable means of expanding students' knowledge, vocabulary, and love of reading.

1. **A fifth-grade teacher wants to promote comprehension of a content-area passage on the British monarchy. To activate students' schema before reading, which would be an effective activity?**
    A. The teacher asks students to look up "monarchy" in the dictionary, as it is an unfamiliar word to most of the students.
    B. Students discuss in small groups what they liked about the reading and how it relates to a previous passage on the Indian caste system.
    C. The teacher asks students what words come to mind when they think about kings and queens, and she has them draw a picture of what they would imagine a king's palace to look like.
    D. After reading each paragraph, students predict what will occur next.

2. **During a unit study of** *The New Nation* **following whole group instruction and discussion, students read leveled texts matched to student reading levels in small groups. Each small group studies the same content, completes a graphic organizer to support reading, and then comes back together for whole group wrap up. Which instructional practice is demonstrated?**
    A. scaffolding
    B. conceptual grouping
    C. interpreting author's craft
    D. differentiation

3. **Skimming a passage can be an effective strategy for students to promote which of the following?**
    A. Understanding nonliteral language
    B. Understanding idioms
    C. Previewing text
    D. Decoding unfamiliar words

4. **At the end of fourth grade, students are expected to orally read grade level poems with accuracy, appropriate rate, and expression. Which of the following is an example of a scaffolded activity suitable to promote student ability to meet the standard?**
   A. Read a poem as a class, then in pairs, and finally independently.
   B. Use a graphic organizer while reading.
   C. Review a word that is difficult to decode before reading.
   D. Draw a picture after reading.

5. **In which situation is scaffolding most effective?**
   A. Following up with struggling readers after they tackle difficult text
   B. Increasing interest in unknown texts that contain many unfamiliar words
   C. Providing readers of all levels with a foundation in how to use new comprehension and analysis strategies
   D. Teaching high-frequency words that struggling readers have difficulty automatically recognizing

6. **Which would be effective activities for promoting schema building through a text-to-self connection for a reading on the Civil War?**
   A. Students look at a schema map based on the concept of "war" in a prereading activity.
   B. Students talk postreading about their responses and feelings while reading. They might also discuss what they would do if there were a civil war today.
   C. Students talk postreading about the main events and relate this text and another they have read.
   D. Students visualize a war scene while reading. After reading, they draw a scene from the reading that best corresponded with what they visualized.

7. **A third-grade class is reading a trade book. Before reading, the teacher asks students to read the front and back of the book and talk about what they think the book will be about. What purpose does this serve?**
    A. using metacognitive skills to promote comprehension
    B. making inferences based on close reading
    C. identifying author's point of view in order to analyze development
    D. activating schema to promote comprehension

8. **A teacher does a read-aloud with a second-grade class so students can practice their oral comprehension skills. Which would be a logical and grade-appropriate follow-up to assess their comprehension postreading?**
    A. Ask students to write a paragraph on the main theme.
    B. Ask students to draw the story's main events.
    C. Ask students to look up words from the title in the dictionary.
    D. Place students in small groups and have them discuss their thoughts about the reading.

9. **A teacher wants to incorporate scaffolding into a literary response activity that promotes her students' abilities to make text-to-text connections. Which would be the most effective lesson plan to do this?**
    A. Ask students to use structural analysis for any unfamiliar, decipherable words. Preteach students idioms and foreign expressions that will appear in the texts.
    B. Have students underline any unfamiliar words and new expressions. In pairs, have them complete word maps. As a class, write on the board the main ideas in both texts.
    C. Ask students to complete a Venn diagram. Then, ask them to partner to compare their diagrams with those of their peers.
    D. As a class, start a Venn diagram. Ask students to partner to complete the Venn diagram's outer sections with text differences. Finally, have students individually fill in the diagram's middle section with the text similarities.

10. **In a first grade classroom, the following activities may be observed: explicit instruction in letter sound relationships, a learning center for learning sight words to automaticity, guided reading groups, read alouds of content books, shared writing, and invented spelling in writer's workshop.**
    Which approach to instruction is demonstrated?
    A. phonics approach
    B. language experience approach
    C. basal reading approach
    D. balanced literacy

THEORIES & APPROACHES EXPLANATIONS

1. **C**   The question asks about a prereading activity, which would happen before reading. Choice A would be effective for introducing students to an unfamiliar vocabulary word, but it's a poor choice to get them to talk about what they already know about monarchies. Choice B is appropriate as a postreading activity and encourages text-to-text comparisons. Choice D is a metacognitive strategy for actively engaging in a text while reading to better comprehend. Choice C is the best prereading activity that encourages students to generate associations they already have with the subject, allowing them to go into the reading with an idea of what the passage is about and background knowledge about the topic.

2. **D**   In the scenario described, resources are tailored to maximize benefit to the students. A difference is made in the leveled reading text provided. Scaffolding (Choice A) provides support to students so that they can meet goals. As students achieve, support is gradually removed so that they can complete the task independently. Conceptual grouping (Choice B) is a strategy used to group words based on their shared concepts. Interpreting author's craft (Choice C) is a type of analysis in which readers examine an author's use of language, imagery, symbols, motifs, etc.

3. **C**   Skimming may be used as a strategy to preview text (choice C), get a feel for what it is about, and increase a reader's interest. However, skimming is not an effective tool to understand nonliteral language or idioms, as suggested in choice A and choice B. On the contrary, close reading

(when a student takes time to reread and closely analyze each word) and explicit instruction are beneficial when learning about nonliteral language and idioms. Finally, skimming would also not be an appropriate or helpful strategy for choice D, decoding, which requires modeling and instruction in phonics, structural analysis, or using context cues.

4. A Scaffolding, when a student is provided a range of activities that provide support at each level of the learning process, is best exemplified in choice A. By first reading a text as a class, and then again in pairs before students read independently, students are supported throughout the learning process. All other choices are sound ways to promote comprehension, but alone, they are not examples of scaffolding. Although they could be used as scaffolding, they need to combine additional supportive skills and strategies. For example, a teacher could model how a graphic organizer (choice B) could be used before reading a text in class, then help students fill out a piece of the organizer while reading, and finally ask them to complete the rest of the organizer independently while she continues to read.

5. C Although scaffolding can be helpful for struggling readers as mentioned in choice A, used to increase student interest (choice B), or used to model strategies to read difficult words (choice D), it is most likely to be used to provide readers of all levels with support when learning new reading strategies.

6. B Schema building entails building on information students already know. To promote this knowledge by relating the text to themselves, students must analyze the text and put it into perspective with self-knowledge (choice B). Choice A is a prereading activity for activating schema, but it does not promote text-to-self because students have not read the passage. Choice C involves text-to-text analysis, and choice D is a strategy for promoting comprehension while reading (visualizing).

7. D Activating schema is using background knowledge to comprehend text. In reading a trade book cover, the students will likely be introduced to the content, issue, setting, the characters, or the plot. Readers may be able to draw conclusions about the genre or may recognize the author. The goal in reading the cover is to connect the reader with text, thus activating the schema the student already possesses, so that when reading begins, the student can comprehend. Metacognitive skills (Choice A), close reading (Choice B), and analysis (Choice C) are typically done during reading of the text.

8. B Because this is a second-grade class, the activity needs to be basic enough to ensure students can demonstrate their comprehension skills. Choice A, though an excellent follow-up activity, might be difficult for some students, and some children might put so much effort into the writing piece that the teacher will be unable to determine what they understood. Essentially, the students would be tested on not only their comprehension, but also their writing, and because the skills are not isolated, they might be unable to demonstrate all they know. Choice C would help students better understand unfamiliar words and practice dictionary skills; however, it would do little to demonstrate their understanding of the text. Finally, choice D, though another good follow-up activity, would not allow the teacher to determine what each child understood. Choice B, therefore, is the best answer. Because students are independently drawing to demonstrate their understanding, their answers will reflect their understanding, and writing will not be an issue. The teacher will also be able to see what each child (individually) took away from the reading.

9. D Scaffolding, which is meant to support students in all steps throughout the learning process, is best exemplified by Choice D. Whereas the other choices all involve good literary response activities, only Choice D scaffolds students by providing the most support initially, and then slowly tapering as students become more comfortable with the material.

10. D The activities described demonstrate a balanced approach to literacy. The evidence of explicit letter-sound instruction characteristic of phonics (Choice A), plus shared writing and invented spelling characteristic of Language Experience (Choice B), and small groups characteristic of basal reading (Choice C) combine to provide a balanced literacy approach to instruction.

5.2 Strategies

This lesson is not intended to be comprehensive. It is representative of the strategies and skills of reading development. Explicit instruction is part of promoting every skill.

Description of Common Strategies	Skill promoted
⊙ Substitution: "Mary had a little spider"; "Humpty Dumpty sat on a cow." ⊙ Clap and count syllables in name	Phonological awareness
⊙ What is the first sound in fox? ⊙ "Down By the Bay....Did you ever see a whale with a polka dot tail..."	Phonemic awareness
⊙ Point to book parts (title, beginning, cover, etc)	Book handling
⊙ Following print with finger during read aloud ⊙ Big Books ⊙ Modeling	Print directionality/ Tracking print in connected text
⊙ Label objects in classroom ⊙ Scribing student words ⊙ Environmental print ⊙ Read aloud ⊙ Big Books ⊙ Predictable text books	Print awareness
⊙ Letter poster with pictures of objects that begin with that letter ⊙ Systematic phonics instruction	Letter–sound knowledge
⊙ Tracing multi-sensory letter shapes ⊙ Handwriting	Letter formation
⊙ Sing "Alphabet Song" ⊙ Read alphabet books ⊙ Match upper and lower case letters ⊙ Systematic instruction in letter-sound association	Alphabetic principle

Description of Common Strategies	Skill promoted
⊙ Instruction in spelling patterns ⊙ Write captions on pictures; label drawings ⊙ Write the word chop on the board. Ask student to circle the letters that make the /ch/ sound.	Phonics
⊙ Systematic phonics instruction ⊙ Study sight words	Automatic word recognition/ identification
⊙ Improve decoding skills ⊙ Audio books	Fluency
⊙ Reader's Theater ⊙ Model oral reading	Prosody
⊙ Schema building—brainstorming, KWL chart ⊙ Metacognition—self-questioning, visualizing, rereading ⊙ Graphic organizer ⊙ Preteach vocabulary ⊙ Improve decoding skills ⊙ Student-generated questions, note taking, outlining, summarizing	Comprehension
⊙ Common patterns: CVC, CVCC, CVVC, CVCe	Decoding
⊙ Use words in the sentence to find the meaning of menorah. -- A menorah, an eight-branched candlestand, is a common symbol of Hanukkah.	Context clues: Semantic
⊙ Choose the nonsense word that fits in the blank: Ramona charged ____ toward Susan. (storply, storption)	Context clues: Syntactic
⊙ Read aloud	Oral vocabulary
⊙ Use ask—pair—share (The teacher asks a question, students are paired, and partners share answers with each other, allowing all students frequent opportunities to share ideas, receive feedback, and take part in the lesson.) ⊙ Play "Would you rather..." ⊙ Retelling	Oral language

Description of Common Strategies	Skill promoted
⊙ Structural analysis ⊙ Morphemes ⊙ Latin and Greek roots ⊙ Roots and affixes ⊙ Students contribute answers to the prompt, "Make a list of words with bio in them." ⊙ Break down words into syllables	**Word analysis** **Multisyllable words**
⊙ Paraphrasing ⊙ Semantic mapping ⊙ Read-alouds ⊙ Dictionary ⊙ Read a wide range of texts ⊙ Play "Guess the idiom." Students act out "hold your horses," etc.	**Vocabulary** **Academic language** **Domain-specific words**
⊙ Point of view—1st, 2nd, 3rd person ⊙ Distinguishing fact and opinion ⊙ Multiple accounts ⊙ Reasons and evidence	**Close reading**
⊙ Graphic organizers ⊙ Read a wide range of genres ⊙ Trace plot, theme, character development (literary analysis) ⊙ Identify figurative language (literary analysis) ⊙ Compare/contrast versions or books by same author (literary analysis) ⊙ Text structures (informational text)	**Text analysis (literary and informational)**
⊙ Journal writing ⊙ Making connections	**Literary response**
⊙ Classroom library ⊙ Read alouds ⊙ Make diverse reading materials of varying genres available to students ⊙ Involve families in school or classroom reading events and incentive plans	**Love of reading**
⊙ Provide time, skills, and resources	**Independent reading**

Grouping

As with all strategies, grouping for reading instruction is best when an appropriate balance is struck. As everyone learns differently and students come to the classroom with varied background knowledge, skill mastery, ability to learn new concepts, speeds at which they can learn, and interests, more than one specific type of instruction is typically most effective. The material being taught and the students' levels of need can be considered when selecting whole/large group, small group, or individual instruction.

Large-Group Reading Instruction

Large-group instruction is one option for reading instruction. Note pros and cons below.

Pros

Efficient use of instructional time

All students provided with the same information during one lesson

Positive modeling by peers

Students learn from one another

Students can work with everyone in their class, not only those children in their small learning groups

High-level readers available to help answer questions for low-level readers

Quick assessments may be done to evaluate student understanding throughout the class

Cons

Easy for students to be off-task

Difficult to target specific learning needs

Less frequent teacher feedback per child

Fewer opportunities for each child to answer questions or have a turn during an activity

Difficult to fully assess the extent of student understanding

Small-Group Reading Instruction

As classrooms have become increasingly diverse, teachers have needed to diversify the way they teach. Instructions need to be configured to best meet the entire class' needs. Frequently, heterogeneous or homogeneous small-group instruction can help to meet these varied needs. Note pros and cons of small-group reading instruction:

Pros

Group configurations can remain fluid as students need change.

Students may be grouped by needs and varied goal-oriented instruction delivered.

Students may be grouped based on time required or help needed to master a particular skill.

Cooperative groupings may be used, in which students of different abilities are paired.

Additional on-task time for all students, especially students reading on a lower level.

More frequent feedback provided to each student.

More frequent practice opportunities for each student.

Simpler to assess students' individual understanding.

Ability to remain on topic until students have mastered skill.

Less wait time for students to get instructions clarified or questions answered.

Cons

Can be unclear when a small group becomes too big and smaller groupings should be provided.

Not as much training typically provided about creating and implementing small reading groups.

More difficult to implement, as teachers must manage many things at once.

Because students are often grouped by ability, they do not benefit from learning from all peers.

Benefits of instruction directly depend on teacher's ability to manage the rest of the class.

Though lessons are shorter to plan, several different lessons need to be created.

Additional time must be dedicated to teach students expectations and procedures when they are not in the teacher's small group.

Studies have shown that small reading groups tend to have the greatest impact on high- or low-level readers. Although mid-level readers are not hindered by small-group instruction, they do not typically make as much progress as those in the other subgroups do.

Individual

Individual instruction or tutoring may be provided by specialists, paraprofessionals, teachers, or peers.

Assessment of specific reading skills is often helpful to do individually, particularly in early childhood, with beginning or lower-leveled readers or students with disabilities.

1. **Which of the following is <u>not</u> an advantage to large-group instruction?**
   A. Students learn more from one another's background knowledge.
   B. Positive modeling by peers.
   C. Easier for all students to remain on task.
   D. Direct instructional time is used for all students.

2. **Which of the following strategies is designed to promote reading and understanding multisyllable words?**
   A. Sing and recite lines that rhyme
   B. Paraphrasing
   C. Structural analysis
   D. Provide a wide range of genres

3. **Students in a kindergarten classroom complete a worksheet in which they must match the upper and lower case letters. What reading skill is the worksheet designed to encourage?**
   A. Letter-sound knowledge
   B. Alphabetic principle
   C. Phonics
   D. Print directionality

4. **A teacher provides background knowledge and preteaches vocabulary terms during large-group instruction. What should his next step be before having students read differentiated text in their small reading groups?**
   A. The teacher should launch right into small reading groups.
   B. The teacher can now assume all students approach the text from the same place and, during tomorrow's lesson, can pick up instruction where he left off.
   C. The teacher should conduct a quick assessment to gauge student understanding.
   D. Nothing—because students have been working in a large group, it is impossible to quickly gauge individual student understanding.

5. **Whole-group learning is efficient because of all of the following reasons except one. Which reason is <u>not</u> a strength of whole-group learning?**

   A. All students are provided with information at the same time, and the concepts do not need to be retaught in the same manner to several groups.

   B. Because all students can receive the same material and instruction, differentiated instruction in small groups is not necessary.

   C. Students can learn from all other students.

   D. Whole-group learning does not require successful management of students who are not in the teacher's group.

6. **Which of the following does <u>not</u> address why teachers might find small-group instruction difficult?**

   A. They received insufficient training in this area.

   B. They must manage other groups while teaching their small group.

   C. Time needs to be spent up front to teach students procedures and expectations while teachers are working with a small group.

   D. There are very limited opportunities for teacher feedback to each student.

7. **Which of the following is an appropriate use of partner reading?**

   A. When students will benefit from peer-tutoring opportunities

   B. When assessments will be based on accuracy and individual performance

   C. When a teacher needs to provide specific intervention

   D. When all students need to be formally assessed

8. **A kindergarten class experiments with substitutions in nursery rhymes. Students make up lines such as "Hickory Dickory Dock, the** *moose* **went up the clock." What is the rationale behind this activity?**

   A. Substitution builds attentiveness to attributes of a character.

   B. Substitution builds oral vocabulary.

   C. Substitution strengthens phonemic awareness.

   D. Substitution promotes phonological awareness.

9. **A teacher uses small reading groups to work on students' decoding skills. While working with one group, she has another group complete a new game on their instructional level at their desks and a third group of students answer questions about a passage well above their instructional level. The teacher finds herself frequently interrupted by students from other groups. Why are her small groups likely ineffective?**
   A. Games are disruptive for small group activities.
   B. Student activities are at or above an instructional level instead of at an independent level.
   C. Decoding skills should be taught to the whole group.
   D. Repetitive activities failed to hold the students' attention.

10. **Which classroom situation is appropriate for a think-pair-share activity?**
   A. Communicating new lesson content
   B. Drilling for mastery of math facts
   C. Soliciting student opinion on a "why" question
   D. Fostering endurance in sustained independent work

STRATEGIES EXPLANATIONS

1. C   Large-group instruction allows all children to benefit from one another's varied background knowledge—whenever one student shares his insight, other students can hear and benefit. Likewise, students act as positive models for one another, and teachers can work with everyone in the class efficiently. The only incorrect choice is choice C. Whole- or large-group instruction does not necessarily make it easier for students to remain on task—especially those having difficulties keeping up with the group or lesson pace or finding the material too simple and becoming easily bored. As a result, some students might find it more difficult to remain on task during large-group reading instruction.

2. C   Structural analysis looks at the parts that make up a word. Analyzing roots, base words, affixes, inflections, etc. helps in decoding and making sense of multisyllable words. Rhyme (Choice A) is helpful to promote phonemic awareness. Paraphrasing (Choice B) is a good activity to promote vocabulary acquisition and comprehension. A wide range of genres

(Choice D) is beneficial to promote a love of reading, text analysis skills, and other reading skills.

3. **B**   Recognizing upper and lower case letters is an alphabetic principle skill. Letter-sound knowledge (Choice A) is awareness of the systematic relationship between letters and the sound they represent. Phonics (Choice C) is method of teaching that promotes understanding of letter-sound relationships. Print directionality is not a specific objective of the activity since letters could be matched right-left or left-right.

4. **C**   After any whole-group lesson, teachers should take the time to quickly gauge student understanding, especially if they have not already done so throughout the lesson. By launching directly into small groups or picking up the lesson tomorrow, the teacher will have little knowledge about where the students are starting and in what areas they require additional instruction. Because there are many quick ways to assess large groups of students (ask for a quick signal - thumbs up/down, nods, exit slips, and so on), there is little reason not to do a check-in with students to help guide future instruction.

5. **B**   Whole-group instruction is efficient because students receive the same instruction at the same time (A), students can learn from all other students, not just the ones in their group (C), and the need for classroom management of students not in the teacher's group is eliminated (D). However, because students learn differently, large-group instruction does not eliminate the need for differentiation. (B)

6. **D**   Choice D is not a challenge of small groups. One benefit of small groups is that students can receive frequent, applicable teacher feedback. Teachers often find small-group instruction difficult. Often, they are not provided with much training in forming and running small groups. Instructional time might be lost while procedures are pretaught; and once the groups are running, teachers must manage several things within the classroom at once. Additionally, teachers must often plan for several activities within various groups while children work in the small group or independently. Finally, groups need to remain fluid, and teachers need to constantly evaluate student placement within groups.

7. **A**   Partner reading is a cooperative learning strategy in which students of different levels can be grouped for peer-tutoring. If an assessment of the reading is required, assessment should be based on teamwork and ability

to reach a team goal (B). Partner reading is not appropriate for individual instruction (C) and intervention since the reading is with a peer. Teachers can circulate during partner reading and conduct informal assessment; however, formal assessment is challenging during partner reading (D).

8. **D**   Phonological awareness is the ability to hear, recognize, and manipulate language. Substituting words helps students identify individual words in a sentence. Substitution is unrelated to character analysis (Choice A). Students would be substituting words they have already internalized as oral vocabulary (Choice B). The activity does not address individual sounds (phonemes) in words, so it does not promote phonemic awareness (Choice C).

9. **B**   To effectively run small instructional groups, teachers must also simultaneously manage other students. Activities for students not in the teacher's small group need to be familiar at student's independent or instructional levels so students can work on their own. Appropriately taught and monitored games are not necessarily disruptive (A). The game in this scenario is inappropriate because it was new. Decoding is appropriate for small group (C) or whole group instruction. The scenario described does not fail to hold the students' attention because it was repetitive (D). It was, in fact, a new activity.

10. **C**   Think-pair-share is a classroom organization method in which a teacher poses a question, students think of an answer, pair up and take turns answering, and share the answers with the group. This method is good for soliciting opinion and giving students all opportunities to speak and listen. It is not an efficient way to present new content (A). There is little reason for partners to "share" the answers of a paired activity in math drill (B). As a paired activity (D), it does not specifically foster independent work.

5.3 Selecting Reading Material

There are a number of factors to consider when selecting materials for a classroom of students, who have considerably different strengths, weaknesses and interests. If readers expend too much effort decoding each word and are unable to read text fluently, they are less likely to comprehend the material and absorb new vocabulary. On the flip side, if material is too easy, students are likely to become bored and tune out; they won't be pushed to develop new decoding, fluency, vocabulary or comprehension skills; they'll simply remain stagnant until given the opportunity to work on a level more appropriate for them.

Challenges to Texts

The following list explains some challenges or supports in texts. Building awareness allows students to make sense of challenges and use supports to their advantage. Ultimately, student background knowledge, level of exposure, or overall ability impacts all interaction with text.

- ⊙ *Content* —Encourage a wide range of core content to build comprehension. Use scaffolding to give all students access to rich content.
- ⊙ *Genre* —Encourage a wide range of genres (short story, epic, novel, biography, etc).
- ⊙ *Decodability*— A decodable text contains a high percentage of words restricted to the sound/spelling correspondences that the reader has learned. Decodable text can also contain previously taught high-frequency sight words. For a child who has only studied consonants and short vowels, decodable text is primarily CVC. For a child who has studied long vowels and diphthongs, the text can include those patterns. Essentially every text is decodable for skilled, adult readers.
- ⊙ *Language* —Consider whether the language is straightforward or complex. Unfamiliar, figurative language adds more challenge. Natural conversational language provides support to text.

- *Length* —Attention span, interest, and situation factor into the length of book that is appropriate for a reader. Young children can enjoy and appreciate challenging text when the text is read aloud. The same text would be beyond their independent reading level.
- *Pictures/Illustrations* —Meaningful illustrations support or add to the print content.
- *Predictability*—A predictable text has repeated language structure. The repeated language often has a pleasant cadence or rhyme. "Goodnight bears Goodnight chairs Goodnight kittens And goodnight mittens." (*Goodnight Moon* by Margaret Wise Brown)
- *Sentence Structure*—Short sentences tend not to require the reader to use as much working memory. Longer sentences include more ideas and complex language that students need to retain while reading.
- *Text Structure/Organization*—The more exposure students have had to the particular text organization (description, cause and effect, problem/solution, etc), the more likely they are to pull information and make sense of what they read.
- *Vocabulary* — Students who have previous exposure to terms within the text have a clear advantage in comprehension and appropriate use of context clues. When vocabulary remains a mystery, students are not as likely to engage in higher-level thinking skills, and the passage is not as meaningful. General academic and domain-specific vocabulary are both vital. Vocabulary in trade books, while typically age and level appropriate, is less controlled than vocabulary in text and decodable books.

When equipped with key tools and exposed to a variety of text, students can use text challenges as supports.

Texts, Readers, and Situations to Consider

Understanding where students are in their reading development is essential. Because reading skills are interrelated, build upon one another, and can progress simultaneously (i.e. the more fluently children read, the better they are able to comprehend), students need to be met and taught at their instructional level. Text leveling is a way to effectively choose readings that will be best for the learner's level. A one-size-fits-all approach simply won't be as effective for multiple reasons.

Often, students will be stronger in one aspect of reading than in another. Typically, children are able to understand material well above that of which they can read independently. At an instructional level, students may be stronger in decoding than in comprehension or vice versa. Teachers must identify areas of strength and weakness so instruction may be targeted to address deficits.

Text Leveling

- ⊙ Consider the text decodability, vocabulary, sentence length, passage organization, grammar and overall difficulty. For beginners, texts should consist of many repeated, common words, and they should contain elements that are similar to oral language to help students transition to print.
- ⊙ Many schools rely on a formal leveling system to indicate a book's reading level. Some leveling systems also consider the age appropriateness of materials.
- ⊙ Teachers can align the level of text with the student's independent, instructional and frustration levels (These levels vary between children despite their age and/or grade level).

Age or Reading Level of Students

- ⊙ Is the text content developmentally appropriate?
- ⊙ What stage is the student? pre-reading, emergent, decoding, fluent; beginning, intermediate, or advanced?
- ⊙ What is the student's reading level? These reading levels are important. They need special font or graphics to make them stand out.
  - Independent Level – text is considered simple, the student is able to read with minimal or no errors.
  - Instructional Level – though the student will encounter some points of difficulty and read with some errors, this level is appropriately challenging for guided reading experiences and allows enhancement of skills.
  - Frustration Level – material is clearly difficult and the student makes numerous errors throughout the text. When materials on a student's frustration level are presented, they lead to discouragement. While it is often preferred to select alternate text, such text can be used for read alouds or assisted guided reading material.

Setting in Which Text Will Be Used

- ⊙ Is the text being used for guided or independent reading?
- ⊙ Will the text be a read aloud?
- ⊙ Is the text meant to reiterate knowledge already understood or to introduce and explain new material?

Text Complexity

Whereas text leveling is determined by publishers or outside experts, text complexity is based on several factors including a quantitative measure, a qualitative measure, and a teacher judgement. Quantitative measures include such factors as word length, word frequency, and sentence length. Qualitative measures include levels of meaning or purpose, text structure, and background knowledge necessary for comprehension. Teacher judgement focuses on the individual reader and the task. A text such as a story about a little league team which might be basic to many students may be somewhat complex for new immigrants from a country where baseball is relatively unknown. Using a text as a teacher read aloud, requires a different level of interaction than using a text for reading and completing a graphic organizer independents.

It is the combination of quantitative measures, qualitative measures, and the teacher's unique knowledge of students and task which combine to determine text complexity.

Varied Reading Experiences

One of the most important factors when planning reading lessons is your audience and their prior, current and future exposure to varied types of text. Frequent, extensive and varied reading experiences encourage greater development of reading skills and improved vocabulary and understanding of language. While textbooks and basals have traditionally been the resources

of the classroom, the availability and wide range of reasonably-priced trade books has made the use of commercially-published books a viable option for many students. Trade books are books that are published by a commercial publisher and intended for a general readership. These books would include picture books, series, informational books, reference books, and imaginative literature. They cover a wide range of themes and are less likely to simplify syntax and control vocabulary than textbooks.

Many students have reading preferences; and while they should be able to make their own choices at times, it is also important to provide for them a balanced literary diet. Providing literary and informational texts that are rich, meaningful, and of high-interest engages students, allowing them to further develop higher level thinking skills and understand that reading can be purposeful. Given the importance of exposure to a wide array of materials, it is critical to strike a balance between providing new materials and allowing them to make their own choices.

The organization and selection of reading materials is often key to classroom and lesson success. While high-interest materials that appeal to a variety of classroom personalities need to be available, teachers also need to make available texts that are at student's instructional levels. Books and other reading materials should be presented and organized in a way that is welcoming to students and makes locating particular books simple.

SELECTING READING MATERIAL PRACTICE

1. **Why should a teacher provide students with quality texts from varied genres?**
   A. Students can read simple and repetitive words and phrases.
   B. Students can focus on their fluency and accuracy skills.
   C. Students gain exposure to different types of text structures and explore varied interests.
   D. Students improve metacognitive strategies.

2. **When assessed at the beginning of kindergarten, a student is found to decode on a second grade level. Which of the following is an appropriate conclusion?**
   A. The student has mastered all areas of phonological and phonemic awareness.
   B. The student can comprehend text at a second grade level.

C. The student is confident in his phonological awareness and encoding skills on a second grade level.

D. The student decodes above grade level; nothing more should be assumed.

3. **What is the relationship between text selection and student age and reading level?**

   A. Text should be age and developmentally appropriate as well as the correct level.

   B. Choosing materials designed for a specific grade level is the efficient and preferred way of selecting texts.

   C. Students' instructional levels tend be similar to those of other children also in their grade making consideration of reading level unimportant.

   D. Priority should be given to a student's reading level as his age is of little consequence.

4. **A third grade teacher plans to introduce a unit on space travel in guided reading groups using non-fiction books about a famous astronaut. Given this information, the books should be at which level?**

   A. Independent Level

   B. Instructional Level

   C. Frustration Level

   D. Interest level

5. **A teacher determines a reading group to be too high for one of her new students. She is likely able to tell the reading materials are at the student's frustration level due to all of the following except:**

   A. The student makes numerous errors reading the text.

   B. The student appears to be discouraged throughout the reading group.

   C. After reading aloud, the student continues to have difficulties comprehending.

   D. The student's few decoding errors do not interfere with comprehension.

6. **When considering the amount of choice students are given in selecting reading material, which statement is the most reasonable?**
   A. Highly proficient readers should always be allowed to select their text.
   B. Students should not be allowed to select the texts for guided reading.
   C. A balance between teacher-selected texts and student-selected texts is critical.
   D. Students should always be allowed to select their own independent reading text.

7. **Decodability refers to**
   A. Text composed of CVC and familiar high-frequency sight words.
   B. Text with a high percentage of regular decodable words containing the sight-sound patterns the student has learned.
   C. A student's ability to decode a list of regular words.
   D. A student's ability to spell words using sound-spelling patterns that have been learned.

8. **When teachers consider text genre, content, sentence structure, language, and student background, they are making evaluations about which of the following?**
   A. Text complexity
   B. Text level
   C. Age appropriateness of text
   D. Text placement in classroom library

9. **A reader has the following characteristics: enjoys picture books, recognizes some words and letter patterns, recognizes some letters and some corresponding sounds, reads 1-2 lines per page pointing to each word, and enjoys sharing the same book repeatedly. What is this reader's stage of reading development?**
   A. emergent
   B. early
   C. transitional
   D. fluent

10. **What is the purpose of using leveled text in a diverse classroom?**

   A. Leveled texts are books for general publication, enjoyable for all readers.

   B. Leveled texts can be aligned to students' independent and instructional reading levels.

   C. Leveled texts are textbooks for content areas that are readable within a grade level.

   D. Leveled texts are predictable, decodable books appropriate for beginning readers.

SELECTING READING MATERIAL EXPLANATIONS

1. **C** It is important for teachers to use, model and teach with a variety of quality texts so students are able to learn how various texts are structured and used. Varied, quality texts also engage students and exposed them to text they may not otherwise read. Selecting varied texts does not typically allow students to read simple and repetitive words (Choice A), focus on their fluency skills (Choice B), or reinforce metacognition (Choice D).

2. **D** Though students may be highly proficient in decoding upon entering kindergarten, it should not be assumed they have phonological and phonemic awareness skills (Choice A), comprehension skills (Choice B), or encoding skills (Choice C). Teachers should use additional formal or informal assessments to determine stage of reading development in all areas.

3. **A** A student's age does need to be taken into consideration when selecting reading materials to ensure the text is age and developmentally appropriate. Often, children may have the ability to read at a level much higher than what is expected for their grade. When this is the case, text needs to be carefully previewed to ensure content is appropriate; just because they can read the material, doesn't mean they should (Choice D). Additionally, some children read below grade level expectations and the opposite problem occurs. Often in these situations, students become frustrated, as the books they are able to read seem juvenile. In this situation, text that is of high interest and engaging needs to be located to

keep students motivated and interested in reading. Material designated for a specific grade level may not meet the diverse needs in the classroom (Choices B and C).

4. B Text used during guided reading should be at instructional level. While students may encounter appropriate challenges in decoding and comprehension, this level will not serve to frustrate (Choice C) and will allow for maximum reading growth (Choice A). Because the book will be used for guided reading, selection need not be restricted to interest level (Choice D).

5. D When students work at frustration level, they may make numerous errors, become easily discouraged and/or have difficulties comprehending the material. Choice D is the only incorrect option; if the only difficulty the teacher observed was a few errors while reading, the text would likely be at the student's instructional level.

6. C It is important to give students choice in their selection of reading materials; this increases their motivation and keeps them engaged. However, students also need to be exposed to materials they would have otherwise not read so they can broaden their interests and understanding of other genres. Struggling, on level, and highly proficient readers should be balanced between teacher and student choice in both guided and independent reading.

7. B Decodability is a designation given to text. It refers to text that has a high percentage of words that use sound-spelling patterns that the student has learned. A text's decodability depends on student knowledge, as a given text may be decodable for a fourth grader, but not for a first grader.

8. A Text complexity is a term that refers to how difficult a text is for a student at a particular level. Consideration is given to the features listed as well as other features. Text level (Choice B) does not consider student background. Age appropriateness refers to the suitability of content for readers at a particular age or developmental stage (Choice C). Organization of a classroom library is significant for student enjoyment of reading; however, it cannot encompass all features listed in the question (Choice D).

9. A While the designations and descriptors of reading stages show some variations, designations of emergent, early, transitional, and fluent are common. The characteristics listed are typical of an emergent reader. An early reader recognizes most easy high-frequency words, self-monitors, uses illustrations, and reads longer stories (Choice B). A transitional read reads silently, reads many words with automaticity, uses phrasing, and reads text with many lines from multiple genres (Choice C). A fluent reader reads to learn, analyzes text, sustains interest, and uses a variety of reading strategies for word analysis and comprehension (Choice D).

10. B Formal leveling systems assign a level to books based on the books' language, sentence structure, illustrations, etc. The leveling system crosses grade levels and helps align readers with a text suitable for instruction or independent reading. The description in Choice A defines trade books rather than leveled texts. While textbooks are typically written for a specific grade level, they are not considered leveled readers (Choice C). Beginning leveled texts may be predictable and/or decodable books (Choice D); however leveled readers also include books appropriate for mature readers.

5.4 Promoting Reading Development

Promoting Close Reading

Close reading refers to a way of reading that focuses on forming a deep and nuanced understanding of the style, content and author's intentions. Close reading usually requires rereading the passage several times to closely examine the symbols, character development, larger meanings, etc. From here, readers can connect the text to other pieces of literature and concepts. Close reading also allows students to evaluate the quality and content of the text.

Promoting a Love of Reading

In addition to instructing the mechanics of reading and comprehension, teachers also promote a love for reading. Several strategies can encourage a love for reading.

- ⊙ Allow students some **choice** in the selection of the text for group or independent reading. Giving students ownership of text selection can make them more inclined to *want* to read and to read purposefully.
- ⊙ Provide **access** to books. Time to browse the shelves of a class library, school library, and public library allows students to be reacquainted with favorite books and find new books of interest. Making books available to students from their early days of learning book handling and on throughout life encourages a love for reading.
- ⊙ Provide students **time** to read, not for a specific content objective or to prepare for a particular assessment, but to relax and enjoy anything from magazines, non-fiction, fiction, comics, etc.
- ⊙ Engage students with **proficient readers**. The mature readers may be reading buddies, parents, community members, etc.
- ⊙ **Read aloud** to students. Although all students can benefit from the experience, read alouds provide a way for struggling or lower-level readers to enjoy a selection that might have otherwise been too difficult for them to read, comprehend *and* enjoy. Simultaneously, it allows higher-level readers to have reading modeled with appropriate pause, inflection and inquiry.
- ⊙ Develop school-wide **motivational plans** to foster an environment that encourages reading. Similarly, smaller incentives can be offered within a class or grade level.

Promoting Independent Reading at School and Home

Ultimately, independent reading should be the goal. The best way to encourage independent reading is to provide appropriate opportunities and motivation at school and home.

Suggestions for school and home

Explore varied genres

Maintain a well-organized, easy-to-use home or classroom library that includes texts from several genres and exposes children to different types of writing. Visit the local public library and encourage children to make varied selections.

Provide students with necessary skills

Investing time to teach students strategies that allow them to decode and comprehend text enables them to enjoy independent reading even when they do stumble on something they do not know. These higher-level thinking skills also help students to make connections that make reading more meaningful. Students gain reading skills through modeling, direct teaching and guided (and eventually independent) practice.

Make reading a priority

Allow time - and work hard to preserve the time - for independent reading every day.

Allow students to share what they have read

Students are empowered when they can share what they have read with teachers or peers. Create and make available a variety of follow-up activities (write a few sentences about the book, illustrate your favorite part, create a book jacket, participate in a book club, interview a character, etc.).

Instill ownership in students

Giving children a voice in what they read and working with them to set their own reading goals provides ownership. For example, if students are working to improve their fluency, help them set a goal of the number of words per minute they read at their independent level. Provide a bar graph or chart for them to record how many words they read each week. By tracking their progress, they are more likely to remain motivated. Guide students to selections at their independent reading level, but allow them to take ownership of their selections.

Encourage parent involvement

Make reading a common buzzword between home and school. Encourage parents to get involved by inviting them to school events that highlight reading – book fairs, read in's, read and record events, etc. Teachers should offer to share resources at home or provide families with other ways to obtain quality texts for children. Teachers might also explain to parents that research supports reading at home – students who read at home are usually linked to higher reading achievement, increased vocabulary, fluency and overall academic achievement.

Using Instructional Technologies to Promote Reading Development

Teachers are often able and encouraged to use technology to promote reading development. Technology can be a rich source of materials and programs that model skills and provide practice at all levels of reading and language arts development.

Benefits of Instructional Technologies

Increased active learning time

Even when not being directly taught, technologies provide opportunities for students to continue practicing specific skills or have skills modeled. Many programs also allow progress to be saved so teachers can track progress later.

Custom curriculum

By tailoring technology use to the specific needs of individual students, each child can have an individualized reading experience. Students can make the most of independent time by working on reading with texts specific to their level and interests.

Increased student motivation

Because activities using technology can be matched to each child's instructional level, students remain engaged and motivated to learn.

Every year, additional reading programs that use various technologies are created – computer programs, apps, etc. Many programs allow one or more of the following:

- ⊙ Phonics, phonemic awareness and alphabetic code practice
- ⊙ Fluency practice
- ⊙ Word analysis practice
- ⊙ Text-to-speech or speech-to-text software
- ⊙ Text in alternative formats
- ⊙ Techniques or scaffolding to help students organize thoughts or ideas in text or their writing

Though technology provides an abundance of resources, opportunities, and motivation, it is not a substitute for explicit classroom instruction and peer interaction. Purposeful use of technology for all students balanced with instruction, small groups, independent reading of print, etc., offers the best approach.

PROMOTING READING DEVELOPMENT PRACTICE

1. **While creating a classroom library or providing advice to parents regarding reading materials for children, teachers should encourage which of the following?**

    A. Materials focused exclusively on topics students are interested in and want to learn about.

    B. A varied collection of age-appropriate literary and informational materials.

    C. Materials of the same genre (i.e. comic books, fiction, magazines, etc.).

    D. Materials at a student's instructional level or higher.

2. **While learning about the Underground Railroad, a reader engaged in close reading may look like which of the following?**

    A. Because reading materials are at the student's frustration level, he/she simply closes the book.

    B. Upon completion of the unit assessment, the student receives an unsatisfactory grade.

C. As a result of paying close attention to the text, the student comprehends, discusses, makes connections, and evaluates.

D. Based on pre-reading and post-reading activities, the student is able to retell the purpose of the Underground Railroad.

3. **Which of the following strategies is <u>not</u> designed to promote a student's love and appreciation for reading?**

A. Allow students the opportunity to choose their reading materials.

B. Provide motivation through classroom or school-wide reading programs, incentives and support from home.

C. Provide opportunities for read alouds during class.

D. Incorporate spelling instruction.

4. **A classroom contains a number of ELL students, students with disabilities and students who read below grade level. The teacher often uses text-to-speech software. All of the following are benefits of instructional reading technologies except for which of the following?**

A. Increased motivation

B. Increased active learning moments

C. Appropriately leveled materials

D. Learning from peers

5. **A second-grade teacher provides daily instruction in decoding and comprehension skills, designates a time for silent reading, sets individual and class reading goals, and directs parents to quality resources available in the community. These combined actions are designed to promote which of the following?**

A. Independent reading

B. Awareness of environmental print

C. Development of oral vocabulary

D. Close reading

6. **Students in a third-grade class demonstrate the ability to decode fluently; however, overall, they fail assessments that test comprehension of grade-level academic reading selections. What strategy could the teacher best use to adjust her instruction in the future to meet her students' comprehension needs?**

   A. Focus attention primarily on narration until comprehension improves.
   B. Provide additional instruction on word analysis skills.
   C. Model how to engage in close reading.
   D. Regroup students into heterogeneous reading groups.

7. **Which strategy is most likely to foster a child's independent reading at home and in school?**

   A. Provide students with the genre and subject they prefer and permit them to read only these texts.
   B. When they're ready, students begin reading independently for their own enjoyment.
   C. Wait until students enjoy reading on their own and then begin providing them with strategies to help them decode and comprehend text.
   D. Make reading a daily priority both at home and school. Provide reading materials and strategies to involve parents with their child's reading.

8. **At some schools, text-to-speech software is available to support student learning. What motivations reflect appropriate use of the technology in the classroom?**

   A. The software allows teachers to focus on classroom management instead of direct teaching of reading skills.
   B. The one-size-fits-all nature of technology unifies diverse student needs.
   C. The software allows students to focus on comprehension skills when engaging with text beyond their instructional reading level.
   D. The software diminishes motivation for beginning readers to learn new skills.

9. Fifth-grade students read accounts of colonial America from three different perspectives. Students are able to answer literal questions but lack the skills to evaluate the texts through comparison and contrast past the literal. The teacher selects one of the texts, guides students in re-reading and asks nuanced questions calling attention to the author's point of view. Students then reread the other accounts, looking for similar information. The teacher has modeled and practiced which strategy with the students?

A. Close reading
B. Differentiation
C. Selecting meaningful reading material
D. Sequencing by text complexity

10. Instructional technology is likely to have the least impact on which area of reading instruction?

A. assessment
B. reading classic print literature
C. practicing reading strategies
D. curriculum resources

PROMOTING READING DEVELOPMENT EXPLANATIONS

1. B   It is important to encourage interaction with a wide range of literary and informational materials that are rich, high-interest and meaningful. While students should be allowed some choice in what they read (and choice can be quite motivating), an appropriate balance needs to be found where students are also encouraged and purposefully introduced to other genres and subject areas. Text at varying levels should be provided; text at the student's independent level will allow for children to read on their own and gain confidence, text at the student's instructional level may be read with an adult and will encourage further skills, and text at a student's frustration level may be appropriate to be used as a read aloud and allow students to be exposed to materials that would otherwise be too difficult for them to read on their own.

2. C   Close reading refers to a reader's ability to understand text. A reader is said to be engaged in "close reading" when he/she takes the time to re-read, participates in engaging discussions, and/or further processes and evaluates the text. Close reading goes beyond one's ability to retell a story or chain of events (Choice D) and becomes obvious when the reader develops a sense for the author's purpose and organization of the text. When this happens, students are better able to connect the text to other materials and experiences and form an opinion regarding the quality of what they have read.

3. D   Providing students with necessary skills for reading is an important component of reading instruction. Spelling instruction does reciprocate with improved reading skills, however it is the weakest answer. Student choice, motivation, and read alouds are all strategies that promote a love for reading.

4. D   Technology does not facilitate cooperative learning with peers. Because activities using technology can be matched to each child's instructional level, students remain engaged and motivated (Choice A). Even when not being directly taught, technologies provide opportunities for students to continue practicing specific skills and/or having skills modeled (Choice B). Finally, by tailoring technology use to specific needs of individual students, each child may have an individualized reading experience catered to his/her level and interests (Choice C).

5. A   Giving students the skills, opportunities, motivation, and resources for reading are all actions teachers can do to promote independent reading. These actions are not specifically related to noticing every day or environmental print (Choice B) or oral vocabulary (Choice C). While the actions may support close reading, they are not close reading strategies that lead to nuanced understanding of material (Choice D).

6. C   Since students are struggling with comprehension, the teacher should demonstrate how to interpret and process materials they read. Rather than focusing predominately on one type of literature (Choice A), teachers should work to expose student to a variety of text types. This will expand student's vocabulary, develop higher level thinking skills, and promote interest in other types of literature. While practicing word analysis (Choice B) and regrouping (Choice D) may provide some help, their greatest need is specific instruction in and modeling of close reading.

7. D It is important for reading to be a priority at home and school. It is especially motivating when students are able to see that their families are working in conjunction with school to ensure reading is a priority. Additionally, while it is important to give students some choice in what they read, a wide range of genres and subjects should also be provided to encourage them to broaden their reading interests. Purposeful instruction at all levels of reading development encourages progress. Students learn to decode before reading independently.

8. C Text to speech software presents a unique opportunity for teachers to have text read aloud to a student. While such programs are frequently used for students who have difficulties decoding and/or reading text fluently, they can also be used to assist students when they are reading text higher than their instructional level. By being able to simply listen to text, comprehension skills can be targeted and those skills isolated. As a result, teachers will have a better idea of how well students comprehend material slightly above their instructional level, without being concerned that the information was not understood due to a lack of fluency and/or decoding skills. Technology is not a substitute for direct instruction (Choice A). Technology is not one-size-fits-all and can be customized to the student (Choice B). Software can be used to improve phonological awareness, vocabulary, and enjoyment of text—all skills and motivations that encourage reading development (Choice D)

9. A Close reading refers to a way of reading that focuses on forming a full understanding of the material. Rereading, highlighting, questioning, and engaging with the text are common strategies for close reading. The teacher's strategy does not model differentiation for small groups or individuals (Choice B). It does not consider either selection or sequencing of the reading material (Choices C and D).

10. B Nearly all areas of the reading classroom are impacted by technology. Holding a print book in hand and reading classic literature is still part of reading instruction. While many books are available in digital formats, choice B specifically references print. Reading assessments on the computer have become commonplace (Choice A). A wide range of resources are available to practice reading strategies from print awareness to literary analysis (Choice C). Whereas classrooms in previous years relied heavily on traditional textbooks, online textbooks and sources are changing classroom curriculum (Choice D).

5.5   Individual Learners

Differentiation is individualized, variable instruction. Teachers differentiate to maximize the learning experience by tailoring their teaching for individuals or small group. Differentiation is necessary to meet each child's needs and to maximize learning time and strategies. To differentiate well, reading instruction must be based on ongoing assessment and appropriately leveled for individuals or reading groups.

ELL/Struggling Readers

Teachers and reading specialists differentiate materials for ELL and struggling readers. Because reading encompasses so many smaller skills, determining where a student's particular deficit lies is important. Once a weakness is found, the targeted interventions can be delivered.

Phonological and phonemic awareness

- ⊙ At-risk students often have lower levels of phonological and phonemic awareness. They might not enter school with the same knowledge base as other children do. Though these skills can be taught, they might take longer to be acquired.
- ⊙ ELL or struggling readers may not know English sounds.
- ⊙ Students might have difficulties distinguishing among sounds.

Phonics and Print Awareness

- ⊙ Instruction needs to involve varied rich texts, and teachers must be mindful that phonics skills are developed in conjunction with comprehension skills.
- ⊙ For ELL students, consideration must be given to a student's native language. Was the student exposed to a non-alphabetic language? (Alphabetic languages use a specific set of letters to compose words,

unlike non-alphabetic languages such as Chinese.) Does the language have the same print directionality? Such factors might make it more difficult for students to recognize letters.

- ⊙ Students might learn to pronounce and use sounds before gaining the ability to connect the same sounds to letters and blends.
- ⊙ Multiple spellings of the same sound, as well as words with multiple meanings can be especially confusing.
- ⊙ Sound to text technology and audio books can be useful as a scaffold, but not as a replacement for written text.

Fluency

- ⊙ Repeated readings of familiar text, read alouds, reader's theater, etc. will help to increase reading fluency and can contribute to oral language development.
- ⊙ Reading in front of peers might be overwhelming, and students might feel embarrassed. Allow students prior access to text to practice ahead of time.

Vocabulary

- ⊙ ELL and struggling readers often start the vocabulary race late. Because these students might not have been exposed to or do not have the capability to retain vocabulary, it might take longer and require additional exposure for them to catch up and learn grade-level material.
- ⊙ When ELL students have difficulty understanding textbooks or other advanced readings, adequate instruction in vocabulary can be helpful.
- ⊙ Adult modeling, picture cues, and word play might be used to increase student vocabulary.
- ⊙ Teach words with multiple meanings, figurative expressions and idioms; provide opportunities to use the words differently (speak, write, read, etc.).
- ⊙ Teach roots, prefixes, and suffixes – when students stumble on a word they do not know, they have a better chance of figuring it out with this knowledge.

Reading Comprehension

- ⊙ Teach that reading is not simply for decoding, but also for finding information or for entertainment.

- Comprehension skills must be explicitly taught. Use graphic organizers for concepts such as cause/effect, problem/solution, and author's purpose, to make them more visual and understandable.
- Use text appropriate for the student's level. If all efforts are put into decoding, comprehension will undoubtedly fall to the wayside.
- Take time to activate prior knowledge and teach necessary background information. Allow students to experiment, preview materials, make predictions, etc.
- Comprehension and language development must be taught in conjunction.
- Provide visuals, practical and interactive opportunities (acting out, creating pictures, gestures, highlighting key terms, providing vocabulary "cheat sheets", etc. to help understand concepts included in text), and organizers to help students process material.

Assessments

In choosing assessments, be mindful of reliability, validity, bias, use of figurative language, cultural relevancy, and reading level. Accommodations and adaptations may be appropriate.

Frequently used accommodations

- Read test aloud
- Ensure understanding of directions
- Extend time
- Allow verbal responses
- Administer in small group or individually
- Allow use of graphic organizers, dictionaries, thesauruses, etc.

Highly Proficient Readers

Although it seems obvious that much effort would go into the planning and instruction for ELL and struggling readers, educators also must know they need to differentiate reading instruction for highly proficient readers. These students, likewise, must stay engaged, interested, and motivated to continually improve existing skills. Though highly proficient readers often begin to read before their peers, might have extensive vocabularies, and be quicker to comprehend grade-level material, they may also exhibit areas of weakness in one (or more) of the particular categories outlined below. For example, if highly proficient students who struggle with decoding skills are strong enough readers, they might be able to compensate for his/her struggles and hide most difficulties. In these cases, areas of weakness should be identified so teachers can target their instruction to fill in these "cracks" and ultimately make the students even stronger.

Phonological and Phonemic Awareness

- Highly proficient readers often come to school with solid phonological and phonemic awareness. They have likely been exposed to more language than some of their other peers have, and they are already strong with rhyming, segmenting, blending, etc.
- It is important to ensure that students have mastered all areas of phonological and phonemic awareness so they can continue to build their existing skills.

Fluency

- It is crucial to ensure highly proficient readers have a solid understanding of decoding and are equipped with the necessary tools to help them read a word they stumble upon and do not know. Without this, students might lack the abilities needed to read at a higher, more engaged level.
- When reading, it is important that highly proficient readers slow their reading enough to comprehend the text.
- Providing motivational activities such as charting one's own fluency goals can help keep students engaged.
- Take time to listen to highly proficient readers or have them record themselves while reading a passage. Are they using appropriate prosody and attending to punctuation?

Vocabulary

- Many highly proficient readers have advanced vocabularies. Help students to further enhance their knowledge by providing instruction on prefixes, suffixes, and root words.
- Challenge students to manipulate words and investigate how subtle changes alter the word's meaning.

- Provide additional word study, spelling words and opportunities (through journaling, dictionaries, thesauruses, etc.) to use the words.
- Have students enhance their writing with content-specific vocabulary, idioms, description, and figurative language.

Reading Comprehension

- If students already know the material at hand, place them on the fast track and allow learning extensions or additional materials to further engage them.
- Nonfiction text can be a good alternative to advanced fiction books which may introduce content that is not age appropriate.
- Create homogenous groups in which children can engage in meaningful discussions or debates about text.
- Pose questions and assignments that do not simply ask students to retell information, but also require them to use higher-level thinking skills to reflect, interpret, hypothesize, and create their own answers or questions.
- Provide materials that include complex characters, problems, and solutions and that can be connected to other text. Include cross-curricular concepts.

Assessments

- Pre-assessments are especially important for highly proficient readers. Should they already know the text or material covered, they should be provided with additional selections that allow them to take their knowledge to the next level.
- To track progress over time, using portfolios might be especially telling for highly proficient readers, enabling teachers to better document progress and further highlight their strengths.
- Providing rubrics for a highly proficient student is also often helpful. Rubrics allow students to self-assess based on the guidelines set forth and to conference with peers or teachers to discuss their thoughts. Both portfolios and rubrics help give ownership to readers and keep them engaged.

1. **Which of the following is <u>not</u> a common way to differentiate reading instruction?**
   A. Use technology to provide additional practice.
   B. Create leveled, flexible reading groups based on frequent assessment.
   C. Use whole group instruction with varied leveled texts and activities.
   D. Use whole group instruction with one text provided for all students with the understanding that struggling readers and English Language Learners will not participate fully.

2. **Differentiation in decoding and fluency instruction should be based on which of the following:**
   A. Common interests among students
   B. Frequent and ongoing assessments
   C. Small groups composed of random combinations of students
   D. A student's ability to work independently

3. **Which of the following is a common challenge for highly proficient readers?**
   A. reading so fast that expression and comprehension suffers
   B. weaknesses in decoding which interfere with comprehension
   C. limited oral vocabulary which impacts decoding
   D. inability to sustain attention on independent reading

4. **Which of the following techniques is the best strategy for strengthening a struggling reader's fluency?**
   A. Repeated readings of familiar text and practicing word recognition in isolation
   B. Frequent "cold" calling on the student to read aloud so he will be given additional practice
   C. Encouraging him to read text which is above his instructional level
   D. Frequently introducing new books, passages and/or paragraphs with little emphasis on word recognition.

5. As an introduction to a fourth-grade unit study on electricity, students will be reading a grade-level biographic sketch about Benjamin Franklin. What is the best approach to reading the sketch?

    A. Give each student a turn to read a paragraph aloud to the class.

    B. Activate prior knowledge and provide students with background knowledge and key vocabulary terms before reading.

    C. To avoid a text that is too high for ELL students, provide an alternate decoding activity.

    D. In preparation for the unit assessment, encourage students to take notes during the read aloud.

6. When working with beginning ELL students, consideration of their native language is important for all of the following reasons except which one?

    A. ELL students may have not yet been exposed to some English sounds.

    B. Students may have been exposed only to non-alphabetic languages.

    C. Students may have difficulties distinguishing between phonemes.

    D. Their native language determines their rate of assimilation to American culture.

7. Which of the following is not characteristic of highly proficient readers?

    A. Highly proficient readers may need to be slowed down when reading text.

    B. Without sufficient instruction in decoding, highly proficient readers may lack the ability to read on a higher, more engaging level.

    C. It is important for teachers to listen to highly proficient readers read aloud.

    D. Highly proficient readers work best independently.

8. A fourth-grade student demonstrates excellent comprehension skills after listening to a story read aloud. When asked to read independently, he fails to answer any questions correctly. Which accommodation would be most appropriate for providing subject content necessary to meet standards?

A. Provide the student with various graphic organizers to assist reading.

B. Read the text aloud to the student.

C. Allow the student to say his answers aloud rather than write.

D. Hold the student responsible for fewer standards.

9. **On a recent reading assessment, a highly proficient student exhibited difficulties reading grade level words in isolation. When asked to read an entire paragraph, however, he was able to read fluently at grade level and sufficiently comprehend the material. Which of the following is likely the best explanation for his performance?**

A. The student lacks skills in tracking print in continuous text.

B. The student was uninterested in reading the words in isolation.

C. The student has not had enough vocabulary exposure.

D. The student effectively uses context clues to compensate for any weakness in the area of decoding.

10. **Students in a diverse classroom are beginning a new unit entitled "American Stories: Step into Historical Fiction." Some students complete the following: pretesting at the beginning of a new unit, extensions to standard tasks, complex exploration of a topic, and a teacher-designed cross-curricular project to synthesize learning. For whom are these tasks most appropriate?**

A. beginning language learners

B. struggling readers

C. highly proficient readers

D. all students

INDIVIDUAL LEARNERS EXPLANATIONS

1. **D** While many appropriate ways of differentiation exist, expectations (though possibly altered) for lower leveled readers and English Language Learners should still be high. Simply having students not participate in pieces of a lesson is not acceptable Rather, instruction should be differentiated to meet

every student at his/her level and when whole group instruction is used, accommodations and adaptations need to be in place so everyone is able to participate and benefit from the lesson. Choices A, B and C each suggest appropriate ways to differentiate through the use of technology, leveled and flexible reading groups, and whole group instruction with leveled text and activities created for students at varying levels.

2. B Differentiation is maximized when teachers have current student data, so that instruction can be matched to skill and knowledge levels. While students enjoy learning with peers who share their interests (Choice A) or with a variety of classmates (Choice C), these types of groupings do not necessarily maximize instructional potential. Finally, whereas a student's ability to work independently (Choice D) may impact the types of activities teachers can plan, it should not be the basis for differentiation.

3. A Highly proficient readers typically are skilled in decoding (Choice B), have sound oral vocabularies (Choice C), and read independently with ease (Choice D). The challenge is that because they read nearly every word with automaticity, they may need to slow down to attend to expression and close reading.

4. A Repeated readings of familiar texts on a student's instructional level is a proven strategy to strengthen a struggling reader's fluency. Re-reading improves automaticity and raises confidence levels. Cold calling (Choice B) frequently overwhelms and embarrasses those who are having difficulties. Allowing students prior access to texts they are expected to read aloud will help with anxiety as they can practice ahead of time. Choice C will likely lead to frustration. To maximize reading development, materials should be at a student's instructional level. Finally, practicing word lists/words in isolation builds automaticity and can help compensate for other with fluency deficits.

5. B Activating prior knowledge and explicitly teaching background knowledge and vocabulary are strategies that support English Language Learners. Forcing all students to read aloud (Choice A), replacing an informational text with a decodable text (Choice C), and taking notes during the introduction (Choice D), are not proven strategies.

6. D A student's native language does not determine assimilation. Native language may have a significant impact on reading development. ELL students often have lower levels of phonological and phonemic awareness. They may not enter school with the same knowledge base as other children. Though these skills can be taught, they may take longer to be acquired. It is possible they've only been exposed to non-alphabetic languages and may not be familiar with English sounds and/or have difficulties distinguishing between sounds.

7. D   Highly proficient readers benefit from cooperative learning and small groups. Highly proficient readers may need to be slowed down; if they read too quickly they may run the risk of missing important information or jeopardizing their understanding of the material. If these readers aren't provided sufficient decoding instruction, they will likely lack the ability to read in a more engaged manner as text becomes more difficult. By providing these students with basic decoding skills, they will know what to do when they come across an unfamiliar word. Finally, it is equally important to listen to highly proficient readers so their progress can be monitored and any difficulties noted and addressed.

8. B   By reading the passage aloud to the student, the student can put all of his/her efforts into comprehension and recall. Graphic organizers benefit students (Choice A), but reading provides a greater degree of support. Writing (Choice C) is not addressed in the prompt. This scenario suggests that the student is capable of achieving all standards with support in reading (Choice D).

9. D   Highly proficient readers may be higher in some aspects of reading than others. By using their strengths – in this case, the student's ability to read text fluently - they may be able to compensate for areas of weakness, such as words in isolation. Though the student's decoding skills are weaker, when reading words within text, he is able to use context clues to help him appropriately identify words he may not otherwise know. His ability to read a paragraph demonstrates skill in tracking print (Choice A). There is no indication that the student lacks interest (Choice B) or vocabulary (Choice C).

10. C   Highly proficient readers who demonstrate mastery of the material on a pretest benefit from extensions that include complex exploration and cross-curricular projects. The tasks described would push language learners and struggling readers to work at a frustration level.

5.6 Chapter Review

1. **Third-grade students are preparing to read an expository text on simple machines. Which of the following pre-reading activities is the best strategy to promote comprehension?**

    A. Introduce vocabulary such as *simple* and *machine*.

    B. Assign a journal entry entitled "Characteristics of Simple Machines."

    C. Show pictures of several household simple machines. Invite students to discuss how the devices make work easier.

    D. Ask students to flip through the selection, skim an interesting paragraph, and pair share what they learned.

2. **Which of the following best demonstrates the use of scaffolding?**

    A. A group of highly proficient readers are given multiple accounts of the same event. This group contributes to a Venn diagram comparing two accounts; then students collaborate on a similar task; students complete the final comparison independently.

    B. Students are placed in homogeneous groups based on reading levels. Reading groups receive guided instruction in reading material at their instructional level.

    C. All students are given the same materials. In whole group instruction, students receive instruction on decoding, comprehension, and fluency.

    D. An evaluation is made of the primary language of English Language Learners. Easily confused phonemes as well as sounds that occur in English but not in the primary language are noted.

3. **Students are given a worksheet with questions like the following:**

    Circle the correct nonsense word to fit in the blank.
    The velvety ___ of the cloth would be perfect for the project.
    shrompture   shromptly

    What is the rationale behind this assignment?

A. building oral vocabulary
B. practicing syntactic clues
C. analyzing words with Greek and Latin roots
D. decoding

4. **Which statement best describes the motivation to use small groups for reading instruction?**
   A. Classroom management is simplified when teacher attention is divided between groups.
   B. Small groups provide a consistent, stable union of students across a school year.
   C. Students learn from all peers in extended lessons in which all students efficiently receive the same information.
   D. Students working in small homogeneous or heterogeneous groups receive frequent feedback on differentiated tasks.

5. **Which of the following features does <u>not</u> impact text complexity?**
   A. Qualitative measures such as predictability of text
   B. Quantitative measures such as the number of different words
   C. Retelling which includes a reconstruction of plot features
   D. Individual reader considerations such as background knowledge

6. **Which of the following best illustrates the use of varied reading experiences with new vocabulary?**
   A. English language learners read a predictable text book which has a different animal on each page.
   B. Fifth graders read a non-fiction account, a historical fiction trade book, and a classic poem on Paul Revere's ride noting use of content words that appear in each.
   C. Fourth graders illustrate new vocabulary words from a selection in their reading book, read the text, and complete assessments on comprehension and vocabulary words.
   D. Given the following list of words: *geography, biography, graphic, autograph,* and *photograph,* students analyze various uses of the root *graph.*

7. **Which of the following describes the use of trade books in a reading classroom?**
    A. Students read textbooks and outline content to promote comprehension.
    B. Students use technology to read passages and answer multiple choice questions.
    C. Students publish their own writing and share their publications with the community.
    D. Students read high-interest, leveled books which may include books in a series and selections for diverse learners.

8. **Teachers should apply which of the following strategies in reading instruction?**
    A. scripted instructions that can be applied to all readers
    B. exclusive use of books designated by a reading program
    C. balanced and differentiated reading, writing, and language arts
    D. limited genres with preference given to informational text

9. **A selection which is at a student's independent reading level is defined as which of the following?**
    A. A selection which a student can read with few errors and with comprehension
    B. A selection in which a student experiences no challenges and can lose interest
    C. A selection at which a student becomes discouraged because of the difficulty of the text
    D. A selection in which topics are appropriate to the reader's age

10. **A fourth-grade teacher uses the following strategy when interacting with new texts with highly proficient readers: read a selection aloud as students follow along using their own copies, interrupt reading to discuss unfamiliar words and phrases, reread, consider interpretations and implications, and reread. These sorts of experiences allow for which of the following:**
    A. activating prior knowledge through repeated reading.

B. modeling and helping students engage in close reading.

C. conducting ongoing informal assessments to guide instruction.

D. collecting data and samples for student portfolio.

11. **What is the primary motivation behind establishing a classroom library?**

   A. providing small group instruction differentiated to learners

   B. giving explicit instruction on book handling

   C. promoting a love for reading through making familiar books available

   D. building content specific vocabulary

12. **A teacher reads aloud to her class regularly. This practice promotes each of the following aspects of reading development except which one?**

   A. automaticity in word recognition

   B. increased vocabulary

   C. love of reading

   D. fluency: reading accurately, quickly, and with expression

13. **Which of the following strategies contributes most to a student's becoming a lifelong independent reader?**

   A. Utilize a schoolwide reading motivational plan

   B. Equip students with skills, resources, and time for independent reading in and out of school

   C. Focus reading efforts on high interest, low readability books

   D. Provide explicit instruction on text features

14. **Which statement does <u>not</u> reflect current research on the uses of instructional technologies for managing and creating leveled activities for reading centers?**

   A. Instructional technologies often increase student motivation.

   B. Instructional technologies allow for increased learning time.

   C. Instructional technologies allow for a custom fit curriculum for students.

   D. Instructional technologies are more effective over time than whole group instruction.

15. **Which description summarizes the best uses for instructional technologies?**
    A. Replacing classroom instruction in the area of test preparation
    B. Eliminating issues with student participation during cooperative learning
    C. Using passage reading with multiple-choice questions to promote student elaboration on a text
    D. Balancing classroom instruction with brief, regular computer-based lessons

16. **Students are preparing to look at a new assigned text in reading class. Which of the following illustrates appropriate differentiation?**
    A. Provide picture cues for key vocabulary terms for a small group of struggling readers
    B. Pre-teach the same words with multiple meanings to all students in small groups
    C. Select a graphic organizer to guide student comprehension
    D. Based on the illustrations of the selection, ask students to "think, pair, share" their predictions about the topic.

17. **How should an ELL teacher select guided reading materials for lessons and assessments when working with first graders who are below grade level?**
    A. Choose predictable text fiction in place of academic nonfiction.
    B. Focus on reading word lists with accompanying pictures rather than reading whole sentences or stories.
    C. Choose texts which are at student's independent or instructional level and which contain repeated words and phrases.
    D. Use the same grade level text with all students, including the ELL students.

18. A first grader has demonstrated the ability to comprehend grade level text and higher when the text is read orally. The student also reads a grade level passage aloud with appropriate prosody and expression; however, she is unable to answer any comprehension questions about the passage she read. Which of the following is the best strategy to include in reading instruction?
    A. practice decoding using phonics rules
    B. slow down, visualize, and ask questions
    C. use syntactic clues when reading
    D. pre-teach vocabulary

19. A second-grade class includes a number of English Language Learners who can decode grade level text, but often struggle to understand key terms and/or expressions. Which of the following activities would be most helpful for them when trying to understand unfamiliar vocabulary used in an upcoming unit about the thirteen original colonies?
    A. Pre-teach the meaning of key words and expressions that will be in the text. Provide students with index cards and time to illustrate what each term/expression means.
    B. Have students find and underline a pre-determined list of words within the text and then copy the sentences containing the words in their notebooks.
    C. Have students practice decoding vocabulary words before they are introduced to the actual text.
    D. Read the text aloud to the students.

20. Which text challenge or support is defined as using words which follow sound-spelling correspondence that the reader has learned?
    A. predictability
    B. graphic support
    C. decodability
    D. glossary

1. C Activating background knowledge (schema) is the best strategy for promoting comprehension for a topic that students have experience with such as simple machines. Defining *simple* and *machine* as two separate words will not lead students to a working concept for the topic (Choice A). Before reading, students may be unfamiliar with characteristics of simple machines, making the topic unsuitable for a pre-reading journal entry (Choice B). Skimming and pair share are strategies that work well during reading (Choice D).

2. A Scaffolding is an instructional method that provides support for students before and during a lesson so that they are able to succeed in learning challenging skills. All levels of students benefit from scaffolding on lessons that would otherwise be at a frustration level. Provision of appropriately leveled reading material (Choice B) describes differentiation. The whole group instruction described in Choice C does not show a process of providing support until students are able to achieve independently. Scaffolding refers to an instructional method, not an evaluation of primary language (Choice D).

3. B This activity promotes looking at word parts of various parts of speech. The blank in the sentence is best filled by a noun. *–ture* is a noun suffix; *-ly* is an adverb suffix. Nonsense words are not intended to build oral vocabulary (Choice A). The nonsense words do not contain Greek or Latin roots (Choice C). The words in the sentence suggest that the student is a mature reader, not still practicing decoding (Choice D).

4. D Students can be grouped in a variety of ways including the same level, different levels, work habits, and support needed. The short lessons can target each group. Students can receive frequent feedback which encourages them to stay on task. Classroom management is not necessarily simplified by small groups as the group not working with the teacher must be able to stay on task (Choice A). Small groups can be flexible and changed frequently to reflect ongoing assessment or learning goals (Choice B). Small group lessons are typically short lessons in which students receive different instruction (Choice C).

5. C Retelling is an assessment tool that can be used with texts of various complexities. Retelling is not an indicator of text complexity. Text complexity is typically determined by qualitative measures (predictability, decodability, illustration support, etc) (Choice A), quantitative measures (word count, number of high-frequency words, sentence length, etc) (Choice B), and reader and task (variables specific to the reader such as background knowledge, interest, motivation, etc.) (Choice D).

6. B Allowing students to see vocabulary in a variety of texts reinforces the meaning and usage. Equally important, students receive a varied reading experience by interacting with fiction, nonfiction, prose, and poetry. While a predictable text book (Choice A) is a means of building vocabulary, it does not itself provide a varied reading experience. Similarly, noting the vocabulary in a reading selection (Choice C) is not a varied reading experience. The word analysis activity (Choice D) does not include reading.

7. D Trade books are books published for general readership. Because they are leveled and diverse, readers often find them interesting. Substantial time spent reading trade books generally improves overall reading performance. Textbooks (Choice A), passages (Choice B), and student publications (Choice C) are not considered trade books.

8. C Teachers should strive to deliver reading programs that provide varied, rich experiences for all students. A well-balanced diet in reading, writing and language arts that incorporates varied genres, subject areas and high-interest materials will encourage students to become independent readers. Allowing students to select some reading material encourages their love of reading. No reading program is a one-size-fits-all model, and students and curriculum need to be closely and frequently monitored to ensure individual needs are met.

9. A Reading material which is at a student's independent reading level is easily comprehendible and decodable text which can be read with fluency. It is not overly simple so that the student becomes bored (Choice B). Text which is challenging yet provides opportunities for growth is at an instructional level. Text which is so difficult that the student becomes frustrated or discouraged is at a frustration level (Choice C). Choice D refers to text that is at a student's interest level.

10. B Close reading is a strategy that helps student interpret literature. Re-reading sections of text, drawing students' attention to difficult vocabulary or phrases and providing the opportunity for text to be re-read while students participate in meaningful discussions allows for reading to be taken to the next level. Such activities and modeling of these strategies allows students to better understand the author's organization of the text and intentions. Then, students are able to make connections between the text and other pieces of literature and/or concepts they've learned. While such activities may activate prior knowledge (Choice A) this was not the teacher's purpose. Assessments (Choices C and D) are not the purpose of this teacher's lesson.

11. C A classroom library gives students access to favorite books, authors, genres, topics, etc. While the library may be used for small group instruction (Choice A), for explicit instruction (Choice B), or for vocabulary building (Choice D), those benefits are not the primary motivation for establishing a classroom library.

12. A Listening to a read aloud does not include students following written text; as such, it does not provide practice in automatic word recognition. Listening to oral reading of a book gives the student access to text which is beyond his reading level. The reading can increase vocabulary (Choice B), give pleasure (Choice C), and model fluency (Choice D).

13. B Students who have the skills to decode and comprehend with fluency, who have access to well-crafted content- and idea- rich books, and who have consistently read independently stand to become lifelong independent readers. In the absence of skills, resources, and time, a school-wide motivational plan (Choice A), a selection of hi-lo books (Choice C), or explicit instruction on any reading skill (Choice D) will be insufficient.

14. D Current research does not indicate that technology is preferred to classroom instruction of a group or individuals by a teacher. Choices A, B and C are each valid reasons to incorporate instructional technologies into reading instruction. Students are often motivated to use technology, and many programs allow for activities to be matched to a child's instructional level thus providing a custom-fit curriculum. This combination keeps students engaged.

15. D Research indicates that technology is best used to supplement traditional classroom instruction. Choices A, B and C are pitfalls of technology. Technology should not replace traditional instruction in test preparation or any other area. It does not eliminate the problem of students with poor skills being overly dependent on technology or classmates so that they avoid reading and writing tasks. While some multiple-choice questions are written in such a way that they require higher-level thinking, others provide students with limited options that require little comprehension or engagement with the text.

16. A Differentiation is individualized, flexible instruction designed to maximize learning opportunities for all students. The indication is that the picture cues are provided only for struggling readers. In this case, the teacher has made a difference in instruction for struggling readers. She has differentiated. Pre-teaching the same words (Choice B), choosing the same graphic organizer (Choice C), and asking the same prediction question (Choice D) are not examples of differentiation.

17. C Beginning level readers benefit from reading text that contains repeated words and/or phrases. All readers benefit from reading material at their independent level (to gain fluency and accuracy) and instructional level (during reading group times to improve vocabulary and comprehension). ELL students can learn from all genres and benefit from academic content texts. (Choice A) While using pictures to support reading is helpful (especially for ELL students), this should not be their entire focus (Choice B). Though ELL students should be provided with quality reading materials like their peers, all students learn best when instructed at a level appropriate for them (Choice D). Differentiation within classrooms remains important so all students are able to progress appropriately.

18. B Highly proficient readers may have areas of difficulty. In this case, the student has the ability to recognize words in grade level material with automaticity and to comprehend material read aloud. The student's abilities do not suggest a need to practice decoding (Choice A), using syntactic clues (Choice C), or acquiring vocabulary (Choice D); however, perhaps because of her rapid pace or weak metacognitive skills, s/he is unable to comprehend the material. By slowing down, visualizing, and self-questioning, s/he can improve comprehension skills.

19. A   Because the students can read grade level text, they do not need to have everything read aloud (Choice D) nor do they require decoding practice prior to reading (Choice C). While finding key vocabulary terms in the text and using context clues to determine their meaning may be helpful, having them simply copy sentences will do little to help (Choice B). By pre-teaching the meaning of key words and expressions and providing an opportunity for students to create a picture to associate with each word and refer back to, students will begin reading with appropriate background knowledge and the text will make more sense. When they come across words and terms they are familiar with while reading, the experience becomes more meaningful and they are able to begin making connections to the text.

20. C   Decodability refers to texts which have a high percentage of words that follow sound/spelling correspondences that students have learned. Predictability (Choice A) in text refers to repeated language structure which allows the reader to anticipate the next word. Graphic support (Choice B) refers to pictures, graphs, maps, etc. A glossary (Choice D) is an alphabetical list of words found in a text with definitions; a small dictionary at the end of a text.

Chapter 6:
Assessment

Lessons

6.1   Characteristics & Uses of Assessments

Reading is a complex process of decoding for the purpose of comprehension. It is an interaction between the text and the reader with his background, aptitude, and attitude. Fluency is the ability to accomplish the reading process with speed and accuracy.

Assessment is the act of gathering information to make decisions about a student or group of students. Given the complexity of the reading process and the diversity of texts and readers, no single assessment will be right for every child and every skill. A wide range of efficient, systematic, purposeful assessment tools is available to support teachers and schools with the task of assessing.

Uses of Assessment

Teachers can rely on a variety of formal and informal assessments to judge overall performance, compare students to peers, identify strengths and weaknesses, manage instruction, determine effectiveness of instruction, and gauge progress. Assessment informs teacher decisions on groupings, instruction, and strategies. Educators evaluate and use test results from the individual level up to the national and international levels. Students need to be assessed regularly (formally or informally) to determine where skills break down and to monitor their progress.

Concepts of Validity, Reliability, and Bias

Validity

Test validity is the extent to which a test measures what it is intended to measure.
Is the assessment measuring the concepts it's meant to measure? Do any factors interfere with test results? If an assessment is meant to assess student comprehension, but the text is too difficult for students to read fluently, is it a good gauge of comprehension?

Reliability

Test reliability is the consistency and stability of the results. Reliability is explained in terms of test-retest (Do tests given by different administrators yield the same results?), parallel forms (Do different forms of the test yield the same results?), and inter-rater reliability (Do different observers rate the skills the same?)

Bias

A test bias occurs when a test design or results systematically yield higher or lower scores when administered to specific criterion groups (for example, students from lower-income backgrounds or students not proficient in English.)

Bias occurs when the content of a test is comparatively easier or more difficult for a group. Language used or specific test questions that are more familiar for one group over another may indicate test bias and should be taken into account. Bias in an assessment would affect an entire criterion group, not individuals. Does this assessment produce differences among groups of test-takers (that is, specific genders, cultures, race, etc.)?

Formal and Informal Assessments

Formal assessments, also known as standardized measures, may be administered at individual, classroom, district, state, and national levels. They have data which is mathematically computed and summarized. Assessment results compare students to peers and include percentile, stanine, and standardized scores. Formal assessments have set directions that may specify time limits or other circumstances. Formal assessments may be criterion-referenced or norm-referenced.

Informal assessments measure content and performance skills. Informal assessments can give results in the form of a rubric, yes/no, 22 of 25 correct, etc. They have flexibility in how they are given. They may be constructed by teachers and are most often given at individual, classroom, or grade level.

Criterion-referenced and Norm-referenced Tests

Criterion-referenced tests measure student performance against specific criteria or standards. Students are tested on specific content objectives or benchmarks. Typically, a student is deemed proficient in a given area or level if s/he passes the assessment. Performance based assessments and chapter tests are examples of criterion-referenced assessments. Criterion-referenced tests may be formal or informal.

Norm-referenced tests are designed to show distribution and ranking of students in terms of their own performance and that of their peers. A norm-referenced test is a common way to assess performance of a school compared with other schools. Because specific norms or factors provide a constant, comparative assessments can reveal differences in particular areas. Iowa Tests, ACT, and SAT are examples of norm-referenced tests. Norm-referenced tests are formal assessments.

Assessment	Criterion or Norm	Formal or Informal
ACT	Norm	Formal
Iowa Achievement Test	Norm	Formal
Performance Based & End of Year high stakes tests	Criterion	Formal
Portfolio	Criterion	Informal
Informal Reading Inventory	Criterion	Informal

Group and Individual Assessments

Reading assessments may be administered to a group or to an individual, depending on the type of assessment and the student(s) being assessed.

Group assessment is defined as an assessment that students take collectively as a group. Group testing provides the advantage of efficiency for the teacher. Group testing is sometimes a screening that determines if individual testing is necessary. Individual assessment is defined as an assessment that a student takes one-on-one with an administrator. Individual assessments to assess reading skills of early childhood students are widely used. A common individual assessment is an Informal Reading Inventory.

1. Within a school district, rankings must be made that compare school results at each grade level. Which of the following assessment types has traditionally been used to collect data for whole group comparison?
    A. Criterion-referenced assessments
    B. Norm-referenced assessments
    C. Authentic tasks
    D. Portfolio Assessment

2. After receiving the scores for his student's recent criterion-referenced assessments, a teacher noticed that an English Language Learner who reads on grade level, did not perform as well as expected. What should the teacher do next?
    A. Question the reliability of the test.
    B. Change the student's reading group because his instructional level needs be adjusted lower until he is able to meet the test standards.
    C. Review the test to see if it contained unfamiliar vocabulary.
    D. A wait and see approach is preferred to making adjustments based on assessment, especially given that the validity of this particular test should now be in question.

3. Statewide, standard-based assessments are examples of which of the following type of test?
    A. Criterion-referenced assessments
    B. Norm-referenced assessments
    C. Informal assessments
    D. Biased assessments

4. **The following prompt was used on a district writing assessment.**

   Describe what you would do on a snowy day.

   For students who are recent immigrants from tropical countries, this prompt is likely to raise questions regarding which of the following?
   A. Validity
   B. Reliability
   C. Testing bias
   D. Control of variables

5. **The reliability of an assessment refers to which of the following?**
   A. consistent, accurate results
   B. biases associated with the text
   C. measurement of the specified criteria
   D. comparison to students in other classrooms

6. **A formal, statistical examination of a standardized state test revealed that students with greater life experience performed better than students with less life experience. If the test did not assess academic achievement, which it claimed to do, which test feature was lacking?**
   A. reliability
   B. validity
   C. consistency over time
   D. cultural bias

7. **After administering an Informal Reading Inventory, teachers are concerned about the test's reliability. This means teachers are worried about which of the following?**
   A. Does the assessment test what it's meant to measure?
   B. Does the assessment include any testing biases?
   C. Does the assessment provide consistent results?
   D. Does the test provide data to compare students with their peers?

8. **Which of the following is not a common use of assessment?**
    A. determining effectiveness of instruction
    B. identifying student strengths and weaknesses
    C. keeping students in small groups on task
    D. comparing students to peers

9. **Results of a criterion-referenced test indicate that 70% of the class achieved at or above expectations. 30% performed below the standard. How should the classroom teacher proceed with instruction?**
    A. Emphasize whole group instruction relying on the responses of strong students to help weak students
    B. Repeat instruction on criteria missed with all students, knowing that all students benefit from review
    C. Rely on published teacher guides to inform instruction rather than assessments
    D. Continue to follow the yearly plan while reviewing and re-teaching missed standards to select students in small groups

10. **Which of the following is not an informal assessment?**
    A. A publisher's test over a chapter in the reading book
    B. An exit question following group instruction
    C. A criterion-referenced end of year test administered under state guidelines
    D. A classroom writing assessment scored with a predetermined rubric

CHARACTERISTICS & USES OF ASSESSMENTS EXPLANATIONS

1. B   When looking to compare students in terms of their own performance and that of their peers, educators have traditionally depended on norm-referenced assessments (Choice B) that are designed to show a distribution of scores across students. Choice A, criterion-referenced assessments, measure how a student performs against specific criteria or standards, and can be used to determine student proficiency in a given area. Choice C, authentic tasks are assessments that replicate real life.

Authentic tasks are not formatted to provide data in and across large groups. Finally, portfolio assessments (Choice D) provide a sampling of formal and informal student work samples and assessments. They demonstrate individual student progress over time.

2. C   Given that many English Language Learners need additional support to learn vocabulary, it would make sense to first refer back to the assessment and see if the vocabulary possibly caused the student to have difficulties. While the student may be able to read grade level texts, additional vocabulary instruction and pre-teaching key words before reading grade level text may be necessary. In the case of the assessment, pre-teaching was not a possibility and so the student may have lacked the prior knowledge necessary to being successful.

3. A   Statewide, standard-based assessments are examples of criterion-referenced tests. This form of assessment measures how a student performs against specific criteria or standard. Choice B, norm-referenced tests, refer to assessments that show a distribution of performance and rank students in terms of their own performance and that of their peers. Choice C, informal assessments, may be used daily or even several times throughout a lesson, as teachers gauge student understanding. They are typically planned and used by teachers to guide the remainder of a lesson's instruction or the following days' activities.

4. C   This particular test question is biased as it is particularly difficult for students who have not experienced snow. Because the teacher has students who recently moved from tropical countries, it is unlikely the children have a great deal to contribute to this subject, making Choice C the best answer. The validity of the test (Choice A) refers to if the test measures what it is supposed to test. The test's validity could be impacted due to limited student vocabulary and experience; however, it is the bias that creates the validity issues. Reliability (Choice B) refers to if the test provides accurate results in various testing situations over time. Control of variables (Choice D) refers largely to testing situations that can impact results, an issue which is not a concern on this assessment.

5. A   The reliability of an assessment refers to its consistency in providing accurate results. Choice B, bias, refers to aspects of the test that favor or disadvantage groups of students based on gender, creed, culture, etc. Choice C refers to the validity of an assessment, which indicates if the assessment is a solid measure of what it is supposed to test. Finally,

Choice D refers to norm-based assessments that measure student's performance against that of their peers.

6. B   Validity refers to the degree that a test accurately assesses what it claims to measure. Consistency over time (Choice C), also known as reliability (Choice A), is not in question as the test may have consistently offered different results for students with greater life experience. The test may have some bias (Choice D); however, the question asks specifically about the tests ability to measure what it claims.

7. C   Reliability is the degree to which the test results are consistent over time, in different settings, and with different evaluators. Choice A, which questions if a test is measuring what it is meant to assess refers to a test's validity. Choice C, testing biases, refers to concerns that may be raised if and when a test produces different results among groups of test-takers (i.e. specific genders, cultures, race, etc.) due to language or specific test questions. Reliability is not related to student ranking (Choice D).

8. C   Classroom management would be a poor use of assessment. Various assessment are well suited to indicate the effectiveness of instruction (Choice A) and student strengths and weaknesses (Choice B). Norm-referenced tests compare students to peers (Choice D).

9. D   With 70% of the class demonstrating proficiency, instruction must proceed for all students. However, students must be taught the criteria to mastery. The re-teaching can continue with small groups or with specialists. Published teacher guides are not a substitute for using assessment to guide instruction.

10. C   An assessment administered across a wide range of students with specified, regulated guidelines is likely a formal assessment that will provide statistics to compare students and perhaps districts. By contrast, a publisher's chapter test (Choice A), an exit question (Choice B), and a rubric-scored composition (Choice D) will not be administered under specified set guidelines or provide statistics to compare students to peers.

6.2   Techniques for Assessing

In choosing an assessment, the instructor can ask, "What do I want to know about my students?" This lesson covers a sampling of reading skills aligned with assessment tools.

Skill or Area of Reading Development	Assessment Tool
Phonemic awareness	⊙ Do *dog* and *run* begin with the same sound?
Concepts of Print	⊙ Given a book, point to a letter, word, or space between words.
Letter/sound recognition	⊙ Shown a letter, what letter is this? What sound does it make?
Fluency	⊙ Given an appropriate passage for the student to read aloud, complete a running record and determine words correct per minute. Compare student proficiency to norms.
Accuracy	⊙ Given an appropriate passage for the student to read aloud, note words read correctly and incorrectly. Informal Reading Inventories and running records facilitate accuracy evaluations.
Sound/spelling	⊙ Dictate a list of regular, decodable words. Students write the words. Analyze errors and patterns of errors using a miscue analysis.
Comprehension	⊙ Provide a selection for the student to read and then reconstruct. Retelling or other methods may be used to evaluate comprehension at literal, inferential, and evaluative levels.
Productive Skills	⊙ Rubrics are lists of specified criteria than can be used to evaluate student productive skills. Rubrics are divided into levels which either teachers or students can evaluate.

Skill or Area of Reading Development	Assessment Tool
Growth over time	⊙ Guide students in selecting samples of their work over time. Evaluating student work which is kept in a central location helps students, parents, and educators recognize and measure growth.
Real world skills	⊙ Provide students with authentic, original tasks such as acting as a guide to a tourist attraction. Assess their ability to interact with the text. Rubrics are often used to evaluate authentic tasks.
Vocabulary	⊙ Vocabulary may be measured through a multiple choice type test or through reading and analysis of a passage.
Reading grade level	⊙ Students are given an appropriate passage. Miscues and comprehension are measured. Results are compared to a norm. From the results, the reading grade level can be assigned.
Word recognition	⊙ Student reads from a list of age-appropriate words. Words may be sight words or decodable.

Tools for Assessing

A wide range of assessment tools is available to measure student progress in reading development.

Informal Reading Inventories

Accurately discerning a student's reading level is critical to effective reading instruction to make sure that all students become fluent readers. The most common means of determining reading level is with an Informal Reading Inventory. Results can be used to determine reading grade level as well as a student's **independent, instructional and/or frustration level.**

Students are screened for approximate reading development and given appropriate passage(s) to read aloud. Students read a passage on their instructional level aloud while teachers record errors. If the passage is too easy or hard, the student should be stopped and another passage provided. Teachers may choose to time the passage to determine the child's fluency rate. When the passage is completed, teachers may have the child retell the passage or may ask specific comprehension questions commonly provided by the publisher.

The inventory results provide word recognition and comprehension scores. By timing the reading passages, teachers can also determine student fluency (words per minute). Assessments are conducted one-on-one. Typically, a baseline is done at the beginning of the school year or at the start of a reading program and then re-tested regularly. An IRI measures grade level reading, fluency, comprehension, vocabulary, and oral reading accuracy.

Miscue Analysis

A miscue analysis is a glimpse of what a student does when making errors in reading. By having students read text aloud, recording and analyzing their mistakes, teachers learn whether students are omitting, miscalling, or substituting letters, sounds, or entire words. The process allows teachers to determine targeted instructional strategies to help students become more successful readers.

Running Record

A running record is a tool used to record miscues (omissions, substitutions, etc.) and behaviors (pauses, rereading, self-correction) in oral reading. A running record typically has a copy of the text to be read. The teacher records behavior and miscues on the running record. The running record can be analyzed using a miscue analysis. It can be coupled with comprehension testing to measure reading level. It is a piece of the Informal Reading Inventory. In itself, it is not an assessment. It is an observation tool used in assessment.

Teachers use a code in order to record student reading behavior quickly. Codes vary somewhat from system to system. This code is a sample that could be used.

Reading Behavior	Code	Error
Accurate Reading	√	No error
Substitution	Underline substituted word	1 error per substitution
Repetition	R	No error
Self-correction	sc	No error
Omission	-	1 error per omission
Insertion	^	1 error per insertion
Told by teacher	T	1 error per word
Long pause	//	No error

Rubrics

A rubric is a list of specified criteria for grading. Rubrics often help teachers differentiate because they allow various levels to be established. They provide clear expectations for students, they are easy to use and to understand for teachers and parents, provide good feedback, and they can be used to guide instruction. As a shared document, rubrics involve learners in the process.

Portfolio

A portfolio is a selection of student work. Portfolios may be simple or intricate. Like rubrics, portfolios provide a way to engage students in self-management. Dated samplings of select student work are kept in one central location and comprise the portfolio.

Authentic tasks

Authentic tasks are classroom activities or assessments that encompass real-life settings, experiences, or tasks. Student products demonstrate skills or knowledge acquired over the course of study.

Retelling

Retelling is an oral or written reconstruction of a selection done after the reading. In retelling, students demonstrate their comprehension. Teachers may assign various kinds of retelling including plot, setting, problem/solution, inference, and evaluation. Retellings are open-ended and require student responses without the scaffolding of short answer questions.

TECHNIQUES FOR ASSESSING PRACTICE

1. **During kindergarten screenings, students with solid phonemic awareness would be able to do which of the following?**
    A. Blend the sounds /f/ /a/ /s/ /t/ to say the word *fast*
    B. Read a list of kindergarten sight words
    C. Use knowledge of word patterns to spell unknown words
    D. Point to and name letters of the alphabet

2. **Which of the following assessment tools provides students with a clear set of expectations, allows for both self and teacher evaluation, utilizes scaffolding and differentiation, and informs future instruction?**
   A. a running record
   B. a portfolio
   C. a rubric
   D. a miscue analysis

3. **Upon entering first grade, a student is asked to complete the following tasks:**

   A student is asked to write the following dictated words.
   1. mask
   2. sharp
   3. cooked

   What information will this type of assessment tell a teacher?
   A. the student's level of sound-spelling proficiency
   B. the student's level of phonemic awareness
   C. the sorts of errors a child is making in his/her reading
   D. a baseline for the child's fluency and accuracy rates

4. **A teacher decides to use a rubric to assess student performance on a recent language arts project. What is a rubric unable to do?**
   A. Give clear expectations for students
   B. Provide information to guide future instruction
   C. Differentiate for varied levels
   D. Give a quick snapshot of student fluency rates

5. **A teacher is concerned one of her fourth grade English Language Learners is omitting or substituting phonemes when reading connected text. Which of the following assessments would provide the best information regarding what the student is doing and how the teacher can best guide future instruction?**
   A. Phonemic awareness assessment
   B. Portfolio assessment
   C. Oral retelling
   D. Miscue analyses

6. **A school system uses portfolios to assess kindergarten, first and second grade student reading progress. A portfolio assessment allows for all of the following except:**
   A. The opportunity for students to participate and take ownership in their assessment
   B. Consistency across many evaluators within one school system
   C. A sampling of various reading activities and assessments maintained in one central location
   D. Demonstration of a student's progress over time

7. **A teacher wants to quickly assess reading levels, word recognition and comprehension skills as well as gather data for fluency rates and determine if there are any error patterns for specific students. Which of the following assessments would be the most appropriate for these needs?**
   A. an authentic task
   B. a norm-referenced test
   C. an Informal Reading Inventory
   D. work graded with a rubric

8. **During miscue analyses, a teacher documents the following while one of her students reads aloud:**
   Last week, my sister and I walked to the park. We wanted to see the swans at the lake. The weather was beautiful so we went running down to the bank. My sister accidentally fell and tumbled into the water.
   Based on the recorded errors, what area of language can the teacher target to meet this student's needs?
   A. blending
   B. content-area vocabulary
   C. self-monitoring for comprehension
   D. base words, roots, inflections, and other affixes

9. **How should teachers use assessments to create and maintain reading groups?**
   A. Students should be assessed frequently using formal and informal assessments to monitor their progress; reading groups should remain fluid throughout the year.

B. All reading assessments should be norm-based so teachers know how their students measure up against other students in the same grade throughout the school year.

C. Assessments should be done at the start of the year to form reading groups; once groups are formed informal assessments may be done to measure individual student progress; however, groups should remain the same as students have already grown comfortable with one another.

D. Reading assessments should always be informal; students are likely to perform higher when under less pressure. Classroom management is a higher priority than assessment results when organizing reading groups.

10. **Which of the following questions for retelling would be appropriate to assess students' literal comprehension of a passage from a historical fiction read aloud?**

A. Choose the correct answer to the following: Based on the context, what can you conclude that the word *rampart* means? a. wall, b. starboard side of a boat, c. explosion

B. Use events in the selection we just read to explain how does this selection differ from the journal entry we read yesterday about the same event?

C. Look back through your reading folder. Choose your favorite selection.

D. Use key events in the story to tell in your own words what the prisoner was watching throughout the night.

TECHNIQUES FOR ASSESSING EXPLANATIONS

1. A   Kindergarteners who have a solid sense of phonological and phonemic awareness are able to rhyme, segment, blend, etc. For example, they may be able to blend the sounds /f/ /a/ /s/ /t/ to say the word *fast*. Reading sight words (Choice B), decoding (Choice C), and identifying letters (Choice D) are not phonological awareness skills. They are skills that are typically acquired after phonemic awareness.

2. **C** Rubrics list specified criteria for grading. They naturally provide scaffolding and differentiation, may be used by students and teachers, and provide an outline for future instruction. A portfolio (Choice B) does not provide the specified criteria found in a rubric. Running records (Choice A) and miscue analysis (Choice D) are not designed for self-evaluation.

3. **A** Asking students to encode phonetically regular words demonstrates the level of sound-spelling proficiency. It is not the appropriate assessment for determining phonemic awareness (Choice B). A miscue analysis is a better assessment for determining types of errors (Choice C). An Informal Reading Inventory is intended to assess baseline fluency and accuracy rates (Choice D).

4. **D** Choices A, B and C are all benefits of rubrics – rubrics provide clear expectations for students at the beginning of an assignment, provide valuable feedback that parents and teachers can use to guide future instruction, and assist teachers to differentiate by allowing for various levels to be established. However, rubrics do not provide a quick snapshot of fluency rates, as suggested in Choice D. To assess student fluency, Informal Reading Inventories or running records would be better choices.

5. **D** Letter/sound omission or substitution is a common area of difficulty for English Language Learners. By having students read words and/or passages aloud, recording and then analyzing the mistakes made, teachers can diagnose specific areas of difficulty. Choice A, phonemic awareness assessments are typically used with younger students and/or emergent readers. Choice B, portfolio assessments, allows educators to view formal and informal work samples over a period of time. However, they do not help to identify specific decoding issues. An oral retelling (Choice C) is a reconstruction of a selection that can be used to evaluate comprehension.

6. **B** Choices A, C and D are all true. Portfolios are an excellent way for students to become involved and take ownership over their own assessments. They also provide a central location for a sampling of various work samples and assessments to be maintained and, as a result, demonstrate growth over time. However, Choice B is incorrect - portfolios do not guarantee consistency across varied evaluators. Because grading is more subjective than other forms of assessment, there is a risk involved with how evaluators interpret standards and judge student growth.

7. C   Informal Reading Inventories use word lists and passages to determine a student's independent and instructional reading levels. These assessments allow teachers to gather data regarding a student's word recognition, fluency and comprehension skills, and types of errors. Depending on how the assessment is administered, words per minute and accuracy rates may also be obtained. Authentic tasks (Choice A) and rubrics (Choice D) do not provide systematic feedback on student performance in all areas of reading development. Choice B, norm-referenced assessments are not a quick assessment. They are intended to show a distribution of achievement and rank students in terms of their performance compared to their peers.

8. D   By recording errors, the teacher was able to note the student repeatedly left off word endings. This information can help guide future instruction to target word endings in isolation and within text, as well as to verify student understanding of the differences in word meanings when various endings (-ed, -ing, -s) are added. The running record does not show a pattern of errors in blending (Choice A), vocabulary (Choice B), or comprehension (Choice C).

9. A   To appropriately manage reading groups and instruction, teachers should rely on a variety of formal and informal assessments to determine appropriate targeted reading instruction and gauge progress. Data allows for teachers to best determine reading groups, levels, instruction and strategies. Students need to be assessed frequently (formally or informally) to monitor their progress and groups should remain fluid throughout the year or program.

10. D   A retelling is an oral or written summary of a reading. Retelling is a tool students can use to monitor comprehension. A multiple choice question (Choice A) is not a retelling. A question that asks students to make comparison to a different text is at an evaluative comprehension level (Choice B). Student selection of favorite work is designed to be an evaluative skill. Also, the selection is likely for a portfolio, not a retelling (Choice C).

6.3 Chapter Review

1. **A student is given the following sentence to read:**

    The dentist wears a mask and protective goggles when he treats each patient.

    Which of the following miscues is an example of substitution?
    A. *The denis wore*
    B. *and protection goggles*
    C. *dentist wears mask*
    D. *a mask on and*

2. **Each year a school administers a standardized test in a controlled environment in which the teacher uses scripted directions. The results provide data that shows how students compare to a control group of students of their same age or grade. What is this type of testing called?**
    A. a norm-referenced test
    B. a reliable test
    C. a criterion-referenced test
    D. a miscue analysis

3. **Students are given a reading comprehension test with a passage about baseball followed by several multiple choice questions. The results indicate that students with a thorough knowledge of baseball perform substantially better than students with little knowledge of baseball. Because the test assesses knowledge of baseball instead of reading comprehension, which of the following features could be questioned?**
    A. appropriateness
    B. bias
    C. reliability
    D. validity

4. A teacher has assigned a group project requiring students to work together to research a particular continent. Next, students must independently write a paragraph regarding a specific topic – the continent's weather patterns, native animals, food, culture, etc. Finally, students work together to use what they have learned and create a short presentation about their continent. Which of the following assessments would be best to use to determine individual student performance for group work, written work and oral presentation?

   A. Retelling
   B. Portfolio
   C. Running Record
   D. Rubric

5. An informal assessment is given in which students are asked to write down a list of regular decodable words dictated by the teacher. This type of assessment is intended to test what skill?

   A. phonological awareness
   B. print awareness
   C. sound-spelling relationship
   D. fluency

6. At the end of each quarter, a student is guided to review his writing for that quarter and choose a favorite selection to keep in a writing folder. These selections over the school year are intended to show the student's growth. What is the assessment type being used?

   A. portfolio
   B. running record
   C. rubric
   D. miscue analysis

7. At the beginning of a project, students are given a list of criteria with levels of achievement for each criteria. This guide will be used by teachers and classmates to assess the project. At the conclusion, the student can reflect on his achievement in each criteria. What is the assessment type being used?

A. running record
B. rubric
C. portfolio
D. retelling

8. Following the reading of a classic tale, students are given puppets and asked to retell the story. Which of the following features of the retelling would <u>not</u> likely be assessed when evaluating comprehension?

A. Were phonemes omitted? (e.g. The three bear walk in the forest.)
B. Was the retelling in chronological order?
C. Were puppets used correctly to represent the coordinating character from the tale?
D. Was significant vocabulary used appropriately? (e.g. straw, sticks, bricks)

9. A teacher is evaluating whether it is necessary to give a group of second-grade students reading assessments that include both lists of words and passages. Which statement gives an accurate method of testing reading development?

A. Give only the assessment on reading passages because it provides a complete report on decoding, comprehension, and fluency.
B. Give only the word list assessment because students who can read a list of words with accuracy have evidenced reading mastery.
C. Choose the appropriate assessment for each child so that there is not excessive time spent testing and the necessary data is collected.
D. Give both assessments so that a complete picture of decoding, use of context clues, comprehension, and fluency can be taken.

10. Which of the following is not a common use of student assessment?

A. to inform instruction

B. to evaluate student skills

C. to provide explicit instruction

D. to identify strengths and weaknesses

11. Which of the following statements best characterizes formal assessment?

A. ongoing assessment constructed by a classroom teacher which measures skill or knowledge progress

B. reading assessment which records student miscues and is used to guide instruction and grouping

C. a collection of student work selected by either teacher or student and used to show growth over a specified length of time

D. standardized assessment not constructed by a classroom teacher, administered with guidelines such as time limits, and providing data such as percentile

12. Following whole group instruction, the teacher gives a quick exit ticket question. This activity is an example of what type of assessment?

A. formal assessment

B. informal assessment

C. rubric

D. authentic task

13. Which of the following assessment types measures how a student performs against specific standards?

A. a norm-referenced test

B. a portfolio assessment

C. a criterion-referenced test

D. an Informal Reading Inventory

14. A kindergarten student is shown a big book and asked to point to the beginning of a sentence. This activity is designed to assess which of the following?
    A. phonological awareness
    B. book handling skills
    C. sound-spelling rules
    D. print awareness

15. Which of the following assessments promotes self-evaluation by the student?
    A. retelling
    B. norm-referenced test
    C. formal assessment
    D. portfolio

16. Third grade students are given a mock menu. To demonstrate their comprehension, students are requested to place an order from the menu. What type of assessment was conducted?
    A. assessment with an authentic task
    B. retelling
    C. norm-referenced test
    D. running record

17. Which of the following best describes miscue analysis?
    A. grading a spelling test over words with a specific phonics pattern
    B. examining the types of errors made by a student when orally reading a passage or list of words
    C. noting omissions or changes made in a retelling of the plot
    D. recording mispronunciations of words made by a student when reading a passage

18. **Which assessment is generally used to assess a student's independent, instructional, and frustration levels of reading?**
    A. dictated word list
    B. informal documentation of student behavior
    C. Informal Reading Inventory
    D. norm-referenced test

19. **On a standardized test, students following the belief system of one religion consistently score higher than students with other belief systems. Such a question would be an example of what testing concept?**
    A. bias
    B. reliability
    C. consistency
    D. validity

20. **Through assessments done the previous year, a teacher is aware of several highly proficient readers in her class. In administering beginning of year reading assessments that include vocabulary, fluency, comprehension and decoding components, which of the following should the teacher do?**
    A. For efficiency, allow the highly proficient readers to skip the assessment and place them all in the same reading group to start.
    B. Skim a few points of the assessment with the highly proficient readers so that they are not singled out.
    C. Review the results from the previous year with the former teacher to see if the assessment is reliable.
    D. Give all students the same, complete assessment.

CHAPTER REVIEW EXPLANATIONS

1. **B** The reader substituted *–tion* for *–tive*. The mispronunciation of *dentist* as *denis* (Choice A) is an omission of phonemes. Omission of *a* is a word omission (Choice C). Adding the word *on* is an insertion (Choice D).

2. A A norm-referenced test provides data which compares students to peers in a control group. Results are used for comparison at all levels from the individual to international. The test should be reliable (Choice B); however, it is not called a reliable test. A criterion-referenced test measures the student against a set of standards (Choice C). Miscue analysis (Choice D) evaluates the type of errors a student makes in reading.

3. D Test validity is the extent to which a test assesses what it claims to. A reading comprehension test in which good scores depend on a specific knowledge of a particular subject lacks validity. Appropriateness (Choice A) is not a standard feature evaluated for testing. Bias (Choice B) is the degree to which a certain groups of students are systematically advantaged or disadvantaged. Reliability (Choice C) is the degree to which testing results are consistent and repeatable in various situations.

4. D For this project, a rubric would be the best assessment tool. Because rubrics provide specified criteria for grading, they assist teachers in differentiating as they allow for various levels to be established. They also provide clear expectations for students, solid feedback and can be used to guide future instruction. Rubrics also involve learners in the process and give them a sense of ownership over their project and grade. Rubrics would be particularly useful for this project as they can be broken down by the varied components of the project: student's ability to work within a group, written work, oral presentation, etc. A retelling does not assess this project - retellings allow students the opportunity to orally or in writing recount the events within a particular passage, making Choice A incorrect. Portfolios are a form of assessment used over time and while components of the project may be included within individual student portfolios, this would not help a teacher to assess this project, also making Choice B incorrect. Running records (Choice C) also do not apply; teachers use running records to gauge student fluency and accuracy.

5. C Writing a list of dictated words that follow regular phonics rules will assess a student's skills in sound-spelling relationship. Phonological awareness (Choice A) is a student's ability to hear and manipulate sounds. Print awareness (Choice B) is a student's awareness that print carries meaning, awareness of print direction, and awareness of letters, words, and sentences. Fluency (Choice D) is the ability of a student to read with accuracy, prosody, and expression.

6. A A portfolio is a collection of student work. Students are often encouraged to select the pieces of their work they would like to include in their portfolio and to make evaluations about their work. The portfolio is intended to show student growth. A running record (Choice B) is a script that a teacher uses to record student errors on oral reading. A rubric (Choice C) is a differentiated list of criteria used to assess a work. Miscue analysis (Choice D) is a review conducted of a student's reading or writing which exposes the types of errors being made.

7. B A rubric is a list of specified criteria that is used for grading. It explains levels and provides feedback. A running record (Choice B) is a script that a teacher uses to record student errors on oral reading. A portfolio (Choice C) is a collection of student work. A retelling (Choice D) is an assessment in which a student reconstructs part of the plot or some other element of a selection.

8. A A retelling is a valuable means of assessing a student's oral language; however, this retelling was specifically geared to assessing comprehension. Comprehension can be assessed through retelling of a plot in order (Choice B), using characters appropriately (Choice C), and including significant vocabulary and repeated expressions of characters ("Who will help me bake the bread?") (Choice D)

9. D Different skills are needed to read a list and to read a passage. At the second-grade level, it is necessary to assess decoding without the benefit of context clues through reading a list. Comprehension and fluency can be assessed by the student's reading of a passage.

10. C Assessments can be learning experiences for students; however, they are not tools for explicit instruction. Assessments are used to inform instruction (Choice A), to evaluate and compare student skills (Choice B), and to identify strengths and weaknesses (Choice D).

11. D Formal assessment can be given at any level. It typically has strict guidelines for administration to ensure the reliability of the results. Ongoing assessment (Choice A) is informal assessment. Reading assessment that analyzes miscues (Choice B) can be a formal assessment; however, the immediate use of the results to guide instruction and groupings would be more characteristic of informal assessment. A collection of work (Choice C) is a portfolio assessment which does not provide quantitative data typical of formal assessments.

12. B Informal assessments measure content and performance skills. They may be constructed by teachers and administered with minimal scripted directions. Formal assessments (Choice A) include standardized tests which follow scripted directions and which can compare student results. A rubric (Choice C) is a list of criteria used to assess student work. While the exit question may be an authentic task (Choice D), the question does not provide enough information to draw that conclusion.

13. C Criterion-referenced tests measure how a student performs against specific standards and/or content objectives. These types of assessments are typically used in high stakes testing to assess a students' knowledge and skills in a specified area such as ability to compare and contrast the structure of two texts. Norm-referenced tests (Choice A) refer to assessments that show a distribution of achievement and rank students in terms of their performance compared to their peers. Portfolio assessments (Choice B) are often used to show individual student progress over time; they offer a place for multiple student assessments and/or work samples to be compiled. Finally, informal reading inventories (Choice D) provide information regarding a child's accuracy in reading words in isolation or in passages, fluency, and comprehension.

14. D Print awareness includes knowledge of print direction as well as knowledge that print carries a message, sentences begin with capital letters, and words have boundaries. Phonological awareness (Choice A) is tested through activities such as "Do these words rhyme?" and "How many claps are in this word?" Book handling skills (Choice B) refer to a reader's knowledge of where to begin reading and how to turn pages. Sound-spelling rules (Choice D) refer to the predictable patterns that guide spelling the sounds of regular words.

15. D Student selection of which work to include in a portfolio promotes self-evaluation. The student typically gives some thought to why he would include one piece and omit another. A retelling is a reconstruction done independently by the student; however the student does not necessarily have to evaluate his performance in the retelling (Choice A). Norm referenced (Choice B) and formal assessments (Choice C) provide results to parents and educators which do not include an evaluation by the student.

16. A An authentic task assessment is one in which students are given a real world setting or a near replication of a real world setting. A retelling (Choice B) using the menu might request that the student look at the menu and then list from memory as many items as possible from the menu. A norm-referenced test is a standardized test that uses data to compare students to their peers (Choice C). A running record (Choice D) is a script that a teacher uses to record student errors on oral reading.

17. B Miscue analysis is the examination of a running record which gives insight into the types of errors (omissions, substitutions, miscalling, etc.) being made by a reader. The emphasis is on not just noting the errors, as is done in grading a spelling test (Choice A) or recording miscues on a running record (Choice D). It is on analysis of those errors. Miscue analysis is not typically connected to retelling (Choice C).

18. C An IRI is a test in which a student reads a passage. The student's accuracy and comprehension are analyzed to determine the reading level. A dictated word list (Choice A) is used to test letter-sound knowledge. Informal documentation (Choice B) is valuable but would prove inefficient for gathering information on a class of readers. A norm-referenced test (Choice D) may not give the immediate results needed on student reading level.

19. A A biased question or test is one that is written in a way that it advantages or disadvantages one group of the testing community over another. Biases may be based on gender, race, etc. Reliability (Choice B) and consistency (Choice C) are the extent to which results are the same in various or repeated testing situations. Validity (Choice D) is the extent to which a test assesses what it is intended to assess.

20. D Every student in the class needs to be assessed so instruction can be appropriately targeted. Omitting the test (Choice A), skimming through it (Choice B), and reviewing the previous test (Choice C) will not provide a baseline for the students' current strengths and weaknesses.

Open Response

The open response section of the Foundations of Reading contains two questions that account for 20% of your subtest score. The open response section of the test is designed to evaluate your deep understanding of reading foundations as well as your ability to explain and teach those concepts to others. You should allow no less than 60 minutes to complete the open response questions on exam day.

Your answer should be approximately 150-300 words. You should allow time to plan, write, revise, and edit so that the finished response is a polished, well-developed response written in standard, academic English. Two scorers will review your answer; it needs to be clear and easy to read.

A strong response demonstrates mastery of the foundations of reading development, the development of reading comprehension, and reading assessment and instruction. This lesson provides some strategies for constructing a strong response. The practice section includes sample prompts with strong and weak responses and analyses.

Evaluation Criteria

Open response questions are scored according to a set of standard performance characteristics.

Performance Characteristic	Definition
Purpose	⊙ The extent to which the response achieves the purpose of the assignment
Subject Knowledge	⊙ The appropriateness and accuracy in the application of subject matter

Support	⊙ Quality and relevance of supporting evidence
Rationale	⊙ Soundness of arguments and degree of understanding of the subject area

Score Point	Description
4	**Reflects a thorough knowledge and understanding of the subject matter.** ⊙ Purpose of the assignment is fully achieved. ⊙ Substantial and accurate use of subject matter knowledge. ⊙ Supporting evidence is sound with high quality and relevant examples. ⊙ Response reflects an ably reasoned and comprehensive understanding of topic.
3	**Reflects an adequate knowledge and understanding of the subject matter.** ⊙ Purpose of the assignment is largely achieved. ⊙ Generally accurate and appropriate use of subject matter knowledge. ⊙ Supporting evidence is adequate with some acceptable, relevant examples. ⊙ Response reflects an adequately reasoned understanding of topic.
2	**Reflects a limited knowledge and understanding of the subject matter.** ⊙ Purpose of the assignment is partially achieved. ⊙ Limited, possibly inaccurate or inappropriate use of subject matter knowledge. ⊙ Supporting evidence is limited with few relevant examples. ⊙ Response reflects a limited, poorly reasoned understanding of topic.
1	**Reflects a weak knowledge and understanding of the subject matter.** ⊙ Purpose of the assignment is not achieved. ⊙ Little or no appropriate or accurate use of subject matter knowledge. ⊙ Supporting evidence, if present, is weak; there are few or no relevant examples. ⊙ Response reflects little or no reasoning or understanding of the topic.

Constructing a Strong Response

Address All Tasks

The first listed criterion for the open response question is the extent to which the candidate has completed the assignment. That means that your primary goal is to accurately answer all of the questions asked of you in the prompt. Your first step should be to identify your tasks, and your last step should be to make sure that you have completed all of your tasks.

Identify the Skills Required

After reading through the problem, identify the specific skills and concepts you will need to complete it. An open response question consists of a number of tasks. Look for keywords in each part of the problem to help you quickly figure out the methods required. Typically, the question prompt will include some wording to give you guidance (e.g., *"Use your knowledge of assessment strategies to..."*).

Demonstrate Your Understanding

Much of your score will be based on your ability to show understanding of the subject matter. Explain the reasoning behind your approach to each part of the question. In a sense, the test graders are using this response to evaluate your potential as a teacher. They want to see that you can explain concepts to elementary school children. A strong response analyzes the way that a hypothetical student has responded and substantiates the analysis with insightful observations about the student work.

Write Your Answer Clearly

Two scorers will review your answer, so it needs to be clear and easy to read. Use your scratch paper to make notes and structure your response. When you are happy with your approach, write it as a clear and cohesive solution. The response should be structured to match the order of the tasks.

Using Criteria to Construct a Strong Response

Purpose

Writing a strong response depends on a thorough understanding of the prompt. It is important to take time to read and consider what is being asked in the question. Plot out both the content and organizational structure that will be necessary for an effective response.

Prompts often contain multiple specific requirements. Prompts may require a discussion of both the strengths and weaknesses of a student's work, or a response may be specific to one area of reading (i.e. development, comprehension, assessment, etc.). The key words in the prompt should be appropriately included in the response. The prompt will likely contain more issues than can be addressed in a 300-word response. A strong response focuses on the most important aspects and overlooks the inconsequential. The purpose is achieved by thoroughly and specifically addressing the prompt as it is written.

Your first step is to identify your tasks, and your last step is to make sure that you have completed all of your tasks.

Subject Knowledge

Writing a strong response also depends on knowledge of the foundations of reading. After reading through the problem, identify the specific skills and concepts you will need to include in the answer. An open response question consists of a number of tasks. Look for keywords in each part to help you quickly figure out the response required. Typically, the question prompt will include some wording to give you guidance (e.g., *"Use your knowledge of phonemic awareness to..."*). Prompts are fashioned so that candidates must demonstrate and apply their mastery throughout the response. A strong response will go beyond the obvious and address subtleties. Strong responses avoid ambiguity and generalizations. Judges are looking for candidates who are confident in their knowledge and can draw accurate conclusions based on evidence. One way of demonstrating knowledge of the subject area is to include specific vocabulary. It is crucial that your response accurately use terminology such as phoneme, grapheme, segment, syntax, etc.. The accuracy of your observations and strategies contributes directly to your scores for each characteristic.

If the question is about....	Consider the specialized terminology.
Phonological and phonemic awareness	⊙ Rhyming, segmenting, blending, deleting, substituting, onset, rime, syllables, explicit/implicit strategies, words, phonemes
Print and alphabetic principle	⊙ Letter/sound relationship, environmental print, book handling, letter knowledge, spoken/written language, print directionality, tracking print, connected text, letter formation
Phonics and reading development	⊙ Phoneme, morpheme, consonant digraph, diphthong, consonant blend, sight words, decoding, encoding, semantics, syntax, patterns (CVC, CVVC, CVCe), automaticity, multi-syllable words, fluency
Word analysis	⊙ Affix (prefix, suffix), morpheme, grapheme, base word, homograph, context clues, roots, inflections, structural analysis, analysis/fluency/comprehension, syllabication, word identification, self-correction
Vocabulary	⊙ Oral language, idiom, content-area vocabulary, semantics, syntax, non-contextual strategies, listening, unfamiliar words, academic language, conventions,
Imaginative texts	⊙ Fluency, figurative language, comprehension levels (literal, inferential, evaluative), graphic organizers, story elements, point of view, genres, metacognition, retelling, multiple works, close reading, connections, conclusions, rereading, visualizing, reviewing, self-monitoring, versions
Informational/ Expository texts	⊙ Self-monitoring, preview/review, student-generated questions, outlining, summary, KWL chart, text structures, text features, integrating, multiple sources, comprehension levels (literal, inferential, evaluative), close reading, point of view, fact/opinion, multiple accounts, strategies for reading, skimming/scanning, fluency, graphic features, reference materials, electronic texts

If the question is about....	Consider the specialized terminology.
Formal and informal methods of assessment	⊙ Validity, bias, reliability, miscue, reading inventory, running record, rubric, portfolio, data, standardized criterion-referenced and norm-referenced tests, challenges and supports in a text, student level
Multiple approaches to instruction	⊙ Differentiation, small group, individual, theories, approaches, practices, ongoing assessment, strategies to promote skills, text complexity, balance, environment
Language learner	⊙ Native language proficiency, vocabulary, academic English, distinguish sounds, English phonemes, cognates, oral language, nonverbal support, silent period

Support

Much of your score will be based on your ability to explain the reasoning behind your observations. In a sense, the test graders are using this response to evaluate your potential as a teacher. They want to see that you can explain concepts to elementary school children. Focus on strategies that would promote students' development of skills. This does not mean that you should use child-like language. The grader is an adult and expects to read a well-developed solution written in accurate, academic English.

Every observation must be supported with relevant, substantial evidence. Examples cited should be of high quality. Support can be both paraphrased and quoted directly from the text of the question. The candidate's knowledge of foundations of reading is essential for assessing student responses and for analyzing how and why students responded as they did. Strong responses make the critical connection between reading theory (i.e. word analysis) and student examples (i.e. student miscued *disheartened*). Rather than saying, "Caleb could not read *disheartened*," say, "Caleb's inability to decipher *disheartened* demonstrates that he has not yet mastered segmenting words into roots (*heart*) and affixes (*dis-*, *-en*, *-ed*)." A strong response connects both skills and concepts.

Rationale

The reasoning behind the observations made in the response must be sound and comprehensive. The response must connect any conclusions to the whole picture. Though likely answering several questions such as strengths, weaknesses, and strategies, the response should still be tightly bound to communicate a clear focus. Observations should not contradict or be confusing. A clear strategy should be outlined. Vague notions in place of precise terminology render a weak response. Rather than saying, "She could not read all the words," say, "She substituted digraph /sh/ for /ch/ in the word *chair*."

The Approach

Use the free space on your test booklet to list key terminology, to make notes, and to structure your response. When you are satisfied with your approach, write it on your answer sheet as a clear and cohesive response. The response should be structured to match the order of the prompt.

Complete Steps 1-7 in the free space on the test booklet. You do not need to write in complete sentences until Step 8.

1. Read the entire prompt, circling or otherwise marking each part of your assignment.
2. Identify what category of reading development (i.e. phonemic awareness, imaginative literature, instructional practices, etc.) is being addressed.
3. Identify the terminology necessary to answer the prompt.
4. Identify concepts necessary to assess the student and the specific instances of those concepts.
5. If directed, look for an instructional strategy, preferably one that is specific and student-friendly. Give a detailed description of this strategy. This strategy demonstrates your deep understanding of the foundations of reading and allows you to apply your understanding.
6. If applicable, compare your strategy with the provided student response. Identify weaknesses in the skills and concepts used by the student and suggest methods for developing the student's skills.
7. Make sure that your response is accurate and complete (fulfills all tasks).
8. *Complete response in the online system.* Structure your work to match the order in which the tasks were assigned. Write your cohesive response in paragraph form.

Plan responses for questions about

- ⊙ The role of phonological and phonemic awareness in reading development
- ⊙ The development of alphabetic knowledge
- ⊙ The role of phonics in developing rapid, automatic word recognition
- ⊙ The development of word analysis and strategies in addition to phonics, including structural analysis
- ⊙ The relationship between vocabulary development and reading comprehension
- ⊙ The use of comprehension strategies before, during, and after reading imaginative texts
- ⊙ Knowledge of organizational patterns in informational/expository texts
- ⊙ Techniques for assessing particular reading skills
- ⊙ Strategies for planning, organizing, managing, and differentiating reading instruction to support the reading development of all students

Using your knowledge of the comprehension strategies that are necessary for literary analysis, write a response in which you:

- ⊙ Identify and discuss Kayla's strengths in reading comprehension based on her literary analysis skills.
- ⊙ Identify and discuss Kayla's weaknesses in reading comprehension based on her literary analysis skills.
- ⊙ Identify and discuss an instructional strategy that can help improve Kayla's comprehension.

Kayla, a fourth-grade student, read independently the following passage from Chapter 2 of *Heidi* **and then completed the graphic organizer.**

Meanwhile, Heidi was content to look about her. She discovered the goats' shed built near the hut and peeped into it. It was empty. The child continued her investigations and came to the fir trees behind the hut. The wind was blowing hard, and it whistled and roared through the branches, high up in the tops. Heidi stood still and listened. When it subsided somewhat she went around to the other side of the hut and came back to her grandfather. When she found him in the same place where she had left him, she placed herself in front of him, put her hands behind her, and gazed at him. Her grandfather looked up.

"What do you want to do?" he asked as the child continued standing in front of him without moving.

"I want to see what you have in that hut," said Heidi.

"Come along, then...Bring your bundle of clothes," he said as he entered.

"I shan't want them any more," replied Heidi.

The old man turned around and looked sharply at the child, whose black eyes shone in expectation of what might be inside.

"She's not lacking in intelligence," he said half to himself,

"Why won't you need them any more?" he asked aloud.

"I'd rather go like the goats, with their swift little legs."
"So you shall, but bring the things along," commanded the
grandfather, "they can be put in the cupboard."
Heidi obeyed.

Heidi
By Johanna Spyri

Connection to <u>the world</u>. *Police and scientists do investigations to make discoveries.*	**Connection to <u>the world</u>.** *I saw mountain goats at the zoo. They could climb anything.*
In your words: *Heidi looked all around the grandfather's shed and hut. She wanted to see all around.*	**In your words:** *She wants to be able to run over the hills like the goats do.*
Evidence from text: *"The child continued her investigation…I want to see what you have in that hut."*	**Evidence from text:** *"I'd rather go like the goats, with their swift little legs."*
Character trait: *curious*	**Character trait:** *athletic*

Character: *Heidi*

Character trait: *discontent*	**Character trait:** *obedient*
Evidence from text: *"I shan't want them any more,"*	**Evidence from text:** *"Heidi obeyed."*
In your words: *Heidi doesn't want her old clothes any more. She wants the grandfather to get her different clothes.*	**In your words:** *Heidi obeyed the grandfather when he told her to get her clothes.*
Connection to <u>self</u>. *I like to get new clothes too.*	**Connection to <u>text</u>.** *This reminds me of Laura in the <u>Little House</u> books. She was obedient too.*

During the first week of kindergarten, the following observations have been made of Michael and Tommy based on both formal and informal evaluations.

Michael
⊙ Claps syllables of classmates' names
⊙ Produces nonsense word "zon" to rhyme with Shawn
⊙ Demonstrates knowledge of letter names when independently pretend-reading *Chicka Chicka Boom Boom*
⊙ Points to label of "literacy center" and reads *library*

Tommy
⊙ Responds to question "What did you do today?" with "I cook french fry Michael."
⊙ Produces the word *friend* to rhyme with Michael.
⊙ Pretend reads *Brown Bear, Brown Bear* in what is assumedly his native language
⊙ Points to label of "Art Center" and says "picture."

Using your knowledge of reading development, write a response in which you:
⊙ Identify student strengths
⊙ Identify student weaknesses
⊙ Identify an instructional strategy to promote skill development

Strong response

Kayla's character analysis reveals strengths and weaknesses in her reading comprehension skills. The characteristics *curious* and *obedient* demonstrate her accurate comprehension on a literal and inferential level. After reading a short passage, she is able to select four statements about Heidi (i.e. "Heidi obeyed."), draw her own conclusions to make inferences about Heidi's character traits (if Heidi states, "I want to see what you have in that hut," she must be curious), interpret literally (i.e. "She wanted to see all around"), and connect beyond the text. While some errors are made in comprehension, she has commendable skill reading on literal and inferential levels and uses the text as evidence for character analysis.

Kayla's graphic organizer reveals some weaknesses. She neglects context cues ("Bring your bundle of clothes") and misinterprets the figurative language in which Heidi compares herself to the goats: "I'd rather go like the goats". Kayla was unable to conclude that Heidi wants to go without clothes, as the goats do. With the misinterpretation, Kayla concludes that Heidi wants to run like goats and wants new clothes.

The instructional strategy that can improve Kayla's reading comprehension is guiding her to close reading and using context to interpret figurative language. The grandfather requests that Heidi "bring your bundle of clothes." Heidi obediently gets her clothes, so the context for the conversation is securing her current clothing, not shopping for new clothes or running with the goats. Guiding Kayla to recognize the use of figurative language within the context will improve her ability to interpret accurately beyond the literal level (i.e. "Heidi obeyed.") The strategies of close reading and using context cues to interpret figurative language will be useful for her when analyzing story elements of imaginative text.

Analysis of strong response

Performance Characteristic	Definition
Purpose	**The extent to which the response achieves the purpose of the assignment** **Analysis:** The candidate fulfills the purpose of the assignment by identifying in the stated order strengths, weaknesses, and instructional strategies. The candidate cites evidence from the graphic organizer (i.e. curious, obedient, "I want to see in that hut") to support observations. The response is clear, accurate, and appropriate for a prompt focused on reading comprehension.
Subject Knowledge	**The appropriateness and accuracy in the application of subject matter** **Analysis:** The candidate shows a strong understanding of the strategies for reading comprehension by mentioning literal and inferential levels of comprehension. Use of subject matter terminology is strong (graphic organizer, context, close reading, and figurative language).
Support	**Quality and relevance of supporting evidence** **Analysis:** The support is substantial and relevant. Aware that he could not thoroughly address all points, the candidate makes only passing reference to connections and focuses on comprehension strategies. The specific strategy of using context to interpret figurative language demonstrates an ability to diagnose a student's needs and put a strategy in place to guide the student.

Performance Characteristic	Definition
Rationale	**Soundness of arguments and degree of understanding of the subject area** **Analysis:** This response is well reasoned and presents a unified discussion of Kayla's comprehension as it relates to character analysis. The conclusion aptly broadens to show how comprehension strategies are related to analysis of story elements ("The strategies of close reading and using context clues will be useful for her when analyzing story elements of imaginative text.")

Weak response

Kayla has strengths and weaknesses in reading comprehension. She is able to read at grade level. She knows how to use a graphic organizer to support her comprehension. She is weak in her understanding of the idiom "like the goats." She thinks Heidi wants to run like a goat. Also, she is weak in word analysis. She is unable to read the words well enough to figure out what the story is saying. Kayla has some strengths. She creatively figures out that Heidi is curious. She makes a good connection to a police investigation, to the zoo, to herself, and to other book characters.

There are some instructional strategies that can help Kayla. The most beneficial would be a small group. In the small group, students can do pair readings out loud and discuss their understanding of the reading. Together they can help each other fill out their graphic organizers. In addition to small-group work, Kayla can study word analysis so she can read all the words and comprehend the story.

Performance Characteristic	Definition
Purpose	***The extent to which the response achieves the purpose of the assignment*** **Analysis:** The candidate attempts to respond to the prompt by addressing strengths, weaknesses, and strategies in a general way. Judges are looking for the response to follow the same order as the prompt. This response instead discusses weaknesses and then strengths. While some valid observations are made, the response makes the unsubstantiated observation that Kayla is weak in word analysis.
Subject Knowledge	***The appropriateness and accuracy in the application of subject matter*** **Analysis:** The candidate's knowledge is limited. Figurative language "like a goat" is mistakenly called an idiom. Most importantly, the candidate does not demonstrate knowledge of how to structure a classroom in which students are reading various books. Kayla is reading <u>Heidi</u> independently. She needs strategies to help her comprehension as she reads independently. Certainly, small groups are used successfully in many classrooms, but candidates must be prepared to address the specific issue in the prompt (supporting independent readers), not just depend on general classroom strategies. While the response uses some terminology from the prompt accurately (i.e. graphic organizer, comprehension), additional terminology introduced (idiom, small group, word analysis) is inaccurate or inappropriate for the response.

Performance Characteristic	Definition
Support	***Quality and relevance of supporting evidence*** **Analysis:** The candidate does not demonstrate an ability to draw accurate conclusions. The claim that Kayla has weak word analysis skills lacks support. The graphic organizer gives no indication that Kayla's word analysis skills account for her errors in comprehension. While the statement "She is able to read at grade level" is likely accurate for this fourth grade student, it is unsubstantiated in the response.
Rationale	***Soundness of arguments and degree of understanding of the subject area*** **Analysis:** Rationale is weak because the candidate is unable to connect information about the student skills in the prompt to knowledge of reading development in order to create an instructional strategy for an independent reader. The candidate's observation of Kayla's strengths in making connections ("to a police investigation, to the zoo, to herself, and to other book characters") is not effectively used to develop a unified response to the prompt.

Strong Response

Both Michael and Tommy are making developmental progress toward reading. Both students demonstrate print awareness by pointing to classroom labels and making guesses that fit the context. Both students interact with books and show an understanding of the fact that the text carries meaning. Michael recognizes letters. Tommy's reading of *Brown Bear* demonstrates that he is aware that a story is attached to that specific book, although he does not demonstrate letter name knowledge. Both students show evidence of being at different levels of phonological and phonemic awareness. Michael is able to segment and produce a rhyme. Furthermore, he demonstrates knowledge of the alphabetic principle by naming letters in *Chicka Chicka* and "reading" literacy as library. While his reading is a miscue, he appears aware that the letter "l" produces the /l/ sound. Tommy does not demonstrate knowledge of phonics. He does not connect specific letters of "Art Center" to any sound in the word *picture*. His reading of *Brown Bear, Brown Bear* does not match the English graphemes. There appear to be English phonemes which Tommy does not yet distinguish. His inability to hear English phonemes is demonstrated by dropping word endings like /t/ in cook(ed) and /z/ in fry(s).

While both students can benefit from whole group activities, both students also require differentiated instruction. Tommy will benefit from intensive instruction in English phonemes to enhance his oral language skills, which typically precede reading skills. Michael will benefit from methodical phonics instruction so that he can learn the sound-spelling relationship of all English phonemes. Given a unit study of traditional tales such as *The Three Pigs*, *Three Goats*, and *Three Bears*, Tommy can practice retelling the stories with specific vocabulary including pig*s*, goat*s*, bear*s*, buil*t*, and cross*ed*. Michael can practice letters and sounds he has been introduced to by reading, spelling, and doing close activities with CVC words such as "pig," "big," and "bed." The balance of whole group and small group activities will benefit both students.

Performance Characteristic	Definition
Purpose	*The extent to which the response achieves the purpose of the assignment* Analysis: The candidate fulfills the purpose of the assignment by identifying strengths, weaknesses, and instructional strategies. The response cites evidence from the student evaluations to support his observations (i.e. "Both students demonstrate print awareness by pointing to classroom labels and making guesses that fit the context.") The response is thorough, clear, accurate, and appropriate for a prompt focused on reading development.
Subject Knowledge	*The appropriateness and accuracy in the application of subject matter* Analysis: The candidate shows a strong understanding of the development of reading. (i.e. The response indicates that a student with phonological and phonemic awareness is ready to begin methodical phonics study since once a few letters and sounds are introduced, the student can begin reading. Furthermore, the candidate recognizes that oral language typically precedes reading.) Use of subject matter terminology is strong (grapheme, differentiated, oral language).
Support	*Quality and relevance of supporting evidence* Analysis: The support is substantial. The candidate proves to be aware that it is not possible to thoroughly address all points by making a reference to such skills as segmenting syllables and instead focuses on the skills such as the alphabetic principle and the awareness of /l/ to speak on appropriate instructional strategies appropriate for Michael. The incorporation of popular stories for instruction of both students demonstrates that the candidate knows how to balance whole group and small group activities in an authentic instructional setting.

Performance Characteristic	Definition
Rationale	***Soundness of arguments and degree of understanding of the subject area*** **Analysis:** This response reflects a comprehensive knowledge of reading development in early childhood. The candidate was able to use the evaluation of student skills to identify the level of each student and to create a specific, appropriate strategy for instruction. (Tommy can practice retelling the stories with specific vocabulary including pig<u>s</u>, goat<u>s</u>, bear<u>s</u>, buil<u>t</u>, and cross<u>ed</u>.) The response communicates a unified message that identifies strengths and weaknesses of two students and creates a strategy for classroom use.

Weak Response

Michael and Tommy are kindergarten students. Their language levels were evaluated by their teacher during the first week.

Michael can clap syllables, produce rhymes, and name the letters. Those are his strengths. He cannot read a label. That is his weakness. Tommy can answer questions, and say *Brown Bear, Brown Bear* in his native language. Those are his strengths. He cannot produce rhymes or read labels. Those are his weaknesses. The best instructional strategy is to teach these students separately. Michael is ready to learn sight words like "center." Tommy needs to learn the letters of the alphabet. Tommy needs to learn English vocabulary like "rhyme," "art," "bear," and the colors. Those are words that Michael probably knows, so it is important for Michael to have different lessons while Tommy learns basic vocabulary. By giving Michael and Tommy separate lessons, each student will learn what he needs to to improve his language skills by the end of kindergarten.

Performance Characteristic	Definition
Purpose	***The extent to which the response achieves the purpose of the assignment*** **Analysis:** The candidate attempts to answer by addressing strengths, weaknesses, and strategies in a general way. Approximately 1/3 of the response was a restatement of the prompt with overly simplified observations. While some valid observations are made, the response does not adequately address Tommy's language development as it relates to reading.
Subject Knowledge	***The appropriateness and accuracy in the application of subject matter*** **Analysis:** The candidate's knowledge is limited. While it is appropriate that Michael would learn beginning sight words, "center" is a decodable word that would be learned through a systematic approach to phonics. It is not a sight word. Tommy demonstrates knowledge of basic vocabulary through his use of the words "cook," "french fry," and "friend." Most importantly, the candidate does not demonstrate knowledge of how to structure and organize a classroom. Teach "students separately" is inadequate. Subject matter vocabulary is lacking.
Support	***Quality and relevance of supporting evidence*** **Analysis:** The candidate does not demonstrate an ability to see past the obvious. While the candidate restates general strengths and weaknesses, he fails to use the evaluation to make observations about the students' reading development. (i.e. no mention is made of English phonemes possibly missing in Tommy's native language.) "Michael is ready to learn sight words" is not an adequate instructional strategy.

Performance Characteristic	Definition
Rationale	***Soundness of arguments and degree of understanding of the subject area*** **Analysis:** Rationale is particularly weak. The candidate is unable to connect information about the student skills in the prompt to knowledge of reading development in order to create an instructional strategy for a kindergarten classroom. The response is vague ("needs to learn" and "language skills."). It fails to communicate a unified message that connects the students and strategies.

Diagnostic Exam

1. A teacher says the word *school* aloud and then says, "I wonder what would happen if I replaced /sk/ with /p/." Which phonological awareness skill is the teacher modeling?
   A. Substituting
   B. Blending
   C. Segmenting
   D. Deleting

2. A kindergarten teacher says, "/r/, r" while writing the letter "r" on the board. Students then trace the letter on a piece of paper. This activity is an example of which type of instruction?
   A. Implicit instruction in phonics
   B. Modeling print directionality
   C. Explicit instruction of alphabetic principle
   D. Explicit instruction in phonological awareness

3. A first grader struggles to read the word *drum*. The teacher asks the student to read the word *hum* and use that knowledge to read *drum*. Which skill is the student working on in this activity?
   A. Blending fluency for automaticity
   B. Phonemic awareness skills
   C. Decoding using familiar rimes
   D. Structural analysis skills

4. **A kindergarten teacher begins most days with a morning message written in large print. One day, the message said the following:**

> Good morning, Starfish,
> Today is Tuesday, December 9, 2014. We have been in
> school _____ days. After lunch, we will go to art.
> Love,
> Ms. Kelly

Which aspects of reading development is a morning message designed to promote?

A. Word boundaries, letter formation, print directionality, environmental print

B. Print directionality, word boundaries, tracking print in connected text, print carries meaning

C. Decoding, phonemic awareness, segmenting, word boundaries

D. Letter formation, phonemes represented by letters, print carries meaning, word analysis

5. **Which question assesses beginning phonemic awareness?**

A. How many words are in the sentence, "He ate rice"?

B. What is the first sound in *cow*?

C. Show a letter. What letter is this?

D. What are all the sounds in *o-ver*?

6. **A kindergarten teacher asks students to say the word** *football* **and then say it again without saying** *foot*. **This activity is appropriate for students who can do which of the following?**

A. Given the phonemes /p/, /o/, /t/, the student can blend to form the word *pot*.

B. Given the sentence "I love rice," the student can count the three words.

C. Given the letter cards *d, g, o,* the student can form the word *dog*.

D. Given the words *set, pet,* and *pass,* the student can identify *set* and *pet* as rhyming words.

7. **A first grader decodes the words** *trap*, *flip*, **and** *talk*, **but miscues the words** *seat*, *found*, **and** *school*. **Which assessment accurately describes the student's reading abilities?**
   A. The student successfully decodes words that follow the CVC pattern.
   B. The student struggles to decode consonant blends.
   C. The student struggles to decode diphthongs.
   D. The student successfully decodes monosyllabic words.

8. **A student claps the number of sounds heard in the following words. The teacher records the number of times the student claps in the chart below. Based on the information given, this student would most benefit from which activity?**

Word	Sounds Clapped
sat	3
top	3
scoop	3
scream	4

   A. Divide words into onset and rime and count the number of sounds in each.
   B. Use alliteration to create words with the initial consonant in *scoop*.
   C. Model how to create words by substituting an /l/ for the /p/ in *scoop*.
   D. Ask the student to clap the number of syllables in *scoop* and *scream*.

9. **A fourth-grade student struggles to comprehend the word** *proactive*. **The teacher asks the student to break it into** *pro* **and** *active* **and then think about the meaning. Which word analysis skill for unfamiliar words is the teacher promoting?**
   A. Semantic cues
   B. Alliteration
   C. Word order
   D. Structural analysis

10. **Which activity could a teacher do to promote comprehension of a text that contains difficult idioms?**
    A. Model how to use idioms in context
    B. Ask students to look up the expression in the dictionary
    C. Provide note cards with words and ask students to divide them into similar sounds
    D. Teach students how to look at affixes

11. **Students are given the following activity.**

    Matching: Draw a line to match the two words that make a new word.

yard	brush
water	stick
tooth	ground
play	bell
door	melon

    This activity is intended to promote which of the following:
    A. Apply knowledge of roots and affixes
    B. Use knowledge of Latin and Greek roots
    C. Identify homographs
    D. Understand the concept of compound words

12. **Which of the following statements best describes the role of fluency in reading development?**
    A. Fluency develops naturally as a student engages with a variety of texts.
    B. Fluency improves enjoyment in reading, but it has little impact on comprehension.
    C. Fluency is evident in a student who reads accurately at a rate that helps comprehension and with intonation and expression that sound similar to the student's speech.
    D. Fluency is improved by incorporating context clues into decoding and word identification.

13. **Which of the following blanks is the best fit for a word with the suffix** –able/-ible?

> The ____(1)____ pilot ____(2)____ the plane ___ (3)_____ down the runway and toward the ____(4)____.

A. (1)
B. (2)
C. (3)
D. (4)

14. **A fifth-grade social studies teacher has selected the following vocabulary words: racism, integrate, segregate, riot, march, boycott. Which strategy was used to select these words?**
   A. Identify cognates
   B. Select representative words with high utility
   C. Use structural analysis
   D. Promote use of semantics

15. **During a read aloud, a preschool teacher follows with her finger, pointing to each word read. How will this activity most likely help reading development?**
   A. It promotes an awareness of print directionality.
   B. It promotes book-handling skills.
   C. It promotes phonological awareness.
   D. It promotes awareness of environmental print.

16. **A second-grade student has been assessed as having limited oral language. How does limited oral vocabulary usually affect the student's reading?**
   A. The student has trouble with letter-sound patterns.
   B. The student has difficulty comprehending decoded words.
   C. The student miscues high-frequency words.
   D. The student still reads with age-appropriate fluency.

17. **A sixth-grade class is starting a unit on American presidents. Before reading a passage on George Washington silently, the teacher asks students what they already know. How does this activity promote reading comprehension?**
    A. It promotes structural analysis.
    B. It promotes literary analysis skills.
    C. It promotes schema building.
    D. It promotes literary response skills.

18. **A fourth-grade teacher reads aloud to model good reading practices. The following is a sample of the reading:**

    Doctor Dolittle, by Hugh Lofting
    Oh, I watched a movie about Dr. Dolittle. I wonder whether the movie came from this book.

    "He was very fond of animals and kept many kinds of pets. Besides the gold-fish in the pond at the bottom of his garden, he had rabbits in the pantry, white mice in his piano, (I wonder why he lets mice in his piano) a squirrel in the linen closet and a hedgehog in the cellar. (I can just see that hedgehog in the linen closet.)"

    Which strategy of good readers is this teacher promoting?

    A. Internalizing the alphabetic principle
    B. Metacognitive strategies
    C. Decoding to facilitate fluency and comprehension
    D. Using semantic cues to help identify words

19. **A fourth-grade class is directed to take notes while silently reading a textbook chapter. How does this reading activity promote comprehension?**
    A. Note-taking can be an effective strategy for schema building.
    B. Note-taking allows students to work on literary response skills.

C. Note-taking provides a chance for students to use oral metacognitive strategies.

D. Note-taking encourages active reading and promotes summarizing skills.

20. **In a fifth-grade class, students are reading a text on the battles that occurred during the Revolutionary War. Which of the following graphic organizers would be best to promote comprehension?**

A. A semantic map

B. A KWL chart

C. A story map

D. A timeline

21. **A sixth-grade class is reading a high-interest trade book. Which activity promotes development of literary analysis skills?**

A. Students use text features to answer questions.

B. Students use metacognitive strategies while reading.

C. Students write an essay on the symbolism used in the book.

D. Students use semantic word maps.

22. **Base your answer on the selection given from "The Pied Piper."**

Into the street the Piper stept,
Smiling first a little smile,
As if he knew what magic slept
In his quiet pipe the while,
Then, like a musical adept,
To blow the pipe his lips he wrinkled,...
And ere three shrill notes the pipe uttered,
You heard as if an army muttered;...
And out of the houses the rats came tumbling.
Great rats, small rats, lean rats, browny rats,
Brown rats, black rats, grey rats, tawny rats,
Grave old plodders, gay young friskers,
Fathers, mothers, uncles, cousins,

Cocking tails and priking whiskers,
Families by tens and dozens,
Brothers, sisters, husbands, wives—
Followed the Piper for their lives...
Until they came to the river Weser'
Wherein all plunged and perished.

After reading "The Pied Piper" aloud in class, fifth-grade students give the following oral retelling.

"A man has a magic pipe. When he blows it, an army of people comes out of their houses to follow him. There are so many that they are like rats. The families think they are going to be saved by the music, but in the end, they all die when they get thrown in the river."

This retelling demonstrates that the student

A. Comprehends accurately on a literal level but not on an inferential level.
B. Comprehends on an evaluative level but not on the literal level
C. Misinterprets figurative language in a way that interferes with comprehension.
D. Lacks essential vocabulary to comprehend the account.

23. **Which activity demonstrates what might occur in an oral retelling used to assess comprehension?**
    A. A student reads a passage and then orally relates to the teacher what he or she understood.
    B. A student reads a passage and then writes a response summarizing what he or she understood.
    C. A student explains what he or she knows about the passage's main topic before reading it.
    D. A student reads aloud a passage with another student and then discusses it.

24. **An English Language Learner can comprehend high-interest trade books in English but demonstrates difficulty comprehending material in a content-area textbook. Which describes the likely source of difficulty?**
    A. Insufficient academic vocabulary
    B. Weak skills in decoding unfamiliar words
    C. Deficiency in automatically recognizing phonetic patterns
    D. Failure to master analytical skills

25. **Which assessment tool is effective for tracking a student's independent, frustration, and instructional levels of reading?**
    A. Re-telling
    B. Scoring rubric
    C. Informal Reading Inventory
    D. Norm-referenced survey

26. **In a third-grade class, after students read an excerpt from a short story called "A Mouse's Life," the teacher asks the students, "What would you do if you were Morton?" Students discuss their answer to the question in pairs for a few minutes and then report their answers to the class. This activity is beneficial for which reason?**
    A. Students contrast the author's viewpoint with their own viewpoint.
    B. All students verbalize their analysis of character development with a partner before benefiting from the whole-group discussion.
    C. Students discuss answers and learn evaluative comprehension skills from peers' responses.
    D. The teacher can informally assess all students' various comprehension levels.

27. **Which student would most likely need intervention and explicit instruction based on the difficulties presented?**
    A. A third-grade student with difficulty comprehending figurative language
    B. A kindergartener with limited phonemic awareness skills
    C. A second-grader with trouble decoding regular monosyllabic words
    D. A first-grader with trouble decoding low-frequency multisyllabic words

28. **A teacher thinks that a particular assessment tool might not provide consistent results if repeated several times. Which factor is the teacher questioning?**
    A. Validity
    B. Reliability
    C. Bias
    D. Predictability

29. **Two elementary schools want to comparatively measure their students' reading skills. Which assessment type would be effective for doing so?**
    A. Miscue analysis
    B. Informal oral response
    C. Written retelling of a passage
    D. Norm-referenced survey test

30. **Which activity would be the best fit for a fifth-grade teacher who wants to plan a reading activity that allows differentiation?**
    A. Students illustrate selected vocabulary from a short story and explain in small groups why that word is significant.
    B. Students listen to the teacher read a passage and answer written comprehension questions.
    C. Students complete tiered activities with varying levels of support and challenge.
    D. Students write in a journal a response to a prompt provided by the teacher.

1. A   Substituting is part of manipulating sounds and sound combinations to create words. Blending, choice B, involves saying the word school slowly to show how the consonants and vowel sound blend. Segmenting, choice C, divides a word into sounds or syllables. Deleting, choice D, entails taking out a sound, such as deleting the /s/ in school to come up with cool.

2. C   Alphabetic principle can be explicitly taught with kinesthetic activities that encourage students to draw the letter while watching the teacher model the letter and say the sound associated with it. Phonics, choice A, is more advanced, and it deals with knowledge of common letter-sound correspondences to decode print words. Choice B, print directionality, is more basic than letter names and refers to an understanding that print in English reads from left to right. Choice D, phonological awareness, deals with spoken language and manipulating sounds, not letter names and print.

3. C   The student is working on reading a print word, which involves decoding, or figuring out how to read a word based on knowledge of specific patterns. In choice A, the activity does not involve stretching sounds and joining them to form words with automaticity. In choice B, phonemic awareness involves manipulating spoken language, not printed words. Structural analysis, choice D, means looking at the root or parts of the word drum to understand its meaning. Structural analysis is used for comprehending a word's meaning, not necessarily the pronunciation, because some roots, prefixes, and suffixes can have stable spellings but differ in pronunciation, depending on the word.

4. B   A morning message promotes skills in print directionality, word boundaries, tracking print, conveying that print carries meaning, letter formation (A), segmenting (C), and phonemes represented by letters (D). It is not a strong activity to promote environmental print (A), which is print such as store signs and menus found in the world. This message has a few words decodable (C) for a kindergarten student, but many of the words are high-frequency words that do not follow regular letter-sound rules. Word analysis (D) examines parts of a word such as affixes and roots. Word analysis is not a typical part of kindergarten instruction.

5. B Phonemic awareness is a specific phonological awareness skill that addresses phonemes, the basic unit of sound in a language. Asking a student to identify an initial sound is a way of dealing with the student's level of awareness of phonemes in words. Counting words (choice A) is a phonological awareness skill. Asking a student to identify a letter (choice C) assesses a student's knowledge of the alphabetic principle. Asking a student to identify all the sounds in a word assesses advanced phonemic awareness (choice D).

6. A Phonemic awareness skills often follow a hierarchy of comparison: rhyming (choice D), segmenting (choice B), syllable segmentation and blending, onset-rime segmentation and blending, phonemic segmentation and blending (choice A), deletion (say football without foot), and manipulation. Using letter cards to form words (choice C) follows phonemic awareness skills.

7. C The words *trap*, *flip*, and *talk* contain consonant blends, which the student successfully reads. The words the student struggles with contain diphthongs, or two or more vowel sounds together, such as the *ea* in *seat*. Choice A is possible if the student can blend consonants, but that information is not explicitly given in the assessment. Choice D is incorrect because the words the student miscues are all monosyllabic.

8. A According to the chart, the student correctly claps the sounds for *sat* and *top*, which is a basic CVC (consonant-vowel-consonant) pattern. The student incorrectly claps the sounds for *scoop* and *scream*, which contain a few consonants in the beginning, and so are more difficult. Choice A, breaking the word into onset and rime, or sc-oop, scr-eam, helps isolate the sounds to better distinguish them. Choice B, alliteration, is helpful to promote phonological awareness, but it does not target hearing the two sounds in the onset of *scoop*. Substituting sounds, choice C, is a more advanced phonemic awareness skill, and it does not help a student still struggling with distinguishing individual phonemes in words. Clapping syllables, choice D, is ineffective because *scoop* and *scream* are monosyllabic, or contain only one syllable. Clapping sounds is more difficult than clapping syllables.

9. D Structural analysis involves looking at word parts to determine meaning. In the word *proactive*, the prefix *pro-* and the root *-active* can be used to understand the meaning. Semantic cues, choice A, involve looking at context cues surrounding the word, not an isolated word. The same goes for choice C, word order, which looks at where the word is in the sentence to figure out the meaning.

10. **A** Idioms are expressions that cannot be understood literally, such as "to drive someone up a wall." Because the dictionary definition of the individual words does not explain the idiom, choice B is incorrect. Choice C, dividing the words into similar sounds, helps in decoding the words, but not with comprehending idioms. Looking at affixes, choice D, involves structural analysis, which means looking at the word parts, which also does not help comprehend the expression. Teaching idioms and showing how they are used can best promote comprehension.

11. **D** A compound word is a word composed of two words. In the activity above, students join two words to form a new word. The words listed do not have affixes—prefixes and suffixes (choice A). Knowledge of Latin and Greek roots is not needed to combine the familiar words listed (choice B). Homographs are words spelled the same, but they have different meanings, and they might be pronounced differently (choice C). Although words such as *water, play*, and *ground* are homographs, the activity is not designed to promote knowledge of homographs.

12. **C** Fluency is the ability to read accurately, quickly, and easily with expression. Fluency is improved with explicit instruction in phonics and decoding skills (choice A). Fluency affects comprehension because a fluent reader can concentrate on the meaning of the text instead of on the mechanics of reading (choice B). Reliance on context clues for word identification can harm fluency because it leads to excessive miscues that interfere with comprehension (choice D).

13. **A** Words ending with the derivational suffix -able/-ible are adjectives (for example, *capable, dependable*). English syntax places adjectives before nouns. In this sentence, *pilot* is a noun, so blank 1 is suitable for an adjective. Blank 2 is the appropriate place for a verb. Blank 3 is a likely position for an adverb. Blank 4 follows a preposition and article, so it is suitable for a noun.

14. **B** The concepts represented by the listed words are critical to understanding the material. Additionally, the words can be transported to other subject areas. The words are not consistently cognates—words such as *night* (Eng) and *nacht* (Ger) that occur in different languages and share a root (choice A). Several words individually can be analyzed by structure (for example, *integrate, segregate*); however, that is not characteristic of all the words (choice C). Using semantics to understand antonyms such as *integrate* and *segregate* can be helpful. Noting that *–ism* is a noun

suffix and –*ate* is a verb suffix is also helpful; however, semantics is not the strategy of the list as a whole (choice D).

15. **A** Print directionality refers to the way English is read from left to right. By following with her finger, the teacher models directionality to students. Book handling skills, choice B, include how to hold a book, how to turn to the cover to begin to read, and how to turn pages. Phonological awareness, choice C, deals with spoken language, not print. Environmental print, choice D, is the print of everyday life found on signs, labels, and menus.

16. **B** Oral vocabulary knowledge is important because it links to a student's comprehension of decoded words. A student might know letter-sound patterns, choice A, if the student has had phonics knowledge; however, with poor oral vocabulary knowledge, the student cannot comprehend the words not in his oral vocabulary. Limited oral language might be sufficient for reading high-frequency words in his oral vocabulary, but insufficient for reading low-frequency words, choice C. Fluency is an indicator that a reader has linked word recognition and comprehension. A student with limited oral language usually cannot read fluently because of his lack of understanding of unfamiliar vocabulary (choice D).

17. **C** Schema building involves activating prior knowledge of a topic to relate it to new information. The students can make associations while they read because they have an idea of what the text will explore. Structural analysis, choice A, involves looking at word parts such as prefixes and roots to comprehend an unfamiliar word. Choices B and D, literary analysis and response skills, are activities completed after reading a literary text; this prereading activity does not yet touch on analysis and response.

18. **B** Metacognitive strategies are strategies such as thinking aloud (I wonder ...), using schema/synthesis (connecting to a movie), inferring, asking questions, setting a purpose, and visualizing (I can see ...). Internalizing the alphabetic principle (choice A) means to understand how letters and sounds are connected. Decoding (choice C) means to sound out words. Semantic cues (choice D) are cues in text that signify meaning.

19. **D** Note-taking can be beneficial for reinforcing active reading skills. Notes that include summaries promote comprehension by requiring the student to think about and write important information. Choice A, schema building, requires relating prior information to the reading, rather than taking notes on the chapter as the question indicates. Choice B, literary

response skills, is for imaginative texts and involves analysis skills after reading. A literary response might be an interpretive response to a text whereas note-taking deals more with noting the important facts detailed in the text. Oral metacognitive strategies are used to promote comprehension while reading; visualizing and predicting, for example, are metacognitive strategies. Note-taking does not constitute an oral metacognitive strategy because it involves writing notes.

20. **D** A timeline is beneficial for comprehending and remembering events that can be chronologically organized. A Venn diagram, choice A, is used to compare two elements, books, authors, and so on. A KWL chart, choice B, maps what a student knows, what a student wants to know, and what a student learns to promote self-directed learning and schema building. A story map, choice C, is effective for imaginative texts to note the setting, different characters, and main events.

21. **C** Literary analysis skills allow students to interpret literary texts, to understand nonliteral language, and to evaluate the author's style. Choice A, text features, includes table of contents, index, and glossary found in informational texts. Choice B, metacognitive strategies such as monitoring one's understanding or performing closed readings, if necessary, also promotes comprehension and an active read. A semantic word map, choice D, is useful in building vocabulary, but it is not a strategy used in literary analysis.

22. **C** When this student misinterprets the figurative language "as if an army muttered," he cannot comprehend the story on a literal level (choice C). He makes a valid inference ("They are going to be saved") (choice A) but does not reflect comprehension on the evaluative level (choice B). The retelling does not indicate a lack comprehension of vocabulary (choice D). He can conclude the meaning of words such as *perish* and *uttered*.

23. **A** An oral retelling is a way to assess comprehension by allowing a student to retell or reiterate what he or she understood. Choice B is not an oral assessment, but a written literary response activity. Choice C involves a prereading activity that promotes comprehension, whereas an oral retelling happens after reading. Choice D is a partnered discussion activity that promotes comprehension and analysis skills, whereas oral retellings are traditionally performed individually.

24. A An ELL student might need help developing vocabulary, especially if English is not spoken at home. If trade books are understood, but textbooks prove more difficult, academic vocabulary could be beneficial. Decoding (choice B) and phonetic patterns (choice C) are not the problem because the student comprehends trade books. Choice D, analytical skills, is too advanced if comprehension is a problem.

25. C An Informal Reading Inventory is the only choice that allows teachers and students an informal look at texts that are too difficult (frustration), of high interest (independent), and suitable for reading instruction (instructional). Choice A, a retelling, provides a teacher a chance to see how a student comprehends a text. Over time, retellings might reveal a student's ability to comprehend, but an isolated retelling does not provide the information needed to track a student's reading levels. A scoring rubric, choice B, is beneficial for involving students in the assessment of their work, but it does not necessarily indicate reading levels. Choice D, a norm-referenced survey, assesses students comparatively among peers, rather than assessing a student's individual reading levels to provide better reading instruction.

26. C This "ask-pair-share" activity is beneficial because it allows all students to work on oral expression in partners, which is difficult in a large-group discussion where only some students respond. By having students report, they can learn from their peers and listen to example answers. A "What would you do if ..." question calls for students to verbalize evaluative comprehension. Author's point of view, choice A, deals with an author's purpose or perspective in writing. The teacher's question is unrelated to the author's viewpoint. Similarly, although students verbalize with a partner before the group discussion (choice B), the question is unrelated to character development. Choice D is incorrect because the teacher might not necessarily be able to assess all students' comprehension. If the teacher walks around and listens to each pair's conversation, an informal assessment could be made, but the question does not provide enough detail to assume as much.

27. C In choice C, a second grader who has trouble decoding words that are regular and can be read using phonics knowledge most needs intervention. Choice A presents a student at a normal stage of comprehension because literary analysis and more complex comprehension questions usually start in fourth grade. The kindergartener in choice B might eventually need explicit instruction in phonemic awareness skills, but students in kindergarten work on phonemic awareness, so the case is not yet indicative of needing intervention. Choice D's student struggles with multisyllabic words, which might be common for first graders who are beginning readers, especially if the words are low frequency and not covered under high-frequency word lists.

28. B The reliability of a test is important because fluctuating results might hinder a teacher's ability to plan effective need-based instruction. Choice A, validity, questions whether a test's results are accurate and reflect the skills assessed. If a test is invalid, its results are not incorporated into instruction. A test might have bias, choice C, if it is written so that it favors one group over another; a teacher could also show bias when administering a test, which puts the test's reliability into question. Choice D, predictability, is a component to consider when creating activities and assessments. It questions how images, headings, and other supports in a text allow students to predict what they will read.

29. D Because the schools want to compare students, a norm-referenced survey would be effective. A norm-referenced survey test compares how well a student or school performs compared with other students. A miscue analysis, choice A, is an assessment that shows teachers what strategies a student uses to decode and comprehend a word. An informal oral response, choice B, is not an effective strategy for a school-wide test because the grading varies from teacher to teacher. Choice C, a written retelling, targets determining a student's levels of comprehension (literal, inferential, evaluative) and is useful for one-on-one assessment.

30. C Differentiation means that reading instruction is tailored to fit the needs of all students rather than taking a one-size-fits-all approach. With tiered activities, all students work with the same skills but with varying support. Choice A does not provide differentiation because the activity is the same for all students. Choice B also does not provide differentiation because written comprehension questions are not leveled or accompanied with supports that help struggling readers. Choice D is an open-ended activity that does not provide an example of differentiated reading instruction because all students are asked the same prompt.

Final Exam

1. **A kindergartener who is beginning to develop phonemic awareness skills is most likely able to do which of the following?**
    A. Identify the beginning, medial and last phoneme in the word "*pan*."
    B. Clap the number of words in the sentence, "*I love apples*."
    C. Segment the syllables in the word "*family*."
    D. Recognize the initial sound in the word "*ton*."

2. **Which of the following activities would be considered an advanced phonemic awareness skill?**
    A. Blending the onset and the rime in "bread"
    B. Segmenting "little" into phonemes
    C. Blending the syllables of the word "super"
    D. Segmenting the sentence "I love cake" into words

3. **A teacher guides a kindergarten class in singing "Fe, fi, fiddly i-o" and then changes the initial sound to /d/ ("de, di, diddly i-o") and /m/ ("me, mi, middly i-o.") What aspect of reading development is promoted in this activity?**
    A. acquiring print awareness
    B. distinguishing phonemes
    C. generating rhymes
    D. strengthening oral vocabulary

4. **Which activity can assess phonological awareness?**
   A. Observe student's ability to recognize the front, back, and title of a book.
   B. How many words are in the sentence "Cows eat grass"?
   C. Ask student to say the words *pan, rap*, and *mop* with a /m/ sound at the beginning. Can student respond with *man, map*, and *mop*?
   D. Give students the letters *f, n, u*. Ask student to form the word *fun*.

5. **A second grade student lacking phonemic awareness would benefit from intervention. Which of the following activities would be appropriate for the student?**
   A. Read and explore an alphabet book such as *Chicka Chicka Boom Boom*
   B. Read and explore Dr. Suess's *There's a Wocket in My Pocket*
   C. Display pictures of familiar environmental print such as restaurant and retail signs
   D. Read and explore countdown books such as *Ten Little Monkeys*

6. **Which of the following activities would be an appropriate small group activity for promoting segmenting?**
   A. Ask students to say *foot*, then *ball*, and then to put the two words together to form the word *football*.
   B. Provide pictures of four common objects such as pen, car, hat, cup. Stretch a word (pppeeennn). Ask students to choose the correct word.
   C. Provide students with a printout of the following sentence: *My fish can swim*. Next, using individual word cards, have them build the sentence and count the number of words.
   D. Create funny nursery rhymes such as "Mary had a little cow."

7. **How should a teacher pronounce the word *late* to encourage her students to divide words into onset/rime?**
   A. Say the word *late*, then pronounce it as /l//ate/
   B. Say the word *late* and then the word *early*
   C. Say the word *late*, then pronounce it as /l//a//t/
   D. Say the word *late* and then provide the following additional words: *relate, later*

8. **Why is it important for teachers of young students to provide numerous activities that promote the ability to blend phonemes?**
   A. Students must learn to blend phonemes before they can segment phonemes.
   B. Blending is required for students to understand the alphabetic principle.
   C. Students need to know how to blend phonemes in order to decode words.
   D. Blending skills are necessary for students to track print in continuous text.

9. **Which of the following activities would promote the development of phonemic awareness skills?**
   A. Identifying onsets and rimes
   B. Clapping the number of words in a sentence
   C. Counting the number of sounds in a word
   D. Drawing letters in the sand

10. **During an informal assessment, a teacher asks a student to do the following tasks:**

    Say the word *lifeboat*. Now say it again without saying *boat*. [life]
    Say the word *pat*. Now say it again without the */p/* sound. [at]

    What specific skill is the teacher assessing?
    A. segmenting
    B. blending
    C. deletion
    D. substitution

11. **Which of the following would best demonstrate a kindergartener's knowledge of phonemic deletion skills?**
    A. The student says the word "*tray*" and then "*gray*."
    B. The student says "*tr*" and "*ay*" to segment "*tray*."
    C. The student says the word "*tray*" and then "*ray*."
    D. The student says the word "*tray*" and then "*trap*."

12. **Which of the following children is demonstrating the highest level of phonemic awareness?**
    A. The student who is able to identify which two words in the group have the same beginning sound: *lit, lap, sag* [lit, lap]
    B. The student who is able to segment each of the sounds heard in the word *let*. [/l/ /e/ /t/]
    C. The student who is able to blend the following phonemes together to form a word: /k/ /a/ /t/ [cat]
    D. The student who is able answer what the word *mat* becomes when the middle sound is changed to /i/. [mitt]

13. **Which strategy could be used to promote mastery of letter names and shape formation?**
    A. tracing spoken letters into shaving cream
    B. painting the letter of the week in the art center
    C. reciting nursery rhymes
    D. singing the ABC song

14. **A first-grade teacher is planning an activity to help promote the alphabetic principle. Which of the following would accomplish this goal?**
    A. The teacher shows a picture of words starting with the letter "m," writes the letter on the board, and asks students to provide the name of the letter.
    B. The teacher reads aloud from a big book and draws attention to the direction of the print.
    C. The teacher labels objects in the classroom.
    D. The teacher reads aloud from a book and places it in the classroom library.

15. **A student with an understanding of the alphabetic principle should be able to do which of the following?**
    A. segment the onset and rime of the word *bill* in spoken English
    B. recognize *set* and *bet* as rhyming words
    C. identify *d* as the letter that represents the sound /d/ in the word *dog*
    D. blend the sounds mmmm-iiii-ssss to form the word *miss*

16. **A kindergarten teacher who labels various areas of the classroom, including "science center" and "literacy corner" is promoting which of the following essential skills?**
    A. decoding
    B. phonological awareness
    C. oral vocabulary
    D. print awareness

17. **A kindergarten student draws a picture of two children on a playground, draws squiggly lines under the picture and says, "James and me played tag." Which of the following can the teacher conclude from this scenario?**
    A. The student is mimicking classmates who draw pictures with squiggly lines.
    B. The student has acquired a knowledge that phonemes of spoken language are written with letters and letter pairs.
    C. The student is aware that print carries a message separate from illustrations.
    D. The student has sufficient oral vocabulary to begin decoding.

18. **When considering alphabetic principle, which statement accurately explains the role of learning letter names in reading development?**
    A. Learning letter names typically precedes learning letter sounds. A solid knowledge of letter sounds is an indicator of reading success.
    B. Learning letter names causes confusion in reading, particularly with vowel sounds. Learning letter names should be delayed until after sounds have been mastered.
    C. Learning letter sounds slows the process of reading development. Students should learn letter sounds but not letter names.
    D. As print awareness skills develop, students naturally learn letter names, making explicit instruction in letter names unnecessary.

19. Which of the following has **not** been strongly tied to promotion of print awareness among students?
    A. Label common objects or places around the classroom (i.e. desk, class library, etc.)
    B. Use big books that highlight letters and words.
    C. Read predictable text that closely follows illustrations provided.
    D. Identify common morphemes in familiar words.

20. A preschool teacher sets up various literacy centers in her classroom. Which of the following centers focuses predominately on developing students' understanding of the alphabetic principle?
    A. In the classroom post office, students are encouraged to "write" a letter to a parent, sibling or friend.
    B. Using pretend hammers and provided with five or six choices, students play "whack a letter" by whacking the letter called out by the teacher.
    C. Students draw a picture and dictate one sentence explaining their picture.
    D. While leading students in choral reading of a short poem written on large chart paper, the teacher uses a pointer to track the print.

21. After returning from a field trip to the fire station, a preschool teacher leads the class in a discussion about what they learned. As students provide different responses, the teacher writes their ideas on the board. How does this encourage literacy development in young children?
    A. Later, the students can try to read the board independently.
    B. The students can refer back to the board at a later time.
    C. The teacher is helping to reinforce that speech may be represented in writing.
    D. Because it is unlikely students can read at this age, writing these statements down does little to promote literacy.

22. **Which of the following is most likely to promote strong book-handling skills in preschoolers?**
    A. Create and maintain an enjoyable classroom library
    B. Model the "return sweep" when reading a big book
    C. Scribe student responses to create a predictable text book for the classroom
    D. Call attention to the book cover and beginning pages when reading a favorite book aloud

23. **Students are assigned an activity to "Write the Room." They carry a clipboard and copy words found in the classroom that meet criteria such as "begins with *s*" or "ends with a *y*." Which statement best describes the strategy behind the activity?**
    A. explicit instruction in patterns in language
    B. implicit instruction using environmental print
    C. explicit whole group instruction
    D. habit-building task for sustaining attention

24. **A third-grade student is given the following sentence to read: "A philanthropist is a wealthy person who gives money and time to benefit the lives of other people." The student reads, "A philantropy is a wealthy person who gives money and times to beenfite the lives of other people." What strategy can be practiced to improve the student's reading accuracy?**
    A. conduct spelling inventory to determine student's skill in encoding graphemes of oral language
    B. recognize the series of discrete syllables in multisyllable words
    C. gain automaticity in reading familiar words
    D. use word analysis to identify Greek and Latin roots

25. **Which of the following shows the most common order for introduction of words using phonics rules?**
    A. cat, cast, coat
    B. can, cane, scan
    C. the, these, them
    D. me, my, mist

26. **Students practice making words for a word family ladder and then reading the words. Which aspect of reading development is not addressed in this activity?**

    A. onset/rime
    B. rhyming words
    C. print directionality in connected text
    D. automaticity of word recognition

27. **On a weekly spelling test, a student spells the word** *ungrateful* **as** *ungratful* **and spells the word** *relaxed* **as** *rilaxt*. **The student shows a weakness in what reading skill?**

    A. using syntactic clues
    B. transferring cognates
    C. encoding morphemes
    D. recognizing onset and rime

28. **A first-grade teacher wants to promote automatic word recognition by teaching common phonics patterns. Based on these objectives, which of the following could be implemented during reading instruction?**

    A. daily read alouds
    B. weekly spelling lists that follow letter-sound patterns
    C. songs that promote letter name knowledge
    D. explicit instruction for structural analysis

29. **Second grade students are given the following sentence and must choose the correct word.**

    Tommy _____ and cheered when his team won.
    (jumps, jumped)

    Which strategy for decoding is being promoted?

    A. use of syntactic clues
    B. identification of homographs
    C. chunking into syllables
    D. recognition of alphabetic principle

30. **A third grade student is experiencing difficulties in decoding unfamiliar, multi-syllable words. Which of the following conclusions is probable?**

A. This student's comprehension skills are likely not affected by their decoding skills because the two skills develop independently.

B. It is likely this student also struggles with oral vocabulary as oral vocabulary is contingent on decoding skills.

C. It is likely the student is lacking basic phonemic awareness skills necessary for reading success.

D. The student likely struggles with comprehension and fluency as these skills are interrelated.

31. **Which of the following statements is true regarding making sense of decoded words?**

A. There is a direct connection between a reader's ability to decode and comprehend. Once a word is decoded, comprehension is automatic.

B. An extensive vocabulary is a prerequisite to accurate decoding. Only words that are part of a reader's vocabulary can be decoded.

C. Decoding a list of words in the same word family is an effective means of building oral vocabulary.

D. While beginning readers can decode unfamiliar and even nonsense words, they depend on their oral vocabulary to assign meaning to words.

32. **Which of the following is the primary cause of fluency difficulties?**

A. Inappropriately leveled text

B. Weak comprehension skills

C. Weak decoding skills

D. Inability to use context clues

33. **A student is given the following sentence to read:** *The chickens pecked at the grain while the sheep grazed out in the field.* **The student read with the following miscues:** *The shickens pecked at the grain wile the cheep grazed out in the field.*
    What type of reading error was made?
    A. digraph
    B. consonant blend
    C. morpheme
    D. diphthong

34. **Which of the following words would be most appropriate to introduce to beginning-level phonics learners?**
    A. trap
    B. bus
    C. stream
    D. girl

35. **Christopher's automatic recognition of high-frequency words has tested below grade level. How would this most likely impact his reading?**
    A. This would likely make it more difficult for him to understand spoken language.
    B. This would likely increase his reading fluency.
    C. This would likely hinder comprehension, especially of longer texts.
    D. This would not impact his reading comprehension.

36. **A teacher wants to provide instruction on phonics. Which of the following activities would be the most logical?**
    A. Hearing the name of a letter and drawing it on a paper
    B. Memorizing a list of irregular patterned words
    C. Learning common letter-sound correspondences
    D. Learning how to break down spoken words

37. **A student in second grade struggles with sight words. Which of the following would likely be the most helpful for the student?**
    A. practice phonics
    B. additional practice to learn to read a list of common sight words using memorization
    C. work on phonemic awareness skills
    D. learn structural analysis skills

38. **The following sentence has missing words.**

    > The ___(1)___ students ___(2)___ entered the library ___
    > (3)___ began searching for ___(4)___ books.

    Based on English syntax, which blank is the most likely place for a word with the suffix –ly?
    A. (1)
    B. (2)
    C. (3)
    D. (4)

39. **Which statement best explains the relationship between word analysis, fluency, and comprehension?**
    A. Decoding is at the base of all reading. While strong decoding skills improve comprehension, good comprehension does not impact decoding.
    B. Word analysis, fluency, and comprehension are interrelated. Automatic recognition of morphemes supports comprehension, and vice versa. Strong comprehension skills improve fluency, and strong fluency skills improve comprehension.
    C. Fluency is the product of word analysis and comprehension skills. Fluency in reading does not improve comprehension or decoding.
    D. Word analysis, comprehension, and fluency are three separate skill areas developed in separate parts of the brain. Improving one area has little impact on the other areas of reading development.

40. **Which of the following is demonstrated by the following words?**

   purged
   painted
   flapped

   A. Though the spelling of suffixes varies, it is more reliable than pronunciation.
   B. Affixes don't indicate the tense of a word.
   C. The –ed suffix is always spelled and pronounced in the same manner.
   D. Suffixes attach to the front of a word and convey important information.

41. **A practice worksheet contains the following question:**

   Choose the correct definition for the word *letter* as it is used in the sentence.

   The **letter** was delivered to the governor shortly before noon.
       a. a written symbol that represents speech and is part of the alphabet
       b. a written message to another person

   This activity is intended to promote students' knowledge of which of the following?
   A. synonyms
   B. structural analysis
   C. homonyms
   D. discrete phonemes

42. **A second grade spelling list has the following words:** *jolly, soggy, silly, shabby, chubby.* **This word list is most likely to promote which aspect of reading development?**
   A. phonemic awareness skills by teaching students to blend sounds
   B. development of academic vocabulary by reinforcing words needed for schoolwork

C. identification of Greek and Latin roots which can extend language skills

D. retention of spelling patterns which promote word recognition

43. **A teacher will introduce Greek roots as a strategy for word analysis. Which of the following word lists is best suited to promote use of Greek roots?**

A. snowflake, mailbox, baseball, tablecloth

B. antibiotic, biology, biography, symbiotic

C. wanted, walked, washed, wondered

D. Pandora, Hercules, Achilles, Odysseus

44. **A teacher is preparing to provide explicit instruction in structural analysis. Which of the following word lists is most appropriate for practicing structural analysis?**

A. the, they, them, there

B. fin, thin, grin, spin

C. viewed, review, viewers, overview

D. ecosystem, omnivore, endangered, predator

45. **Which of the following activities would allow a third-grade class to develop their expressive vocabularies?**

A. Students silently read their favorite story.

B. The teacher reads a high interest book.

C. Students orally state what they liked about a specific book.

D. Students read newspaper headings.

46. **When teaching new vocabulary words, a teacher uses illustrations and brief stories in addition to words and definitions. Which of the following instructional strategies is the teacher using?**

A. Structural analysis

B. Domain-specific vocabulary

C. Contextualized vocabulary

D. Syntactic clues

47. **Students in a second grade class struggle with word identification. Which of the following activities is most likely to promote word identification skills?**
    A. Students use a word map to group domain-specific vocabulary
    B. Students use Elkonin boxes to segment words into phonemes
    C. Students refer to graphic features to derive meaning from the text
    D. Students practice sight words by writing, stamping, and inserting the appropriate words into cloze sentences

48. **To promote comprehension, a teacher has students complete a word map using context clues for an unfamiliar word while they read. How could this activity be modified as a pre-reading activity?**
    A. Students create a word map by generating questions on the reading they would expect to see on a test.
    B. Students create a word map by guessing the meaning.
    C. Students use reference materials such as the dictionary and thesaurus to complete a word map.
    D. Students talk about their associations with the reading's topic.

49. **A fifth grade class is preparing to read a passage about early onset dementia. The passage contains the following sentence: "Dementia can begin to change the life of a person with a *chronological* age of fifty." The teacher most likely chose to preteach *chronological* as a vocabulary word for which of the following reasons?**
    A. The meaning is apparent from the context.
    B. The word has no roots or affixes that students can use to help decipher the meaning.
    C. The word has significance to the content of the reading.
    D. The teacher sees little value in activating student's prior knowledge.

50. In content area classes, fourth graders are given chapter quizzes and tests containing matching sections of vocabulary words and definitions. Several students who had read the chapter with appropriate accuracy and comprehension and answered promptly in oral review activities, struggled with the list of vocabulary words and definitions.
What is a likely explanation for the student's difficulties?

A. The students lack metacognitive skills for self-questioning during reading.

B. The students are able to read words in context but struggle to decode words in isolation.

C. The students lack the oral vocabulary necessary for recall.

D. The students lack the research skills needed to clarify content.

51. Which of the following activities is intended to teach students how to clarify the meaning of an unfamiliar word found in a sentence?

A. Students paraphrase the definition of the unfamiliar word and substitute the paraphrase for the original word in a sentence.

B. Students listen to a read aloud from an idea-rich literary selection. The reader occasionally interjects to ask, "Where did that happen?" or "Can you predict what will happen next?"

C. A time for independent reading is set aside each day.

D. Students add the unfamiliar word to a vocabulary list and then use the word in a free write journal entry.

52. A teacher is selecting vocabulary words to support reading of informational text. Which answer describes words that can be *omitted* rather than selected for study?

A. Low frequency words important to topic of study

B. Representative words that cross curriculum

C. Words which will appear in post-reading writing assignments

D. Regular decodable words integrated into daily conversation

53. **While learning about bibliographies, a sixth grade student observed the expression** *et al.* **in the following citation:**

Brooks, Felicty, et al. *Usborne Children's Encyclopedia.*

Which of the following strategies should the teacher suggest to the student to help him determine the meaning?
A. Rely on oral vocabulary for pronunciation.
B. Use conventions such as punctuation and spelling.
C. Infer the meaning based on word derivatives.
D. Refer to a dictionary. Insert the dictionary definition in the situation and evaluate suitability.

54. **In an assigned reading for a fourth-grade reading group, the proverb** *"Two heads are better than one."* **is used. Which of the following strategies should the teacher recommend to best help her students understand the phrase?**
A. Explicitly pre-teach the proverb with an explanation and several familiar settings where the proverb could be used.
B. Allow students to explore the meaning of the expression without intervention from the teacher.
C. Encourage students to look up each of the words included in the phrase in the dictionary.
D. Encourage students to look for other instances in the text that have the same proverb and to deduce the meaning.

55. **In which of the following ways does a strong oral vocabulary enhance reading development?**
A. Oral vocabulary allows language learners to connect sounds of words in English to sounds of words in their native language.
B. Oral vocabulary allows readers to derive meaning from decoded words. This in turn helps them derive meaning from individual words to comprehend text.
C. Oral vocabulary enables students to analyze morphemes of multisyllable words.
D. Oral vocabulary enables students to hear and generate rhymes.

56. **Third-grade students are learning about weather patterns in their science class. Many are having trouble recalling the meaning of unfamiliar vocabulary in the unit. Which of the following strategies would the teacher most likely use to help students recall the meanings of the various terms?**

   A. Pronounce words multiple times until they become part of the students' oral vocabularies.

   B. Draw attention to the spelling of the words.

   C. Help students to group words conceptually.

   D. Look for cognates for the vocabulary words.

57. **A seventh-grade class is reading Geoffrey Chaucer's** *Canterbury Tales,* **which includes stories of several characters. The "Tales" are told from the perspective of several pilgrims taking part in a story-telling contest during their travels together. Which of the following is the most appropriate pre-reading activity to provide students with the knowledge they'll need while reading?**

   A. Have students look at a timeline while the teacher writes key dates on the board.

   B. Have students skim through the chapter names and discuss different narrators.

   C. Have the teacher preteach the meaning of *Canterbury*.

   D. Assign students to write their own story, pretending to be one of the characters.

58. **While retelling what happened in the final chapter of** *Charlotte's Web,* **a third grade student makes appropriate comments about what he believes will happen to Wilbur (the main character) in the future. This student is demonstrating which of the following?**

   A. How to self-monitor

   B. A literal level of understanding

   C. Strong decoding abilities

   D. An inferential level of understanding

59. **After reading a chapter from** *Alice's Adventures in Wonderland*, **students are asked to choose either Alice or the Mad Hatter, illustrate their selection in a scene from the story, and list two traits supported by quotes from the story. This activity is designed to promote which aspect of literary analysis?**
   A. identifying features of different genres
   B. identifying literary allusions
   C. analyzing character development
   D. connecting elements in the text with prior knowledge

60. **Students listen to classic and modern versions of the traditional story** *Little Red Riding Hood* **read aloud. Additionally, they listen to the Chinese version,** *Lon Po Po*. **Which activity would provide an appropriate structure for comparing and contrasting different versions of the same story?**
   A. In a whole group setting, "Think-Pair-Share" the following: "What aspects of Chinese culture do you see in *Lon Po Po*?
   B. Using the two versions of the story, complete a Venn diagram to record similarities and differences between the two stories.
   C. Retell the story from the grandmother's point of view.
   D. Create a concept map to record the main events of the classic *Little Red Riding Hood*.

61. **Students participate in an activity in which they receive a fictitious letter from a popular storybook character such as** *Flat Stanley* **or** *The Cat in the Hat*. **Based on clues in the reading, students must discover the character's location. This activity is primarily designed to promote which reading skill?**
   A. recognizing literary allusions
   B. making inferences
   C. identifying features of a genre
   D. interpreting figurative language

62. **Often while reading aloud, a fourth grade teacher will pause and explain what he is thinking about. Below is an example:**

> The girl walked quickly through the dark, quiet house, taking care not to wake her mother, father or younger siblings. *I'm imagining a girl tiptoeing through her house, which seems very still and calm.* Upon entering the kitchen, she noticed a soft glow beginning to shed warm light through the large breakfast room window. *I can visualize faint light streaming into the house as the early morning sun begins to rise outside.*

Why does the teacher most likely read in this manner?
A. To demonstrate how to understand text on a literal level
B. To demonstrate how to read fluently and with expression
C. To demonstrate metacognitive strategies for students
D. To demonstrate an understanding on an evaluative level

63. *The Little Red Hen* **is about a hen that asks fellow farm animals for assistance in planting and harvesting wheat and baking bread, however, they all decline the request. After reading different versions of this classic tale, a teacher has students pretend to be the dog and write a letter to the farmer about the incident with the grain. Which of the following aspects of reading comprehension is the teacher most likely promoting?**
A. analyzing point of view
B. analyzing literary allusions
C. oral language proficiency
D. writing summaries

64. **In a first grade unit about plants and how they grow, a teacher reads the following books aloud:** *The Tiny Seed* **(Eric Carle),** *The Magic School Bus Plants Seeds* **(Joanna Cole and Bruce Degen),** *National Geographic Reader: Seed to Plant* **(Kristin Baird Rattini),** *From Seed to Plant* **(Gail Gibbons), and "The Garden" (***Frog and Toad Together***, Arnold Lobel).**
This unit likely utilizes which of the following goals and strategies?

A. knowledge of common idioms, comprehension on an evaluative level, literacy rich environment

B. literacy rich environment, treatment of similar topics in different genres, listening comprehension

C. multiple accounts of the same event, knowledge of text features, love of reading

D. reading for varied purposes, decoding multisyllable words, self-monitoring

65. **Which of the following is an example of close reading for literary response?**

A. Students retell the story plot following oral reading of a classic tale.

B. Students practice common spelling patterns to promote word identification.

C. Students analyze an unfamiliar multisyllable word from the text to gain understanding.

D. Students work collaboratively on classroom posters of popular authors and their different books.

66. **Which of the following activities supports a student's efforts to interpret the craft and structure of imaginative literature?**

A. use text features to locate content to answer literal questions

B. practice correct usage of conventions in written English

C. develop word analysis skills including identification of common morphemes and Latin roots

D. use a graphic organizer

67. **A fourth grade class is preparing to read a book about Rosa Parks. Which of the following pre-reading activities would be most helpful in promoting student comprehension of the book?**

A. Provide students with background information about the time period

B. Pronounce difficult vocabulary words for students.

C. Discuss with students the type of text they will be reading and the differences between fiction and non-fiction.

D. Have students complete a journal entry explaining their reactions to the text.

68. **A fifth grade English class reads several essays about allowing or prohibiting vending machines in school cafeterias. The teacher posts the following questions, asking students to consider them carefully while reading the texts.**

> What does each author believe and how does he support his arguments?
> What is the background of each author?

What is the teacher most likely trying to teach her students?

A. The teacher wants her students to understand the text on a literal level.

B. The teacher wants to help her students distinguish between facts and opinions.

C. The teacher wants her students to analyze and use the author's point of view to better understand and put the texts in perspective.

D. The teacher wants her students to make connections between texts.

69. **A teacher provides her fifth-grade class with both an expository reading passage and guide to complete. The guide contains questions that prompt students to relate the passage to themselves, the world around them, and other similar information they've learned about the topic prior to reading the passage. It also contains multiple questions that encourage students to determine the validity of the author's main points and conclusion. Which of the following is most likely the purpose of the guide?**

A. To encourage students to think on a literal level

B. To encourage students to think on an evaluative level

C. To encourage students to re-read what they do not understand

D. To determine if students had any prior knowledge of the topic at hand

70. **After reading an expository essay on the importance of not texting while driving, the teacher asks, "What did the author suggest?" The teacher is aiming to promote what level of comprehension?**

A. inferential

B. evaluative

C. literal

D. non-literal

71. **A sixth grade teacher has students read a passage for homework. The following day, he has the students spend the first ten minutes of class discussing the passage. Finally, he breaks students into groups to reread the same passage. Why is the teacher most likely having students reread something they've already read and discussed?**

   A. The teacher is concerned some students didn't receive support at home.

   B. The teacher wants students to understand the text on a literal level.

   C. The teacher wants students exposed to the same text again so they can further comprehend the material.

   D. The teacher wants students to complete a graphic organizer.

72. **Students are beginning a research project about animals. Which of the following analysis skills will they have the opportunity to practice that they might not use on other daily assignments?**

   A. integrating information from multiple print and digital sources

   B. integrating knowledge from multiple literary works

   C. analyzing author's point of view

   D. expanding knowledge of standard English grammar and usage

73. **Which of the following are examples of text features?**

   A. emergent, decoding, fluent

   B. chronological, cause/effect, comparison/contrast

   C. table of contents, headings, index

   D. characters, plot, setting

74. **On a criterion-referenced test, students are expected to write a paragraph that explains the impact of the Civil War on America. Which text structure is most appropriate for the assignment?**

   A. chronological

   B. comparison/contrast

   C. description

   D. cause/effect

75. **Which of the following activities is intended to promote comprehension by asking students to analyze text and then record it in their own words by substituting, deleting, and maintaining original information?**
    A. skimming
    B. visualizing
    C. conceptual grouping
    D. note taking

76. **A second grade teacher is introducing a unit on force and motion. She sets up a play bowling set and basketball. As students discuss, she records the following content-specific vocabulary words as they are said aloud:** *roll, bounce, up,* **and** *down.* **She then adds the words** *friction* **and** *gravity* **to the list while casually discussing their meanings. What is the best rationale for the teacher adding these words?**
    A. In addition to the one-syllable words listed, students also need skills in using spelling patterns for multisyllable words.
    B. The students' omission of *friction* and *gravity* suggests that they are not part of their oral vocabulary. The teacher is introducing additional key words to support comprehension.
    C. Students with evaluative comprehension will be able to go beyond the text and analyze the style of the text.
    D. The cause/effect text structure requires understanding of events and the causes of the events.

77. **A fifth grader is beginning an internet research project on sustainable living. In addition to gathering information, online research provides an opportunity for the student to demonstrate which reading comprehension strategy?**
    A. distinguishing fact from opinion
    B. oral language to promote comprehension
    C. self-generated questioning
    D. analyzing character development

78. **A district publishes a school report card in the local newspaper. Included in the report card are student test results. The results referenced are likely from which of the following test formats?**
    A. Portfolio
    B. Norm-referenced test
    C. Authentic tasks
    D. Informal Reading Inventories

79. **Which of the following promotes student reflection of assessments?**
    A. norm-referenced tests
    B. portfolio
    C. re-telling
    D. student-teacher shared journal

80. **Which of the following describes a test on which validity could be questioned?**
    A. Recent immigrants score poorly on a writing prompt which asks how they celebrate the Fourth of July.
    B. Students are permitted to choose a nonfiction or a fiction text for a running record assessment. Though books are the same form, students consistently performed better on the nonfiction test.
    C. Miscue analysis reveals that a student drops word endings.
    D. Compared to their results on the general math test, struggling readers performed poorly on math story problems.

81. **When an elementary principal evaluated the results of a school wide Informal Reading Inventory assessment, she found that results varied widely between test administrators. Which test concept could be called into question?**
    A. bias
    B. validity
    C. reliability
    D. predictability

82. **Which of the following informal assessments would be the most appropriate means to evaluate students' understanding of the alphabetic principle?**
    A. As individual students read aloud, the teacher notes reading behavior on a running record.
    B. A student selects work to include in a kindergarten portfolio.
    C. Given a card with the letter *r*, the student is asked the name and sound of the letter. Results are recorded.
    D. On a norm-referenced year-end test, students are asked to select the letter the teacher says from a multiple choice list of four letters.

83. **A running record is used to record student miscues and behavior while an English Language Learner reads aloud. In analyzing the miscues, the teacher observes a pattern. What strategy can be utilized to improve student skills?**

    Original text: *The rabbit and the turtle lined up for the race.*

    Student reading: *The labbit and the turtre lined up for the lace.*

    A. Provide explicit instruction in discrete phonemes /l/ and /r/.
    B. Enhance instruction of phonics used to decode accurately.
    C. Promote development of oral vocabulary so the student can derive meaning from decoded words.
    D. Look for cognates that transfer between student's native language and English.

84. **Which of the following is an example of the use of an authentic task used for assessment?**
    A. Students are given an informational text accompanied by ten multiple choice questions. Students answer literal, inferential, and evaluative multiple choice questions based on the text.
    B. A teacher sets up a learning center in which students look at a map of a zoo. The students then plan a trip around the zoo, listing the ten animals they most want to see. A rubric is used to score the student responses.

C. In a learning center, students work a puzzle in which they must match together two short words to form one compound word.

D. Students work on a literacy website designed to provide practice in phonics and decoding. Student progress is tracked so that activities are matched to student performance.

85. **Which of the following assessments is most suitable to administer to a group?**
    A. second grade Informal Reading Inventory
    B. preschool retelling of the story line of a traditional tale
    C. third grade norm-referenced vocabulary test
    D. fifth grade writing portfolio

86. **A teacher dictates a list of phonetically-regular words. Students write each word. What is this activity designed to assess?**
    A. phonological awareness
    B. phonemic awareness
    C. concepts of print
    D. letter-sound knowledge

87. **Why would a fourth-grade teacher most likely ask a student to independently read a grade-level passage and then retell what happened?**
    A. Retellings are often the most efficient way to assess a large class of students.
    B. Retellings are an excellent comprehension assessment tool as nothing needs to be created prior to the activity when students verbally recount the events.
    C. Retellings are a good gauge of comprehension, as they require students to think independently and explain the course of events without questions or prompts from the teacher.
    D. Retellings are one of the few easily quantified comprehension assessments.

88. **Analysis of a standard-based assessment reveals that of the twenty-two students tested, seven missed the following question:**

> Choose the correct word to complete the sentence:
> The children left ___ books on the shelves.
> (a). they're
> (b). there
> (c). their

What is the best use of the assessment data?

A. In a small group, provide explicit instruction and sufficient practice of homophones.
B. Teach a unit on homophones to the whole group.
C. Tell students who missed the question the correct answer.
D. Provide implicit instruction in usage of *they're/there/their* as these or other homophones occur in reading.

89. **When provided with age-appropriate, content- and idea- rich texts at their instructional reading level, readers in a fourth grade guided reading group were reluctant to engage. What is a likely cause of and solution for the problem?**

A. Students already have extensive exposure to idea-rich text. Allow students to select their own reading material.
B. Students lack decoding skills for the text level. Select a book at the students' independent reading levels.
C. Students struggle with comprehension on all levels. Model rereading and close reading strategies so that students can access the content and ideas.
D. Students lack the schema to connect to the text. Select high-interest material written for a general audience of fourth graders in place of content- and idea- rich materials.

90. All of the following strategies except one are likely to equip students to become independent readers outside school. Which of the following methods is <u>not</u> likely to promote independent reading?
   A. Provide students with the skills to decode and comprehend with fluency.
   B. Make time for independent reading during the school day.
   C. Provide extrinsic motivation that is intended to become intrinsic motivation for reading.
   D. Limit genres to the favorite and familiar ones until skills are secure.

91. During whole group instruction, students are introduced to new text and are given a graphic organizer to use to find and evaluate the author's use of reasons. The teacher elicits the first reason from the class and writes it on a graphic organizer. Students then think-pair-share a second reason. Finally, students work independently to complete the graphic organizer. This instructional strategy utilizes which practice?
   A. scaffolding
   B. connection to background knowledge
   C. differentiation
   D. ongoing assessment

92. What is the primary reason for text leveling?
   A. to provide age-appropriate content in informational and literary texts
   B. to match books and readers so instruction can be effective without creating frustration
   C. to provide one text which can be used whole group with a heterogeneous classroom of readers
   D. to promote metacognitive skills of visualizing and self-questioning

93. A fifth-grade teacher wants to choose a reading passage that is at students' instructional level. Which of the following criteria should be considered first?
   A. The number of foreign expressions and idioms
   B. The ratio of familiar to unfamiliar words

C. The number of multisyllabic words

D. The genre

94. **Which of the following practices in a fourth grade classroom is intended to promote a love of reading which can lead a student to becoming a lifelong reader?**

    A. using audio books for English language learners

    B. using computer time as a reward for completing literacy activities

    C. placing a favorite read aloud in the classroom library

    D. creating story maps for literary/imaginative texts

95. **When making choices regarding appropriate text for students, teachers consider text complexity. Which of the following best defines** *text complexity*?

    A. The difficulty of reading and comprehending a text with consideration given to the reader and task

    B. The ability to hear and manipulate sounds in spoken language

    C. The designation given when a student is able to read a text with accuracy, prosody, and comprehension

    D. The gradient designation assigned to a book that indicates how easy or hard a book is to read

96. **Reading instruction that relies on schema theory assumes which of the following to be true?**

    A. Readers learn by putting new information in relation to previously learned information.

    B. Readers learn best by learning new vocabulary.

    C. Comprehension skills are impacted by reading fluency.

    D. Reading progresses from whole to part.

97. **Which of the following statements accurately explains how literary and informational texts should be balanced in the classroom?**

    A. Because the language and content of all genres have value, students at all levels should read and have exposure to both literary and imaginative text.

B. English Language Learners benefit first from informational texts written about familiar topics. After basic English vocabulary is acquired, imaginative texts can be introduced.

C. Early childhood should be devoted to imaginative texts so that creativity and free expression can be promoted before the specialized vocabulary of informational texts.

D. Balance of literary and informational texts can be determined by the student. Allowing students to choose their own reading will increase their love of reading.

98. **Why should a fifth-grade teacher be concerned with providing her students with a variety of high-quality text from across literary genres?**

A. Diversified text ensures all students will enjoy the material at some point.

B. Diversified text promotes student's understanding on the literal, inferential and evaluative levels.

C. Providing a variety of text types allows instruction to be diversified for all learners.

D. Providing students with and using diverse text within a classroom exposes students to varied text structures and features.

99. **In a first grade classroom, instruction is flexible and tailored to maximize the learning experience for each child. Strategies include leveled reading groups and modifications that are strategically planned for content, work skills, task, etc. Which term best identifies this methodology?**

A. scaffolding

B. schema building

C. differentiation

D. cooperative learning

100. **Which of the following strategies and reasons is not an accurate reflection of best practices in reading instruction?**
    A. Provide a classroom library where students can develop literary analysis skills.
    B. Read aloud to foster an engagement in literacy.
    C. Offer electronic books with scaffolds to struggling readers.
    D. Read a variety of genres to gain an understanding of text structures and features.

FINAL EXAM EXPLANATIONS

1. D Recognizing the initial consonant in monosyllabic words is typically one of the earliest phonemic awareness skills. Choices B and C deal more with phonological awareness since they involve clapping the number of words and syllables; phonemic awareness deals with phonemes, or individual sound units. It is usually more difficult to count phonemes than to count syllables. Choice A is the hardest phonemic awareness skill to develop. Identifying the medial and final sounds in a word is more challenging and is typical of a more advanced level of phonemic awareness skills.

2. B Since the question asks about phonemic awareness skills, we know to look for answers that deal with individual sound units (phonemes). Remember – phonological awareness is an umbrella term referring to an individual's awareness that oral language is comprised of smaller units, such as words and syllables. Phonemic awareness refers to one's ability to hear and manipulate phonemes. Choice A does not involve phonemes since the onset and rime of "bread" include multiple sounds. Choice C looks at syllables while Choice D looks at words, making these choices incorrect as well. Choice B, segmenting the sounds in *little* is the best answer. This requires a student to identify the beginning, medial and ending sounds in a word which is considered an advanced phonemic awareness skill.

3. B Changing phonemes in a song is an example of implicit phonemic awareness instruction. The song does not address print as suggested in Choice A. While there are rhyming words (fe, de, me…), the words are not heard together, and the song is not designed to teach students to generate rhymes, also making Choice C incorrect. The song also doesn't contain any words, only nonsense sounds, so it will not strengthen oral vocabulary (Choice D). Choice B is therefore the best answer – by having students replace one phoneme at a time, the teacher is promoting their ability to distinguish between sounds, or phonemes.

4. B   Phonological awareness is an umbrella term referring to an individual's awareness that oral language is comprised of smaller units, such as words and syllables. Choice B requires students to break a sentence down to count words – this is a frequent activity used to assess phonological awareness, making it the best answer. Choice A assesses print awareness, making this choice incorrect. Choice C asks students to manipulate phonemes in a word and Choice D assesses phonics skills and student's ability to use letter-sound relationship to form words. While both of these choices suggest excellent activities, they are geared toward phonemic awareness rather than phonological awareness, also making them incorrect.

5. B   Phonemic awareness is the ability to hear, identify, and manipulate phonemes. A rhyming book such as *There's a Wocket in My Pocket* contains common words in which a phoneme has been substituted, making Choice B the best answer. Phonemic awareness is not focused on the alphabet (such as in *Chicka Chicka Boom Boom in* Choice A). Environmental print can aid students in print awareness and in understanding that print carries a message, but does not address phonemic awareness, also making Choice C incorrect. A predictable text such as *Ten Little Monkeys* (Choice D) builds oral language, but is not the best option for intervention designed to target phonemic awareness.

6. C   Segmenting refers to separating sounds. Sentences, words, and sounds can be segmented. Giving students individual word cards to replicate a sentence and then count the number of words promotes the concept that a sentence can be segmented into separate words, making Choice C the best answer. Choice A, saying *foot* and *ball* separately and then together is a blending activity. Choice B, stretching words, is also a blending activity as students hear the sounds strung together rather than segmented. Finally, Choice D is a substitution activity in which students substitute one word for another, also making this choice incorrect.

7. A Rhyming is typically one of the earlier ways students acquire phonological awareness. Often, students begin rhyming by using the part of the word known as the *rime* (in one syllable words, this would be last part of the word) and changing the *onset*, or the first letter(s) before the vowel. Given the word *late*, the scenario described in Choice A is the best demonstration of how to appropriately separate the onset from the rime (/l// ate/). In Choice B, the teacher demonstrates opposites while in Choice C, the word is segmented by individual sounds. Finally, Choice D demonstrates how adding morphemes (adding the prefix *re-* and the suffix *–er*) can change the meaning of a word. Choice A remains the best answer.

8. C Blending phonemes allows students to take individual sounds and string them together to form words. This skill is necessary for students to decode words and eventually read fluently, making Choice C the best answer. Segmenting phonemes is essentially the opposite skill – it involves taking a word and breaking it down by individual sounds. Though this skill often goes hand in hand with blending and opportunities to practice this should also be provided, blending is not necessarily a prerequisite to segmenting, making Choice A incorrect. The ability to blend and segment sounds eventually allows for fluent reading which in turn, allows for successful comprehension. Choice B, which refers to the alphabetic principle, is also incorrect – though students need to understand there is a relationship between written letters and spoken sounds, blending is not necessary for this to be learned. Finally, there is not a strong connection between blending and tracking print, also making Choice D incorrect.

9. C Phonemic awareness deals strictly with individual sounds, or phonemes. Only Choice C deals with individual sounds – counting the number of sounds within in a word promotes phonemic awareness, making this the best answer. Choice A considers initial phonemes in certain words, but identifying the onset and rime does not necessarily involve identifying individual sounds, making this incorrect. Choice B, clapping the number of words in a sentence, promotes phonological awareness also making this choice incorrect, Finally, Choice D involves letter knowledge, which goes beyond phonemic awareness and spoken language. Choice C therefore remains the best answer.

10. **C** In this particular assessment, the teacher is determining a student's ability to delete individual parts and sounds within a word to create a new word. One of the more difficult phonological awareness tasks, this skill is known as deletion, making Choice C the correct answer. Segmenting, as suggested in Choice A, refers to one's ability to break sentences into words, words into syllables or syllables into phonemes. For example, when segmenting *pat*, the word would become /p/ /a/ /t/. Blending (Choice B) is often understood as the opposite of segmenting and refers to the ability to sequence sounds together to form words – so when the sounds /p/ /a/ /t/ are put together, they form the word *pat*. Finally, substitution (Choice D) refers to changing a sound in a word to create another word – for example, if you replace the /p/ in *pat* with the /k / sound, you will get *cat*. This is likewise one of the more difficult skills and is often developed after a child learns to delete sounds.

11. **C** Phonemic deletion means that a sound is taken out of a word in order to create a new word. Choice C shows the initial sound deleted to make a second word (i.e. *tray* becomes *ray*). Choice A demonstrates substitution skills (i.e. by replacing the *t* in *tray* with a *g*, the word becomes *gray*). Choice B is dividing onset and rime and is indicative of a student's ability to segment. Finally, Choice D is indicative of substitution skills (i.e. *-ay* is substituted with *-ap* to form the word *trap*.

12. **D** The student in Choice D is demonstrating the ability to substitute a sound (/a/ for /i/). Additionally, s/he is able to do this task using the medial sound. Typically children are first able to delete and substitute using the first sound, followed by the last sound, and finally the middle (and most difficult) sound within a word. The other students are demonstrating different skills that are simpler and typically developed before deletion and substitution. For example, the student discussed in Choice A is able to hear similar sounds at the beginning of words, the student in Choice B is showing the ability to segment sounds and the student in Choice C is blending sounds. Choice D therefore describes the most advanced level of phonemic awareness and remains the best answer.

13. **A** Multisensory activities are useful in reinforcing knowledge of letter shapes in conjunction with letter names in an activity where the teacher says the letter and the student draws it. While painting does promote mastery of letter formation, it does not support learning the letter name, making Choice A a better option than Choice B. Because the activity

described in Choice A requires students to hear the name of the letter and then draw it in shaving cream, both letter names and shapes are promoted, making it the best answer. Reciting (Choice C) and singing (Choice D) do not require knowledge of letter names or shapes.

14. **A** The alphabetic principle refers to an understanding that sounds and sound combinations correspond to written letters. Choice A is an example of explicit instruction on letter names and their corresponding sounds and is therefore the best answer. While the other choices are all helpful ideas for a classroom, they do not directly promote the alphabetic principle. Choice B refers to print directionality, or the understanding that print in English reads from left to right. Choice C is beneficial for promoting print awareness by reinforcing that letters make up words and carry meaning. And finally, Choice D would likely encourage a love of reading by providing students the chance to re-read stories they've heard.

15. **C** The alphabetic principle states that phonemes are represented by letters and letter pairs. Only Choice C specifically addresses letters of the alphabet, making it the best answer. Choice A would require segmenting skills, Choice B an understanding of rhyming and Choice D assumes the student knows how to blend sounds to form words.

16. **D** Labeling promotes a student's awareness that print carries meaning and that print represents speech, making Choice D the best answer. It is unlikely that kindergarteners would decode *science, center,* or *literacy*, making Choice A incorrect. Phonological awareness, Choice B, is not connected to print, also making this answer incorrect. Finally, labels are not used to explicating promote oral vocabulary, making Choice D incorrect as well.

17. **C** Given that the student draws a picture with squiggly lines and then communicates the message of those lines, he has likely acquired print awareness and the knowledge that print carries a message separate from illustrations, making Choice C the best answer. Because the student communicates the story orally, he does not appear to simply be mimicking classmates, making Choice A incorrect. As the student does not yet write letters, he may not have developed alphabetic awareness (Choice B). Finally, readiness for decoding is dependent on phonics skills in addition to oral vocabulary and phonics skills are not evidenced by the student's picture, lines, and oral description, also making Choice D incorrect.

18. **A** Research indicates that knowledge of letter names is an indicator of future reading success. Students who know letter names are better able to sequence and blend letters, making Choice A the best answer. As learning letter names actually makes reading easier for students down the line and because teaching letter names actually supports children in their learning of sounds, Choice B is incorrect. Additionally, confusion between letter names and sounds can be minimalized through explicit teacher-led learning and because learning letter sounds actually promotes reading rather than slow development, Choice C is also incorrect. Finally, while students may learn some letter names from environmental print, many students will benefit from explicit instruction, also making Choice D incorrect.

19. **D** Print awareness is an understanding that words convey thoughts and are made of letters, and that spaces appear between words. Students may develop print awareness in varied ways. For example, they may learn through environmental print (such as *Target* or *Subway* signs or through labels on common objects within the classroom), as suggested in Choice A. Using big books that call student's attention to letters and words (Choice B) or reading predictable text that closely follows provided illustrations (Choice C) are other ways teachers may promote print awareness in their classroom. Teachers can also promote print awareness include by putting nametags on desks, using toys based on letters and words, and recording student's thoughts as they voice them aloud. Analysis of morphemes (Choice D), however, is a skill students develop after print awareness and not a way in which teachers promote print awareness. Because Choice D is the only incorrect answer, it is also the best choice.

20. **B** The alphabetic principle, or understanding there is a relationship between written letters and spoken sounds, is an important concept for students to develop. Knowledge of letter names, shapes and sounds are required for a child to successfully learn how to read. Choices A and C, in which students "write" letters or dictate sentences that correspond with their drawings, promote print awareness, not the alphabetic principle, making them incorrect. When students use a pointer to follow along as text is read aloud (Choice D) they develop an understanding of print directionality or that English is read from left to right and top to bottom. This activity also requires students to "return sweep", or move from the last word on a line to the next line and back to the left hand side of the page. Choice B is

therefore the best answer – the "whack a letter" activity allows students to practice identifying letters, part of the alphabetic principle.

21. C   Though it is unlikely the students are able to independently read the poster (Choice A) or refer back to it (Choice B) given that they are in preschool, there is great value in what the teacher is doing (making Choice D incorrect). By writing down the children's thoughts, the teacher is encouraging literary development and promoting the concept that speech can be represented in writing, making Choice C the best answer. Furthermore, the teacher is demonstrating concept of print and how to take notes. She may also use the opportunity to extend the experience and guide students in determining the first sound and/or letter in a word, or point out how writing begins at the left side of the paper, etc.

22. D   Students benefit from explicit and implicit instruction in book-handling skills such as what the various parts of the book are, how to hold a book upright, and knowing where to begin reading, making Choice D the best answer. A classroom library (Choice A) is valuable for creating an environment that promotes enjoyment of reading while "return sweep" (Choice B) is valuable for promoting print directionality. Scribing and creating predictable text books (Choice C) helps communicate that speech can be recorded and that print carries a message.

23. B   The "Write the Room" activity utilizes environmental print. Since students are not being directly taught phoneme and phonics rules, instruction is considered implicit, making Choice B the best answer and both Choices A and C incorrect (furthermore, instruction is not whole group, as indicated by Choice C). While the activity may strengthen work habits, it is specifically a language task rather than a habit-building task, also making Choice D incorrect.

24. B   The words miscued by the student are both decodable by using phonics generalization for multisyllable words. While there is a close link between spelling and reading, a spelling inventory of a student's ability to encode is not the best strategy (Choice A). The student reads familiar words with accuracy, also making Choice C incorrect. The words miscued can be analyzed by word part (phil-antrop-ist, bene-fit); however the analysis skills needed to analyze these words is beyond the normal level of third grade students, making Choice D incorrect as well. This student shows evidence of knowledge of general phonetic rules. S/he miscues only multi-syllabic words, making Choice B the best answer.

25. A Most intensive, systematic phonics programs introduce words in the following order: CVC, CVCC, CVVC, and CVCe. Choice A follows that pattern, making it the best answer. Choice B places the CCVC word before the CVCe word, making it incorrect. Choice C includes sight words that are not decoded and while the words *me* and *my* have a common letter-sound relationship, the rules they follow would typically be taught after mastery of short vowel sounds, also making Choice D incorrect.

26. C Word family ladders are activities commonly used to promote recognition of onset/rime (Choice A) and rhyming (Choice B) and when students practice chunking the rime, the activity also supports automatic word recognition (Choice D). Choices A, B and D are therefore all correct. The words on the ladders, however, are not in connected text that reads from left to right and from top to bottom, making choice C the only incorrect choice and therefore the best answer.

27. C Morphemes are the smallest meaningful unit of language. Ungrateful has three morphemes *un, grate, ful*. Relaxed has three morphemes *re, lax, ed*. The student incorrectly encoded the morphemes, making Choice C the best answer. Spelling lists typically do not apply syntactic rules (rules governing language), making Choice A incorrect. The question does not indicate that the student is a language learner drawing cognates from a different language, also making Choice B wrong. Onset/rime is a way of breaking words into onset (the letters before the vowel) and rime (the vowel and everything after it). The only common rime in the words missed is –ate. This one strategy would be insufficient to correct the spelling errors and so Choice D is also not the best answer.

28. B Weekly spelling lists can help provide a foundation for phonics knowledge that can then be applied to other similar words. Systematic phonics provides instruction in letter-sound relationships following a sequential plan, making Choice B the best answer. Choice A, read alouds, or the teacher reading aloud a text, would not promote automatic word recognition or the ability to decode words quickly by applying phonics pattern knowledge. Choice C includes letter name knowledge, which is part of the alphabetic principle, but not necessarily part of phonics and reading print. Choice D, structural analysis, is the process of examining word parts like roots and prefixes. By breaking the word into parts, the reader can draw conclusions about the meaning. Structural analysis follows phonics knowledge.

29. A Syntax refers to the rules used to create well-formed sentences. It includes inflections, word order, grammar rules, and other rules. Calling attention to syntax supports decoding with accuracy and automaticity, making Choice A the best answer. The word choices are not homographs (Choice B) and are not multi-syllable words (Choice C). Students completing this type of activity likely already have a firm grasp of the alphabetic principle (Choice D), or an understanding that there is a connection between spoken words and written letters.

30. D Reading has a hierarchy of skills. Decoding is a prerequisite for comprehension and fluency. The skills do not develop independently as suggested in Choice A. Though the ability to make sense of a decoded word is contingent on oral vocabulary, oral vocabulary can develop independent of decoding skills, also making Choice B incorrect. Because the question specifies that the student struggles with "unfamiliar, multi-syllable" words, we can assume the reader has the basic phonemic skills necessary to decode one-syllable words (Choice C) and that phonemic awareness is not the primary problem. Choice D is therefore the best answer – because the student has difficulties decoding multi-syllable words, they are also likely to struggle with comprehension and fluency as these skills go hand in hand.

31. D Readers can decode unknown or nonsensical phonetically regular words to derive the pronunciation, making Choice B incorrect. However, the pronunciation alone is not enough to derive meaning as indicated by Choice A. Rather, readers use their oral vocabulary to assign meaning to the decoded words. Furthermore, decoding practice is not viewed as an effective means of vocabulary building, making Choice C incorrect. While students may practice reading *dash, gash, lash*, and *cash*, using the words in isolation to build vocabulary would not likely be productive. The best answer is Choice D – while beginning readers can decode unfamiliar and nonsense words, they depend on their oral vocabulary to assign meaning to words.

32. C Though some fluency problems can be resolved through practice, the primary cause of fluency difficulties is weak decoding skills, making Choice C the best answer. If a child is not able to efficiently and effectively blend sounds to form words, s/he is unlikely to be able to decode in a fluent manner. Though weak comprehension (Choice B) is not to blame for a student's difficulties with fluency, fluency and comprehension do work hand in hand as a child's ability to read at an appropriate pace greatly impacts comprehension, which in turn impacts fluency. Readers with higher fluency typically have higher comprehension and, because these readers recognize words with automaticity they can focus less on sound-by-sound decoding and more on comprehension. Though requiring a student to read text that is inappropriately leveled for him/her (Choice A) would likely cause low fluency and simpler passages would undoubtedly make it easier for a child to read fluently, this is not a primary cause of fluency difficulties. Finally, whereas students can effectively use context clues (Choice D) to determine unknown words within text, a lack of ability to do so is likewise not the primary cause of fluency difficulties. It is important to note decoding difficulties need to be specifically diagnosed and addressed so fluency does not negatively impact a student's ability to read and comprehend material.

33. A The student substitutes /*ch*/ and /*sh*/ digraphs and substitutes /w/ for /wh/. Digraphs are two consonants that produce a single sound--*sh, ch, th, ph,* making Choice A the best answer. In a consonant blend, each of the consonant sounds is pronounced—for example, bl, cl, gr. Because the student correctly reads *grazed*, Choice B is incorrect. A morpheme is the smallest grammatical part of a language that makes a meaningful part of a word—*peck, -ed.* As the student correctly reads *pecked* and *grazed*, Choice C is also not the correct answer. Finally, a diphthong is a sliding vowel combination that changes from one sound to another—*ou* or *oi*, and the student correctly read *out*, making Choice D incorrect as well.

34. B Beginning-level phonics instruction starts with CVC words, or consonant vowel consonant patterns, making Choice B the best answer. The other choices would be more advanced—Choices A and C both have two or more initial consonants, which require blending skills. Choice D has final consonants that can be more difficult since they also require blending at the end of the word.

35. C If a student struggles to recognize words and spends a long time trying to decode, the text can be more difficult to comprehend, making Choice D incorrect. This is especially true for longer texts. Choice A is also not the best answer as the student's difficulties automatically recognizing print words does not mean he cannot understand spoken words. Choice B is incorrect since the difficulties would slow, not increase, a student's fluency. Choice C is therefore the best answer – difficulties automatically recognizing high-frequency words would likely make comprehension more difficult.

36. C Phonics deals with common patterns that readers can apply to unfamiliar words to properly decode them. Choice A, hearing a name of a letter and drawing the letter, would promote print awareness, which comes before phonics instruction. Choice B, in which a list of irregular words would be memorized, would mean these words can not be taught using phonetic rules. Finally, breaking down spoken words (Choice D) would promote phonological awareness, which also comes before phonics. Choice C is therefore the best answer – activities that promote learning common letter-sound relationships would be the most effective when teaching phonics.

37. B Sight words cannot be learned by phonics because they are irregular, making Choice A incorrect. Choice C would also not likely be helpful as phonemic awareness deals only with print language. Choice D refers to a more advanced skill, structural analysis, which is a skill for understanding a word by looking at its prefixes, suffixes, etc. Instruction, practice opportunities and support to learn and a list of common sight words would likely be the most helpful for a student struggling with sight words, making Choice B the best answer.

38. B Words ending in –ly are frequently adverbs. The syntax of the given sentence would likely have an adjective in (1) and (4), making Choices A and D incorrect. Some common adjective endings are –ous and –able. Blank 3 would be appropriate for a conjunction, also making Choice C incorrect. Words such as *quietly, gingerly,* or *rambunctiously* would be suitable for (2), making Choice B the best answer.

39. B All areas of reading development are interrelated. Logically, as readers understand the text, they are better able to anticipate words to be deciphered. Automaticity aids fluency. Fluency also supports word analysis and comprehension. As students struggle less with fluency, they can focus more attention on comprehension. The development of the skills is dependent and reciprocal.

40. A Suffixes are added to the end of words to convey grammatical information such as part of speech, number or verb tense. Though prefixes (which are attached to the beginning of words) and suffixes provide a pattern for decoding new words, the spelling and pronunciation of a suffix can vary depending on its root word. This is especially common with the –ed suffix which indicates verb tense and is demonstrated through the pronunciation of the words listed above (*purged /d/, painted*

/id/, flapped /t/). Choices B, C and D are therefore incorrect as affixes may indicate the tense of a word (Choice B), the *–ed* suffix is *not* always spelled or pronounced the same way (only a *-d* is added to *purged, -ed* is added to *painted,* and the consonant is doubled and *–ed* is added to *flapped (-ped)*), and suffixes attach to the *end* of words (Choice D). The correct answer is therefore Choice A – though the spelling of a suffix varies (as seen in *purged, painted* and *flapped*), it is more reliable than the pronunciation of the words (in which the ending sounds vary between */d/, /id/* and */t/*).

41. C   Homonyms are words that are spelled the same but have different meanings, such as the word *letter*, making Choice C the best answer. Synonyms (Choice A) are words with similar meanings. Structural analysis (Choice B) is a way of analyzing words which analyzes roots and affixes. And finally, discrete phonemes (Choice D) are the individual sounds of a word.

42. D   The words listed have a spelling pattern of a double consonant plus *y*. Learning spelling patterns helps students retain phonics patterns and promotes word recognition, making Choice D the best answer. The spelling list does not promote blending and does not contain academic vocabulary needed for schoolwork, making Choices A and B incorrect. Finally, second grade word studies are not typically geared toward identification of Greek and Latin roots, nor do the words lend themselves to this task, also making Choice C incorrect.

43. B   The Greek root *bio* is found in each of the words listed in Choice B, making this the best answer. The words are likely familiar to students and appropriate to demonstrate how words can be analyzed by Greek root to determine meaning. Choice A is a list of compound words and Choice C includes words with the morpheme *–ed*, This list would be more appropriate when teaching patterns for the pronunciation of the inflected form *–ed*. Finally, Choice D is a list of Greek heroes and does not support a lesson on Greek roots for word analysis.

44. C   Structural analysis is the process of understanding the parts that make up a word. By showing words that share a part (*view*) and demonstrating how the word meaning changes with the addition of other parts, students can gain skills in word analysis. The list in Choice C is best designed for this purpose, making C the best answer. The words in Choice A are sight words which share a phoneme /th/, the words listed in Choice B are appropriate for teaching onset/rime and the words in Choice D are domain-specific vocabulary. In summary, the words in Choices A, B, and D do not share word parts that can be used to introduce structural analysis.

45. C Expressive vocabulary skills involve the words we know how to use when speaking or writing. Receptive skills are practiced through listening and reading, such as in Choices A, B and D. Choice C is therefore the best answer.

46. C Contextualized vocabulary is vocabulary placed into context. Illustrations and brief stories are examples of ways to provide context. Structural analysis (Choice A) focuses on analyzing roots, suffixes, and prefixes. Domain-specific vocabulary (Choice B) is vocabulary that is specifically associated with one subject area, such as science or history. Syntactic clues (Choice D) are clues that focus on the grammatical structure of the word. The question does not indicate that the vocabulary words share the same structure, domain, or part of speech – Choice C therefore remains the best answer.

47. D Word identification or word recognition is the ability to read a word accurately and efficiently. Automatic recall of sight words and automatic decoding of regular words both facilitate word identification and allow students opportunities to write, stamp and insert appropriate words. These are some ways to target this particular skill, making Choice D the best answer. Word maps to group vocabulary conceptually are not designed to promote word identification in second grade (Choice A), Elkonin boxes (Choice B) are used to build phonemic awareness which precedes word identification and graphic features (Choice C) are illustrations, maps, charts, etc. which provide information in addition to the text.

48. C Though student-generated questions (Choice A) are a great post-reading activity, they do not work for word maps in a pre-reading activity. Choice B might work during a class discussion to get students talking, but word maps are typically more effective when students are able to make a logical guess about a word's meaning based on context clues or reference materials. While Choice D targets associations that might be useful in activating student's prior knowledge, the discussion will not necessarily help to complete a word map. When using word maps as a pre-reading activity, Choice C, indicating the use of a dictionary or thesaurus, would be most effective by providing students with accurate and critical background knowledge they can later apply while reading.

49. C Context alone does not make the meaning of *chronological* clear to a reader unfamiliar with the topic, making Choice A incorrect. The roots *chrono* and *logic* can be used to expand vocabulary, also making Choice B incorrect. Additionally, by taking the time to pre-teach vocabulary, the teacher likely places value in activating student's prior knowledge - pre-teaching vocabulary is one way to do this and often helps place students on a level playing field so they all approach the reading with the same background knowledge (making Choice D incorrect). As *chronological* is significant to a reading about age, Choice C is the best answer – the teacher is most likely taking time to preteach this particular vocabulary word so students are able to understand it's meaning when they read it within the text.

50. B The students demonstrate the ability to decode, comprehend and recall vocabulary terms accurately when they come across the terms within text. On the test, however, they lack the ability to decode the words in isolation, making Choice B the best answer. As the students have adequate comprehension, metacognitive skills are not likely the problem, making Choice A incorrect. Also, because the test does not involve an oral assessment or require research skills, Choices C and D are also incorrect.

51. A Students can clarify the meanings of words by substituting a definition or synonym in place of the unfamiliar word in the sentence, making Choice A the best answer. Read alouds (Choice B) promote vocabulary acquisition but are not the best choice for clarifying a specific word. Establishing a time for independent reading (Choice C) builds good habits for independent reading, but does not necessarily provide students with assistance to determine the meaning of unfamiliar words. Vocabulary lists and free-write journal entries (Choice D) likewise will not efficiently clarify the meaning of vocabulary.

52. D If a word is decodable and already integrated into everyday oral vocabulary, it is not a high priority for explicit vocabulary instruction, making Choice D the best answer. Words important to the unit of study (Choice A), cross-curricular words (Choice B) or words necessary to understand in order to complete assignments (Choice C) are priority for selection.

53. D While stopping to consult a dictionary can be distracting, other options for determining meaning of this foreign expression will not work, making Choice D the best answer. The word is phonetically decodable and unfamiliar, so depending on oral vocabulary will not help the student (Choice A). And, because the student is encountering the term for the first time, observing the punctuation will likewise be inadequate to determine meaning (Choice B). Finally, the situation lacks semantic clues, syntactic clues, and derivatives, also making Choice C incorrect.

54. A While some proverbs and idioms can be appreciated through the text, other proverbs should be explicitly taught because of their cultural significance. One successful strategy is to call attention to the expression during pre-reading activities so students will understand the phrase when they come across it in their reading, making Choice A the best answer. Allowing the students to explore does not expressly guide their learning, making Choice B incorrect. And, because looking up each word separately in the dictionary will not provide an appropriate definition of the phrase, Choice C is also incorrect. Finally, in order to avoid redundancy and cliché's, it is unlikely that one text will have the same proverb repeated, making Choice D incorrect.

55. B Once a reader has decoded a word, he can attach meaning to that word if it is part of his oral vocabulary. If the decoded word is not part of his oral vocabulary, then meaning cannot be attached, making Choice B the best answer. Recognition of the connection between the sounds of English words and words in other languages does not require an understanding of the word—that is, the reader does not need to have the word in his oral vocabulary in order to distinguish phonemes, making Choice A incorrect. Furthermore, a student may have a word in his oral vocabulary that he is not able to analyze structurally, also making Choice C incorrect. Finally, oral vocabulary is not related to hearing and generating rhymes, making Choice D incorrect.

56. C Pronouncing words multiple times (Choice A) does help secure words in student's oral vocabulary; however, this strategy will not assist students in recalling the meaning for various terms. Likewise, drawing attention to the spelling of words (Choice B) can support their reading and when taught varied word ending meanings, students may be able to determine word tense or number, however this alone is not likely the best strategy to help students recall meaning. Cognates are used primarily with English Language Learners who can relate an English word to a word in their primary language, also making Choice D incorrect. Helping students to group words conceptually (Choice C), however, will help them categorize terms and thus more easily recall their meanings. For example, when discussing weather-related terms, teachers could lead a class discussion and activity to produce the following:

Moderate Conditions	Harsh Conditions
cold front	blizzard
warm front	tornado
humidity	heat index
mist	hurricane

By helping students to group words conceptually, vocabulary becomes more meaningful, terms become connected and thus easier to recall. Choice C is therefore the best answer.

57. B For this particular book, pre-teaching students the character names will likely help organize the story in their minds and provide background information about each narrator/chapter, making Choice B the best answer. Choice A is likely a good activity to provide students with information about the place in time when the book was compiled, but will not likely help the students better understand each narrator. Choice C, explaining the meaning of *Canterbury*, could likewise be helpful if combined with other pre-reading activities. Alone, however, this exercise will not be as helpful as Choice B. Finally, Choice D is a good post reading literary response activity to promote text-to-self comprehension and analysis, but would not likely help as a pre-reading exercise.

58. D The student is making an inference, or a guess, regarding what will most likely happen next, making Choice D the best answer. Comprehending text on an inferential level allows readers to make logical conclusions based on the information they are given and implied concepts. While the literal level is directed at things that are explicitly stated, the inferential level entails what is *not* said (making Choice B incorrect). Self-monitoring, as suggested in Choice A, is also not evident – this would involve the student self questioning to ensure their own understanding or monitor-

ing if they needed to reread/rehear anything, for example. As the student is not reading aloud, one would also not be able to assume he/she has strong decoding skills, as suggested in Choice C.

59. **C** One aspect of literary analysis is character development. The activity described provides a framework for students to consider a character's appearance and traits, making Choice C the best answer. The activity does not provide an opportunity to interact with a genre other than imaginative fiction, making Choice A incorrect. Also, as no mention is made of an allusion, Choice B is also incorrect. The activity depends strictly on interpretation of one passage and does not require the reader to make connections to self, other texts, or the world around him, making Choice D incorrect as well.

60. **B** A Venn diagram is a graphic organizer used to compare and contrast different concepts and would be the most appropriate activity to help students compare and contrast the two versions of the story, making Choice B the best answer. While the most common Venn diagram has two intersecting circles, the diagram may have more intersecting or concentric circles. Analyzing the culture of *Lon Po Po* does not require comparing the text to other versions, making Choice A incorrect. Similarly, analyzing point of view and tracing the plot are useful literary analysis techniques; however they do not necessitate consideration of other versions, also making Choices C and D incorrect.

61. **B** In this activity, students must take what they know and combine it with what the text says to figure out something the author did not explicitly state, making Choice B the best answer. By providing the students with some information and requiring them to develop their own idea about the setting, they are practicing to make inferences. While the task includes a character from literature, that character is clearly identified, not mentioned briefly or indirectly, so the task is not primarily for the purpose of recognizing allusions (Choice A). The task does not direct students to note specific characteristics of a particular genre (Choice C) or make mention of the inclusion of figurative language such as similes or metaphors (Choice D).

62. **C** Because the teacher's comments go beyond a literal understanding and do not simply restate the facts included in the text, Choice A is not likely the correct answer. Though reading aloud to students does often help to teach how to read with expression (Choice B), this is also not likely the

case as the teacher's comments do not center on his intonation. Though the teacher does appear to understand the passage on a higher level, he is not making comments that evaluate or relate the passage to other text, also making Choice D unlikely to be the teacher's motivation for reading in this manner. Because the teacher is clearly thinking about what he is reading through visualizations, he is most likely demonstrating meta-cognitive strategies for his students, or showing them how to think about what they are reading. Choice C is therefore the best answer.

63. **A**   The activity described requires students to look at the event from the dog's point of view instead of from the hen's point of the view, making Choice A the best answer. The activity does not include analysis of literary allusions or oral language, making Choices B and C incorrect. While it is true that events of the book may be summarized during the activity, it is not necessarily the skill the teacher is targeting, also making Choice D incorrect.

64. **B**   Reading aloud the selected books for the unit would likely promote a literacy rich environment (as mentioned in Choices A and B), treatment of similar topics in different genres (Choice B), listening comprehension (Choice B), love of reading (Choice C), and to some extent reading for varied purposes (Choice D). The unit plan does not promote knowledge of idioms, comprehension on an evaluative level (the plan only mentions read alouds by the teacher) (both of which make Choice A incorrect), multiple accounts of the same event (while all selections include seed growth, they are not an account of the same event), knowledge of text features (table of contents, index, etc.) (both which make Choice C incorrect), decoding or self-monitoring (as all selections are read aloud with no indication of interruption) (which makes Choice D incorrect). Choice B therefore remains the best answer.

65. **C**   Close reading involves many strategies. Analysis at the word level is a close reading strategy in which students work to gain understanding of a difficult passage. In Choices A, B, and D, the tasks do not require students to interact with the text. Oral reading (Choice A), studying spelling patterns (Choice B), and collaborative work on author posters (Choice D) are all activities that have merit; but they do not involve close reading of a text.

66. **D**   Graphic organizers such as story maps, webs, frames, clusters, and charts are useful tools to help students summarize and illustrate both informational and imaginative text, making Choice D the best answer. Organizers can help students recognize the interrelationships and

nuances of a text. Text features such as index, table of contents, and glossary are characteristic of informational text instead of imaginative text, making Choice A incorrect. English conventions such as capitalization, grammar rules, and punctuation (Choice B) are not particularly tied to the craft of imaginative literature. And while word analysis does promote comprehension, it is not typically used to interpret imaginative literature, also making Choice C incorrect.

67. **A** Providing students with information about the time period, as suggested in Choice A, is a schema building activity that activates student's prior knowledge about a topic by helping them recall and connect what they already know to the text. In the event that students lack background knowledge, the necessary information is provided, making this the best answer. Though pronouncing difficult vocabulary (Choice B) for students is helpful to encourage recall, simply repeating individual words will not promote student comprehension of text. Likewise, while it is helpful for students to know and understand the difference between the various genres (Choice C), it will not necessarily encourage their understanding of this particular passage. Finally, Choice D is invalid as it is a post reading activity and the question specifically asks about a pre-reading activity.

68. **C** Through these questions, the teacher is trying to direct student's attention to the author and his/her point of view, making Choice C the best answer. Informational and argumentative texts often reflect the author's perspective. It is important for students to consider the author's background and beliefs in order to put the text in perspective and call attention to how the writer's beliefs may influence information being presented. Understanding text on a literal level (Choice A) involves students reading text and gleaning it for basic facts that are explicitly stated. Additionally, facts and opinions (Choice B), though likely presented in the various texts being read, are not the teacher's focus. Finally, while the teacher likely hopes to have student's make connections between the texts (Choice D) as she has assigned texts about the same subject, her questions do not lead students to discuss the similarities and differences among the essays, but rather to focus on each particular author and what about them may have helped to shape their arguments.

69. B Complex questions that prompt students to learn, relate and assess encourage students to think on an evaluative level, making Choice B the best answer. If the guide prompted students to think on a literal level, it would focus on questions that were conveyed simply through the text and words used in the questions would likely come directly from the text (making Choice A incorrect). Though students may need to re-read when they don't understand something, as suggested in Choice C, this is not the most likely purpose of the guide. Students reading at this level likely already self-monitor and re-read as necessary. Finally, were a teacher trying to determine if students had any prior knowledge of a subject, he would likely engage students in pre-reading activities, not provide them with a guide to use while reading (making Choice D incorrect).

70. A Inferences usually involve looking at what the author suggests or hints at without saying, making Choice A the best answer. The literal level would involve looking at exact words on the page, making Choice C incorrect. Choice B would involve comparing this story to other stories or to a larger question rather than looking at what the author is suggesting. Finally, figurative language (Choice D) is commonly used to analyze literary text.

71. C Though support at home (Choice A) is important, it is unlikely the teacher continues to work with the same text in sixth grade simply because he is concerned some students lack support at home. It is also unlikely the teacher is having students reread the same information multiple times to glean literal information – this type of information is typically simple to gather as it is fact based, making Choice B incorrect. If the teacher wanted students to complete a graphic organizer for the text (Choice D), she would have likely done so earlier as graphic organizers are typically used to support student's understanding of text. Having students reread text they've already been exposed to, however, is often a useful strategy to help them further comprehend material. This allows students to notice more details than before and delve into the reading beyond a basic understanding, making Choice C the best answer.

72. A A research project requires integration of multiple sources. Research is an ideal opportunity for an adult to provide support to a student learning to use online sources in conjunction with print, making Choice A the best answer. A research project on animals would not use literary/imaginative works, making Choice B incorrect. The author's point of view could be practiced through a variety of texts rather than uniquely through the research project, also making Choice C incorrect. Finally, grammar and usage for the research project would not require knowledge in addition to what students have practiced through persuasive or narrative writing, making Choice D incorrect.

73. **C** Text features are supports that provide clarity and allow for efficient use of an informational text. They include things such as table of contents, headings, index, glossaries, and sidebars, making Choice C the best answer. Choice A lists some stages of reading development, while Choice B describes common text structures. Finally, Choice D provides various story elements of imaginative literature.

74. **D** Guiding students to analyze the question and choose the correct text structure for response can strengthen student responses. Cause and effect shows the relationship between an event and what happened because of that event, making Choice D the best answer. While history topics are often written in chronological order (Choice A), this particular assignment is better suited for cause/effect. This assignment does not ask for a comparison and contrast of life before and after the war (Choice B) or of a description of life after the war (Choice C).

75. **D** Activities such as outlining and note taking require students to put the text or oral language in their own words, making Choice D the best answer. Skimming would be insufficient to analyze the text as required in the activity, making Choice A incorrect. Visualizing focuses the reader on creating a mental picture from the words in the text rather than analyzing at the word level, also making Choice B incorrect. Finally, conceptual grouping is a strategy of classifying words based on commonality, making Choice C incorrect as well.

76. **B** Because key vocabulary did not come up naturally in the student discussion, the content-specific vocabulary may be missing from their oral vocabulary. Incorporating the vocabulary in daily conversation prepares the students to comprehend the printed text, making Choice B the best answer. Introduction of the words is not primarily for the purpose of spelling (Choice A). The vocabulary words will first be needed for comprehension on the literal level. Second graders would not be expected to evaluate style (Choice C). The vocabulary may be loosely related to text structure; however, text structure would not be the primary purpose for introducing key content-specific words (Choice D).

77. A Accurate internet research requires that a student be able to distinguish between fact and opinion as he is likely to encounter some factual information alongside blogs and opinion-based pages, making Choice A the best answer. The research project does not require oral language (Choice B). And, while self-generated questions can be a valuable strategy in guiding research, the task can be completed without self-generated questioning (Choice C). Finally, analysis of character development is a skill generally connected to literary texts (Choice D).

78. B Norm-referenced tests rank students according to their performance. The rankings of norm-referenced tests are used to compare students and schools to a peer group, making Choice B the best answer. A portfolio (Choice A) is a collection of student work that shows growth of that particular student over time. Authentic tasks (Choice C) are activities and assessments that replicate real life. Such tasks are not typically standardized to compare students. Informal Reading Inventories (Choice D), as the name suggests, are informal assessments that do not provide stanine and percentile data used in comparison.

79. B A portfolio allows students to assess their work, view progress over time, and choose the pieces that showcase their talents. Because the process strongly involves students, they take ownership in their work and tend to reflect on the pieces of work included in the portfolio, making Choice B the best answer. Choice A, a norm-referenced test does not invite reflection of student work. It is more useful for comprehension and analysis than assessment. Choice C, a re-telling, is purposely open-ended to allow students to demonstrate how they construct meaning from a text, but it is not the type of assessment method that allows students to evaluate their own work. Choice D, a shared journal, encourages students to construct and analyze meaning, but a journal is not necessarily an assessment tool.

80. D Because test scores appear to be tied to reading and/or comprehension of story problems, there may be a question of test validity, making Choice D the best answer. Is the test assessing reading ability instead of math ability? A test in which a discrete group has a specific advantage or disadvantage is said to be biased (Choice A) whereas tests in which two forms yield different results (Choice B) are said to lack reliability. Finally, the miscue analysis results do not indicate a problem with validity (Choice C).

81. C Reliability refers to the consistency of the results, making Choice C the best answer. An assessment should be reliable regardless of tester, form, and situation. Bias (Choice A) refers to test design or results that systematically favor or disadvantage a criterion group. In the example given, however, a criterion group is not advantaged. Validity (Choice B) refers to the degree to which the test assesses what it is intended to test. Predictability is not typically considered a test concept.

82. C An individually-administered assessment in which students are asked to identify the name and sound of a letter and in which results are recorded is an example of an informal assessment to evaluate alphabetic principle, making Choice C the best answer. A running record (Choice A) is an informal assessment; however it is being used in this situation to assess reading behavior. The portfolio described (Choice B) is likewise an informal assessment; however, does not necessarily contain an assessment of the student's knowledge of the alphabetic principle. A norm-referenced test (Choice D) is a formal assessment.

83. A A pattern of /l/ /r/ confusion is evident. The miscue is the result of the student's inability to form the phonemes, making Choice A the best answer. Instruction in phonics (Choice B), acquisition of additional oral vocabulary (Choice C), and recognition of cognates (Choice D), though all valuable for language learners, will not correct the particular error pattern evident in the running record.

84. B Using a zoo map to plan a trip to the zoo is an example of an authentic task—a task that replicates real life. The rubric is the assessment tool used, making Choice B the best answer. Multiple-choice tests to assess comprehension are widely used; however, they do not closely replicate real life, so they are not considered an authentic task (Choice A). Working a puzzle to practice joining compound words (Choice C) is a common activity; however, it is not an authentic task, nor is there indication that it is used to assess student knowledge of compound words. Student practice on a literacy website can be an example of technology use in a classroom. Progress is noted so that lessons stay at the appropriate level. The activity does not replicate real life, so it is not considered an authentic task (Choice D).

85. C While norm-referenced tests can be administered to individuals, they are also designed to be administered to a group, making Choice C the best answer. By contrast, Informal Reading Inventories, retellings, and portfolios are all assessments administered individually, making the other choices incorrect.

86. D A dictated list of phonetically-regular words is a tool to assess students' knowledge of letter-sound relationships, making Choice D the best answer. Can the student hear words such as *chat* and correctly encode the sounds /ch/ /a/ /t/ into the letters *c-h-a-t*? Skills in phonological awareness, phonemic awareness, and concepts of print do not include graphophonemic (relationship between orthography and phonology) skills, making the other choices incorrect.

87. C Retellings prompt students to share their understanding of text without the scaffolding often provided through teacher questions. Instead, student responses are based purely on their own reading and interpretation of text, making Choice C the best answer. Retellings are not likely the most efficient means of assessment, especially if multiple students need to be assessed at once (making Choice A incorrect). Likewise, retellings are not easily quantified, making Choice D incorrect. While Choice B (which suggests that retellings are good tools as they require no prior planning) is true at times, this is not likely why the teacher asked the student to perform a retelling. Furthermore, because retellings are not easily quantified, teachers may choose to create a rubric ahead of time.

88. A A small group of students failed to meet the standard for homophones. Because the question is likely representative of overall use of homophones, explicit instruction on the use of common homophones is appropriate. Since the majority of the group appears to have mastered homophones, a small group can be targeted, making Choice A the best answer and Choice B incorrect. To promote student mastery, students can be given instruction rather than told the answer (Choice C). And finally, while calling attention to homophones that occur in reading is appropriate, it may also be disruptive to the reading and be inadequate to provide mastery of the topic at hand (Choice D).

89. C Exposure to content- and idea- rich text is important at all levels of reading development. By promoting and modeling close reading strategies, students can gain access to and appreciation for well-crafted writing, making Choice C the best answer. Students should have a balance of materials that they have selected and that the teacher has selected, making Choice A incorrect. The question indicates that the book is at the students' instructional level and appropriate for guided reading, also making Choice B incorrect. While some texts are both high-interest and well-crafted, text that students do not find highly interesting because of a limited ability to make connections need not be replaced with high-interest text (making Choice D incorrect as well). Students benefit from mastering the skills needed to read all types of imaginative and informational texts.

90. **D** Because the goal is to develop independent readers of all genres and levels, limiting genres will be counterproductive, making Choice D the best answer. Students will benefit from exposure to a wide range of types of writing. As each genre is explored, students gain the additional knowledge and skills needed to master the genre independently. Having the skills (Choice A), stamina (Choice B), resources, and motivation (Choice C) helps to equip students for independent reading.

91. **A** *Scaffolding* is the use of support to help all students achieve the goal. In the scenario given, the first point is drawn from the whole class; the second point is found as students work in pairs; further points students must find independently. Gradually, the support is removed when the student can reach the goal without it. Choice A is therefore the best answer. This scenario does not include a connection to prior knowledge, making Choice B incorrect. Differentiation is an instructional strategy that tailors content, process, or product for individual students - in this scenario, all students complete the same task (also making Choice C incorrect). Finally, ongoing assessment is used by teachers to guide instruction and assessment is not ongoing or guiding instruction in this situation, making Choice D wrong as well.

92. **B** Leveled readers are intended to match books and readers. By dividing students into groups based on their skill level, instruction can be delivered to improve reading development without using text that is so difficult that students become frustrated, making Choice B the best answer. Age-appropriate content is available in non-leveled books; simply leveling a text does not make it age-appropriate, making Choice A incorrect. Highly proficient readers may be capable of reading leveled texts which are not age appropriate. Text leveling is intended to alleviate the problem of trying to use one text for a diverse class of readers, also making Choice C incorrect. Finally, while leveled readers are an excellent opportunity for practicing metacognitive skills, they are not specifically written for that purpose, making Choice D incorrect as well.

93. B A text that is at a student's instructional level should contain an appropriate ratio of familiar to unfamiliar words so as not to be too easy and cause a loss in interest or be too hard and cause frustration, making Choice B the best answer. Choice A may not necessarily be a factor since foreign expressions and idioms can be easy depending on the context. Choice C is also not necessarily correct since common, high-frequency words that are multisyllabic may not be challenging for a fifth-grade class. While students benefit from being exposed to a variety of genres, as suggested in Choice D, it is not the central component to consider when determining the instructional level since most fifth-graders will have worked with popular genres to a certain extent.

94. C Giving students ready access to favorite books can encourage them to pick up the book and reread a memorable passage – Choice C is therefore the best answer. While audio books can provide support and enjoyment for listeners, they are not a substitute for printed text, making Choice A incorrect. Computer time is best used when scheduled and balanced with formal classroom instruction, also making Choice B incorrect. Furthermore, extrinsic rewards may work only as long as the motivation is there. Finally, story maps facilitate comprehension but may not promote a love for reading, making Choice D incorrect.

95. A Text complexity and text leveling (Choice D) are different in that a book may be assigned a level depending on the text and text features of that particular book. Text level is affixed to the book itself and does not vary depending on the reader or task. Popular leveling systems assign books a level by letter or grade. Text complexity considers the reader and task and how difficult the reading and comprehension will be for that individual, making Choice A the best answer. The ability to hear and manipulate sound in spoken language is phonemic awareness, not a text designation (Choice B). And finally, reading with accuracy, prosody, and comprehension is referred to as fluency (Choice C).

96. A Schema theory says that information is contained in units called schema. We learn by organizing information into this schema and then relating new information to this schema, making Choice A the best answer. Vocabulary acquisition (Choice B), fluency (Choice C) and whole language (Choice D) are not accurate definitions of schema.

97. **A** Students of all levels benefit from imaginative and informational texts. Examining different genres expands student vocabulary and promotes comprehension of a variety of text structures and features, making Choice A the best answer. Language learners may prefer literary or imaginative texts, depending on background and preferences, or they may prefer informational text particularly about topics with which they are already familiar. Both literary and informational texts promote language skills. (Choice B). Informational texts should not be excluded from early childhood. The specialized vocabulary promotes expansion of vocabulary (Choice C). Some choice of reading material can be left to the reader; however, students benefit from interacting with content- and idea- rich text of various genres (Choice D).

98. **D** It is crucial to provide all students with a variety of high-quality text from across genres. By diversifying materials, students will be exposed to varied text structures and features, making Choice D the best answer. While it is likely different students will prefer different genres, diversifying text will not ensure student enjoyment (Choice A) – rather, student enjoyment and engagement needs to be promoted through both quality text, lessons and teaching. Furthermore, the goal of interpreting text on the literal, inferential and evaluative levels is not achieved simply by providing varied materials (Choice B), however, providing multiple opportunities for students to practice such skills with diverse text is helpful. Likewise, while providing varied genres will not address the need to diversify instruction (Choice C), differentiated instruction needs to be planned *using* varied text with student's individual needs in mind.

99. **C** Differentiation is an approach to instruction that matches student needs and abilities with instruction. Scaffolding (Choice A) is support provided at all levels that gives students access to achieve academic goals. Scaffolding does not necessarily modify content, skills, or tasks. It enables students to access the goals that have been established. Schema building (Choice B) is connecting to student background knowledge. Cooperative learning (Choice D) is an educational approach that includes student groupings so that students complete tasks collectively.

100. A Students benefit from explicit instruction and guided practice in developing literary analysis skills. Providing a classroom library fosters a love for reading and interacting with books, but is not likely to contribute to literary analysis skills, making Choice A the best answer. Reading aloud promotes vocabulary development and interest in books (Choice B). Strong oral vocabulary and interest in reading are characteristics of strong readers. Electronic books (Choice C) provide scaffolding in pronunciation and definitions of unfamiliar words. Readers find greater enjoyment in reading books in which they do not struggle with fluency and comprehension. Finally, a strong reading program includes instruction in a variety of genres (Choice D) so that students can recognize and use different text structures and features.

Appendix:
Glossary

Affix

a prefix or suffix; letters added to the beginning or end of a word to change its meaning

Alliteration

repetition of consonant sounds in a series of words, such as "pen, pot, pour"; can be helpful for pointing out the initial sound in words.

Allusion

a brief literary reference to something in history, culture, literature, or politics which is outside the text.

Alphabetic principle

states that sounds (phonemes) correspond to print letters and letter combinations (graphemes); includes knowledge of letter names, shapes, and sounds.

Argumentative essay

a type of text in which the author presents an argument and supporting points in order to persuade the reader.

Assessment

an evaluation of the quality or ability of someone or something.

Assonance

repetition of vowel sounds in a series of words, such as "peak" and "leak" or "hour" and "loud"; can be helpful for pointing out vowel sounds and substituting.

Authentic task

a task that replicates the real world

Automaticity

a behavior that can be done with little effort or awareness. Automaticity is word recognition means that the word is drawn from memory rather than decoded.

Bias

a prejudice favoring one group over another

Blending

the ability to blend together two or more letter or sound combinations; blending is important for developing reading fluency and impacts comprehension

Blends

two or more sounds or letters that blend together; different categories include consonant blends, vowel blends, initial blends (occurring in the beginning of a word) and final blends (occurring at the end of a word).

Book handling skills

skills associated with knowing how to hold a book, looking at the cover, understanding that the story starts on the first page, and knowing to turn pages to continue reading.

CCVC

an abbreviation for a word that follows a pattern of consonant consonant vowel consonant such as "step." CCVC has an initial consonant blend and thus can be be more challenging than CVC patterned words.

CVC

an abbreviation for a word that follows a pattern of consonant vowel consonant like "bun." Phonics instruction often begins with teaching CVC patterned words.

CVCC

an abbreviation for a word that follows a pattern of consonant vowel consonant consonant such as "milk." CVCC has a final consonant blend and thus can be more challenging than CVC patterned words.

Close reading

a way of reading text for understanding

Cognate

words having the same etymological origin. Considering cognates between language (such as the English word "organization" and the French word "organization") can support language learners in acquiring vocabulary.

Compound word

a word made of two independent words

Context clue

information in pictures or surrounding words or sentences that may be used to identify or understand an unknown word

Cooperative learning

students working in pairs or small groups on a clearly defined task

Criterion-referenced test

a test that measures how well a person has learned specific knowledge or skills in an area of content

Decode

the ability to change a word from print to speech; the ability to sound out a word

Deletion

the phonological skill of deleting a sound(s) to create new words; deleting "s" from the word "star" results in "tar."

Differentiated instruction

instruction that is tailored to fit all students' needs by modifying assignments to fit students' instructional levels; differentiated instruction can be used in classrooms with students at different reading levels and to provide more effective activities for struggling readers, English Language learners, or high-achieving learners.

Digraph

a pair of letters used together to represent one phoneme; (e.g. "sh," "th," "qu")

Elkonin boxes

an activity for promoting phonemic awareness skills; students write each sound in a given word in a box.

ELL

English Language Learner

Encoding

to change spoken language to print letters

Environmental print

the print of everyday life; it includes such print as street signs, logos, food labels.

Evaluative

a level of comprehension in which the reader forms an opinion; the reader looks outside of the reading or assesses a text's argument.

Explicit instruction

teaching a concept or skill by first presenting information on it and following up with an exercise that practices that concept or skill; an example of explicit instruction includes teaching learners how to segment into syllables and then practicing segmenting a list of words provided by the teacher.

Expository text

a type of text that informs the reader and makes some type of claim or argument; a newspaper article on the need for political reform is an example of an expository text.

Expressive vocabulary

all the words that a person can use in spoken or written communication.

Faulty logic

the use of poorly supported examples, false assumptions, generalizations, etc.; important for evaluating the argument in a text.

Fiction

a text that is in part or in whole imagined and not real

Figurative language

language used to describe something by comparing it to something else; language that must be "figured" out and is not literal

Fluency

the ability to read with accuracy, rate, and prosody

Frustration reading level

level that requires extensive scaffolding because the reader does not have adequate background knowledge or skills for reading with accuracy and appropriate pace.

Genre

word to describe the category a literary text belongs to according to its form or content, such as a short story, novel, poem, detective novel, science fiction, etc.

Grapheme

letter or letter combination that spells a phoneme such as o, au, and aw.

Graphic organizer

a written activity that promotes comprehension by organizing ideas, characters, events, etc.; examples include a timeline, a schematic map, a character map, and a Venn diagram.

Homographs

words that are spelled the same but have different meanings and may be pronounced differently (e.g. tear/tear)

Imaginative text

a type of literary text that comes from the author's mind; Imaginative text may be poetry, prose, or drama.

Implicit instruction

instruction in which the information or problem is presented and students draw their own conclusions, rather than instruction in which explanation is given first. Phonics implicit instruction moves from whole to part. An implicit way to practice substituting is to use songs with rhymes.

Independent reading level

level at which a student can read and comprehend accurately without support

Infer/inference

to gather details from a text by looking at what the writer suggests or hints at rather than explicitly states.

Inflection

a change in the form of a word to express different grammatical category such as tense or number (e.g. give/given; reptile/reptiles)

Informational text

a type of text that informs the reader how to do something or that provides explanatory details; one example of an informational text is a how-to list or a manual for a device.

Instructional reading level

level of reading that requires assistance of teacher; however, error rate is 2-5 words/100 with good comprehension. This is the level at which students can make good progress in reading.

KWL chart

a chart with three columns for "what I know," "what I want to know," and "what I learned"; allows for student involvement in choosing topics to explore and self-assessment; effective for differentiated instruction.

Letter formation

the ability to distinguish and write upper and lower case letters; letter formation may be practiced with paper and pencil, on sandpaper stencils, in flour, etc.

Levels of comprehension

the different levels at which a reader constructs meaning from a text; includes literal (what is explicitly stated), inferential (what is suggested), and evaluative (how the reading relates to readers' lives, other texts, or larger questions about society).

Literal

a level of comprehension based on what the text says explicitly; opposed to nonliteral or figurative meanings and inference.

Literary analysis skills

the ability to analyze a text by looking at the genre, character development, figurative language, etc.

Literary response skills

ability to do written activities that target comprehension and the ability to relate a text back to a reader's life, to other texts, or to a larger question related to society, history, etc.; also includes the ability to use evidence from the text to support one's ideas.

Literary text

in its broadest definition, literary text includes all writing whether fiction or nonfiction, poetry or prose.

Long vowel

a vowel sound that sounds like the letter name; the "a" in "ape," the "e" in "each," the "i" in "ice," "o" in "open," the "u" in "unicorn."

Metacognition

the general term for thinking about what is being read; students can be taught to use metacognitive strategies while reading in order to promote an active engagement with the text and to promote comprehension.

Metacognitive strategies

strategies used while reading a text to promote an active engagement with the text and to promote comprehension; examples include visualizing, predicting, and self-questioning.

Miscue

an observed response that does not match what the person listening to the reading expects to hear.

Morpheme

the smallest unit of meaningful language (e.g. book, un, thank, ful)

Nonfiction

a type of text that is based on true events; examples include documentaries, reference material, or autobiographies.

Norm-referenced test

an assessment over specified content that compares the individual to a group

Note-taking

recording information from a source; effective strategy to promote comprehension while reading instructional or expository texts.

Onset and rime

a common way to divide words by breaking the initial sound before the vowel into the onset and the vowel and remaining sounds in the rime; in the word "bus" the onset is "b" and the rime "us." In the word "stream," the onset is "str" and the rime is "eam."

Oral vocabulary

all of the vocabulary that a student understands when listening and speaking.

Outlines

a hierarchical list; an effective strategy to promote comprehension of instructional or expository texts.

Paraphrase

to restate something in other words

Phoneme

smallest sound unit; there are about 44 phonemes in English. Phonemes can be represented by one or more letters; the sound /f/ corresponds to both "f" in "far" and "ph" in "graph."

Phonemic awareness

awareness that spoken language can be broken down into phonemes or individual sound units; phonemic awareness is a more specific aspect that falls under the larger term phonological awareness.

Phonics

instruction concerning the correspondences between print letters and sounds; based on common patterns and associations that readers use to decode unfamiliar words.

Phonological awareness

umbrella term for awareness that spoken language can be broken down into smaller parts; sentences can be broken into words; words can be broken into syllables; and syllables can be made of one or more phoneme.

Phonological processing

an auditory processing skill that involved detecting and differentiating phonemes

Point of view

the position or perspective of a literary text as presented by the author, narrator, or character. Narrative text can be described as first-, second-, or third person.

Portfolio

a collection of student work used to document student learning

Predicting

an oral or metacognitive strategy used to promote active reading and to relate prior schema to the text by logically makes guesses as to what will happen.

Predictability

the extent to which a text is predictable based on illustrations, repetitions in lines, and frequency of words used.

Pre-teaching

teaching difficult or unfamiliar vocabulary words or concepts before the main lesson in order to promote comprehension.

Previewing

a pre-reading activity that involves looking at illustrations, titles, headings, sub-headings, and other information in order to promote comprehension by providing readers details on what they will be reading.

Print awareness

an understanding that print carries meaning; develops in a child's environment (in the home and in public) and in the classroom; often demonstrated with young children by pretend reading and writing; encouraged in the classroom by labeling classroom objects and creating a print-rich environment.

Print directionality

knowledge that print in English reads from top to bottom and from left to right.

Prosody

the expression used in oral reading. It includes the timing, phrasing, emphasis, rhythm, intonation, and pitch that give meaning to oral language.

Receptive vocabulary

all the words that a person can understand; involves words one can understand by reading and hearing.

Reliability

the extent to which a test is consistent; a test feature that describes a test created so that it can be administered repeatedly with minimal errors

Re-telling

a method to assess a student's reading comprehension; the student reiterates what s/he understood after reading a text.

Rubric

a guide listing the criteria for scoring an assignment; rubrics typically have a table with various descriptors and various levels of achievement

Running record

a reading assessment tool that tracks the errors made by a student in oral reading; the record may also note fluency.

Rhyme

a correspondence in ending sound (e.g. caught, bought, tot)

Semantic clues

hints within a text that give cues about the meaning; clues may be synonyms, antonyms, definitions, etc. Semantic clues give meaning to words that can mean different things in different contexts

Scaffolding

instruction that introduces new concepts by building off of previously learned concepts gradually and incrementally; may involve presenting a less difficult version of a text followed by a more difficult one.

Schema building

instruction that puts new information into relation with prior knowledge of the topic; involves activating prior knowledge by asking students what they associate with certain ideas or events and why; based off of schema theory.

Schema theory

theory of learning that aims for schema building, or relating new knowledge (or new schema) to prior knowledge (or prior schema) because the brain organizes knowledge into units; a schema building example for a unit on Abraham Lincoln could include a pre-reading activity that asks students what they know about Lincoln before reading, and then a post-reading activity that assesses new information learned.

Segmentation

the ability to break spoken and print words into smaller parts; readers can segment phonemically a spoken sentence into words, a spoken word into syllables, or spoken syllables into phonemes; segmenting is learned at the beginning stages of developing phonological awareness skills and is one of the easier skills (out of blending, deleting and substituting).

Self-directed learning

learning opportunities where students participate in what or how they will learn; a KWL chart promotes self-directed learning by having students choose a text based off of what they want to learn; important for choosing texts that students are interested in reading and for promoting a desire to keep reading.

Self-monitoring

a metacognitive strategy used to monitor one's reading and to re-read or look again at difficult parts; also involves knowing when to skim information in a text.

Self-questioning

an oral or metacognitive strategy used to promote an active reading by asking questions about what has been read in order to assess one's comprehension.

Semantic map

a type of graphic organizer for promoting schema building and comprehension by organizing different ideas or events into logical groups based on association.

Short vowel

a vowel sound that doesn't obstruct the flow of air; the short vowels are a in apple, e in egg, i in igloo, o in ostrich, and u in umbrella.

Story elements

the way content and events are organized; (e.g. setting, characters, plot, theme)

Story map

a graphic organizer for mapping out the characters, setting and/or main events in a story; promotes comprehension and analysis skills.

Student-generated questions

a post-reading activity where students write questions that would elicit the most important information in a text.

Structural analysis

using the meaningful parts of a word to read and understand the word (football-foot/ball; transport-trans/port)

Substitution

a phonological skill that involves substituting the sound(s) with another in order to make a new word; in the word "mast," /m/ can be replaced with /f/ to make "fast."

Summarizing

oral or written overview that captures all of the main points; often uses the same terminology

Syllable

a word part that contains a vowel (e.g. bas-ket-ball)

Syntactic clues

the grammatical relationship between words and phrases (i.e. subject/verb) Syntax involves word order as well as inflections for various parts of speech (Compassion is a noun; compassionate is an adjective; compassionately is an adverb.)

Text complexity

the difficulty of reading and comprehending a text as related to the reader and task

Text features

the components of a story that are not in the main body; index, glossary, table of contents, headings, sidebars, etc.

Text structure

organization of a text; examples include cause/effect, sequences (chronological), comparison/contrasting.

Theme

the main idea or message about life in a piece of literature

Timeline

a type of graphic organizer that is beneficial for mapping out events

Validity

the accuracy of an assessment to measure what it was supposed to measure (instructional objectives)

Venn diagram

a type of graphic organizer for comparing and contrasting two or more ideas, authors, characters, etc; shows similarities and distinguishing traits of each concept being compared.

Visualizing

a metacognitive strategy used to promote active reading and comprehension by visualizing the information.

Word ladders

a tool to teach substitution skills; shows readers how one letter that changes to another makes a new word.

Word part

affixes, base words, and roots; many English words have a basic word to which affixes are added. A root word can stand alone: slowly has the root word slow and the suffix –ly; a root does not typically stand alone: biology has the Greek root bio which means life.

Word root

words from other languages that are the basis for English words; 60% of English words have Latin or Greek origins

Written vocabulary

all of the vocabulary that a student understands when reading print and that a student knows how to use when writing.

51908598R00223

Made in the USA
Middletown, DE
05 July 2019